The Critique of the State

What kind of political order would there be in the absence of the state? Jens Bartelson argues that we are currently unable to imagine what might lurk 'beyond', because our basic concepts of political order are conditioned by our experience of statehood. In this study, he investigates the concept of the state historically as well as philosophically, considering a range of thinkers and theories. He also considers the vexed issue of authority: modern political discourse questions the form and content of authority, but makes it all but impossible to talk about the foundations of authority. Largely due to the existing practices of political and scientific criticism, authority appears to be unquestionable. Bartelson's wide-ranging and readable discussion of the suppositions and presuppositions of statehood will be of interest to scholars and upper-level students of political theory, social theory and the philosophy of social science.

JENS BARTELSON is Professor of International Relations at the University of Copenhagen. He is the author of *A Genealogy of Sovereignty* (1995), as well as articles in journals such as *Political Theory, Review of International Studies* and *International Sociology.*

The Critique of the State

Jens Bartelson 2001

CAMBRIDGE
UNIVERSITY PRESS

PUBLISHED BY THE PRESS SYNDICATE OF THE UNIVERSITY OF CAMBRIDGE
The Pitt Building, Trumpington Street, Cambridge, United Kingdom

CAMBRIDGE UNIVERSITY PRESS
The Edinburgh Building, Cambridge CB2 2RU, UK
40 West 20th Street, New York, NY 10011-4211, USA
10 Stamford Road, Oakleigh, VIC 3166, Australia
Ruiz de Alarcón 13, 28014 Madrid, Spain
Dock House, The Waterfront, Cape Town 8001, South Africa

http://www.cambridge.org

First published 2001

Printed in the United Kingdom at the University Press, Cambridge

Typeface Plantin 10/12 pt.   *System* LaTeX 2$_\varepsilon$ [TB]

A catalogue record for this book is available from the British Library.

Library of Congress Cataloguing in Publication Data
Bartelson, Jens.
The critique of the state / Jens Bartelson.
    p.   cm.
Includes bibliographical references and index.
ISBN 0 521 80665 8 – ISBN 0 521 00140 4 (pbk.)
1. State, The.   I. Title
JC11 .B37 2001
320.1 – dc21   2001035277

ISBN 0 521 80665 8 hardback
ISBN 0 521 00140 4 paperback

To the memory of my father

Contents

Preface

This book is a treatise on political criticism and its consequences. As such, it is an inquiry *into* criticism and its conditions as much as it is an exercise *in* criticism of its consequences. As the title indicates, the book's main object of inquiry is the concept of the state and the changes this concept has undergone in political discourse during the past century, largely as a result of the critical attention it has received within political science over this period. Since the concept of the state has been crucial to the identity of the discipline, this book can also be read as a study in disciplinary history. To the extent that the discipline of political science can be suspected to define the boundaries of our political imagination, this book can be read as a study in political theory. To the extent that we believe that political theory has political implications, this book can also be read as an inquiry into the politics of the modern state.

This project has grown out of two convictions. The first is that criticism is a constitutive feature of modernity, and the second that the state concept has been foundational to modern political discourse. From Kant to Marx and far beyond, criticism has been the main instrument in fulfilling the promises of the modern age. By chasing premodern ghosts out of political institutions and political inquiry, criticism would emancipate us from everything that had previously stopped us from realizing our full potential as social beings. From Rousseau to Hegel and far beyond, the modern state has been envisaged as the place where such expectations were to be realized. Replacing premodern conceptions of political authority and community, the discourse on the state created a new home for man in a new world. Now that this world has come of age, some would even say that this home is about to crumble.

From these two convictions a question arises: what is the precise relationship between political criticism and the concept of the state? In my attempts to answer this, I was led to question the conditions of criticism as much as the concept of the state itself, gradually discovering that far from being inherently opposed to authority, criticism ought to be understood as conducive to its smooth functioning, not because of what it says, but rather because of what it does by saying what it says. So when somebody says that the modern state is withering away, that may well be seen as a way of breathing new life into it.

The attempt to answer this question has resulted in a book that tries to repoliticize the question of the political by rescuing the state and its authority from the paralysing spell of conventional modes of political criticism, by insisting on the need for historical *and* philosophical inquiry into the foundations of political authority and political criticism alike. As such, this book is based on the assumption that far from being exclusive, historical and philosophical approaches should be more closely integrated within political theory.

Many institutions and individuals have contributed to the completion of this book. A generous grant from the Swedish Council for Research in the Humanities and Social Sciences (HSFR) made it possible for me to do much of the research needed. A pleasant term at the Swedish Collegium for Advanced Study in the Social Sciences (SCASSS) made it possible for me to devote myself to writing, unencumbered by other duties. Many people have read and commented upon individual chapters or in other ways provided me with crucial input. During the initial phase of this project, Ronnie Hjort, Per Jansson, Torsten Nybom and Olof Ruin all contributed with valuable suggestions. While I was at SCASSS, Barbro Klein, Göran Therborn and Björn Wittrock all patiently took part in long discussions, as did John Broome and Sven Danielsson. Chapter 2 was graciously commented upon by Kari Palonen, Wyger Velema and Peter Wagner. Chapter 5 was read and commented upon with considerable acumen by Fredrika Lagergren and Johannes Lindvall. In the end the entire manuscript was subjected to thorough review by Terrell Carver, Henrik Enroth, Kjell Goldmann, Peter Hallberg, Bob Jessop, Sofia Näsström-Skold, Magnus Reitberger and Tomas Tranæus, all of whom suggested fruitful revisions. Finally, Alexandra Segerberg read the manuscript with meticulous attention to intellectual content and details of language.

1 The spirit of criticism

Today there is a widespread conviction that the sovereign state is unlikely to remain the main source of political authority in the future. It is challenged by new forms of authority and community which transcend the inherited divide between the domestic and the international, and it will therefore ultimately be replaced by new forms of political life which know nothing of this distinction and what once followed from it. As a result of the corrosive effects of globalization, the state will eventually enjoy a fate similar to that of the tribe, the city republic and the empire.[1] To this contention an important qualification is sometimes added. Our ability to understand this ongoing transformation and its possible outcomes is limited since our basic concepts of political order are conditioned by the distinction between domestic and international political life, and these concepts make modern politics intelligible only in terms of the state. As Hedley Bull once remarked, 'one reason for the vitality of the states system is the tyranny of the concepts and normative principles associated with it'.[2] That is, we simply seem to lack the intellectual resources necessary to conceive of a political order beyond or without the state, since the state has been present for long enough for the concept

---

[1] For different versions of this argument see, for example, Stephen Gill, 'Reflections on Global Order and Sociohistorical Time', *Alternatives*, vol. 16, 1991, no. 3, pp. 275–314; Timothy W. Luke, 'Discourses of Disintegration, Texts of Transformation: Re-Reading Realism in the New World Order', *Alternatives*, vol. 18, 1993, no. 2, pp. 229–58; *The Contemporary Crisis of the Nation-State, Political Studies*, special issue, vol. 42, 1994; Bertrand Badie, *La Fin des Territoires* (Paris: Fayard, 1995); Jean Baudrillard, *The Illusion of the End* (Cambridge: Polity Press, 1992); Ian Clark, 'Beyond the Great Divide: Globalization and the Theory of International Relations', *Review of International Studies*, vol. 24, 1998, no. 4, pp. 479–98; Philip Cerny, 'Globalization and the Changing Logic of Collective Action', *International Organization*, vol. 49, 1995, no. 4, pp. 595–625; Hendrik Spruyt, *The Sovereign State and its Competitors: an Analysis of Systems Change* (Princeton, NJ: Princeton University Press, 1994), ch. 9; Yale H. Ferguson and Richard W. Mansbach, *Polities: Authority, Identities, and Change* (Columbia, SC: University of South Carolina Press, 1996), esp. pp. 3–31; Zygmunt Bauman, *Globalization: the Human Consequences* (Cambridge: Polity Press, 1998), pp. 55–76.

[2] Hedley Bull, *The Anarchical Society: a Study of Order in World Politics* (London: Macmillan, 1977), p. 275.

1

to confine our political imagination. Thus, what might lurk beyond it is not simply unknown to us, but also effectively hidden by our statist intellectual predispositions.[3]

There is something disturbingly familiar about this critique of the state and the ensuing proviso. The end of the state has been proclaimed many times during the twentieth century, and has usually been supported in the same way. By pointing to an apparent mismatch between political theory and political practice, political philosophers of different persuasions have decided that since the state is about to wither away, the problem of political order needs to be reconceptualized in order to better capture new realities; yet this problem has been very resistant to such reconceptualization. It is therefore fair to describe these efforts as both propelled and frustrated by the logic of the problem: the state has not only constituted a recurrent problem, but has also been perceived as an obstacle to its solution.

This book is not another attempt to declare the state obsolete or to celebrate its permanence. To write a good book on such a topic would require exactly what is lacking today: a fundamental agreement about what the state is. But as Agamben has pointed out, '[t]here is a moment in the life of concepts when they lose their immediate intelligibility and can then . . . be overburdened with contradictory meanings'.[4] I think this is a fair description of the status of the concept of the state today. In such a situation, another kind of analysis is called for: an analysis of the contradictory meanings of the state concept, and above all an analysis of its remarkable staying power within political discourse, despite its contradictory nature and the recurrent celebrations of its demise. This book is an attempt in this direction. It is less a book about the state proper than a book about the presupposed presence of the state within modern political discourse, as it is manifested in the function of the state concept within this discourse. In other words, it is a book about the phenomenon of statism and its implications for political theory. Consequently, it will have very little to say about whether we are about to see the end of the state or not, but all the more to say about the possibilities of conceptualizing political order beyond or without the state.

In the course of doing this, the book investigates the concept of the state historically as well as philosophically, and focuses on existing attempts to escape the intellectual limits posed by this concept. It is intended as

---

[3] Cf. R. B. J. Walker, 'From International Relations to World Politics', in J. A. Camilleri, A. P. Jarvis and A. J. Paolini (eds.), *The State in Transition: Reimagining Political Space* (Boulder, CO: Lynne Rienner, 1995), pp. 21–38.

[4] Giorgio Agamben, *Homo Sacer: Sovereign Power and Bare Life* (Stanford, CA: Stanford University Press, 1998), p. 80.

a diagnosis of how we have got into our present and quite confusing predicament with respect to the state; that is, how it became possible and prima facie equally reasonable to argue both that we have reached the end of the state and that the theoretical means at our disposal for understanding this process and its possible outcomes are limited by the state concept and what goes with it.

The phenomenon of statism reflects a basic ambivalence concerning the question of authority which prevails in modern political discourse. On the one hand, modern political discourse ceaselessly questions the form and content of authority, its legitimacy and proper boundaries. On the other, modern political discourse makes questions about the ultimate foundations of authority difficult to ask, let alone answer. So while the state is usually thought to be *the* institutional expression of political authority, there is a strong tendency to take its presence for granted, while its actual manifestations in political theory and practice are criticized from a variety of ideological viewpoints.

The ultimate source of this ambivalent attitude to authority is to be found in modern political discourse itself, and in the critical spirit animating it. Above all, modern political discourse is critical in so far as it relentlessly questions authority; yet it poses an inner limit to this criticism. Since this limit also functions as a principle of identity of that discourse by defining it as political, it simultaneously conditions the terms of criticism. It is perhaps no coincidence that the philosopher who is commonly believed to have inaugurated critical thought was also eager to define its limits. As Kant stated in his *Metaphysik der Sitten* (1797),

[t]he origin of supreme power ... is *not discoverable* by the people who are subject to it. In other words, the subject *ought not* to indulge in *speculations* about its origin with a view to acting upon them ... Whether in fact an actual contract originally preceded their submission to the state's authority, whether the power came first and the law only appeared after it, or whether they ought to have followed this order – these are completely futile arguments for a people which is already subject to civil law, and they constitute a menace to the state.[5]

But if the ultimate sources of authority cannot be discovered, why is it necessary to prohibit speculation about them? Why forbid something that is impossible? One obvious answer would be that since it is indeed fully possible to question the foundations of authority, it is necessary to make such questioning impossible by forbidding it, since if the ultimate sources of authority cannot be discovered, any such questioning cannot but lead to

---

[5] Immanuel Kant, 'The Metaphysics of Morals', in Hans Reiss (ed.), *Kant's Political Writings* (Cambridge: Cambridge University Press, 1991), p. 143. Quoted and discussed in Slavoj Zizek, *For They Do Not Know What They Do: Enjoyment as a Political Factor* (London: Verso, 1991), p. 204.

civil discord. But this answer merely invites a paradox, since it would then take authority to enforce the prohibition against questioning authority, an authority itself unquestionable. Thus, in order for authority to remain authoritative, it must be unquestionable, yet authority itself lacks the authority to impose such an unquestionability. Such an unquestionability has to be imposed from within political discourse, not from without. As I shall argue, such imposition has been one of the main functions of criticism within political discourse: it is precisely the recurrent discursive transgression of the prohibition against questioning the ultimate origins of authority that makes it impossible to question these.[6]

This book is about how this transgression has been mediated through critical gestures within political discourse, and how this mediation has been integral to the authority of the modern state.[7] According to the main argument of this book, the state concept has indeed been foundational to large parts of modern political discourse, and attempts to emancipate political reflection from its influence have largely been futile, at first glance testifying to the relative success of the discursive prohibition against questioning the ultimate origin of authority. Thus, in order to exist and remain operative as a source of authority, the state has to enforce a silence about its ultimate foundations by opening its surface up to ceaseless critique. It is this critique and its consequences that form the topic of this book.

As I shall argue in subsequent chapters, throughout the twentieth century the state concept has conditioned the ways in which the core problems of modern political science have been phrased, despite the numerous efforts to rid the discipline of what has frequently been perceived as an ambiguous, opaque or obsolete concept, thus eliciting what has been made to look like its absence. The presupposed presence of the state is thus a historically limited phenomenon, resulting from a specific function of the state concept within those parts of political discourse that have attained scientific status. What makes these different discourses in any recognizable sense political or relevant to the concerns of political science is precisely their – logical as well as historical – dependence on the state concept as their foundation.

Phrased differently, the state has been second nature to political scientists: if not inescapable, the concept has remained sufficiently powerful to set limits to the theoretical imagination – but only as long and in so far as we remain committed to existing disciplinary identities and existing divisions of intellectual labour. Consequently, one important source of the confusion that today surrounds the question of the future fate of the

---

[6] I owe this suggestion to Henrik Enroth.
[7] See Zizek, *For They Do Not Know What They Do*, pp. 204–5.

state is an underlying tension between the state conceived as an object of theoretical and empirical knowledge and the state conceived as a transcendental condition of that knowledge. Within large parts of our legacy of political theorizing, the state is both posited as an object of analysis *and* presupposed as the foundation of such analysis. This makes it inherently difficult to take political theorizing out of its statist predispositions.

The rest of this chapter is devoted to the question of how to go about this undeniably laborious task. First, I shall begin with a brief sketch of the philosophical argument of this book, arguing that the historical trajectory of the state concept must be understood against the backdrop of its ambiguity, and its ambiguity against the backdrop of its conceptual limits. Second, I shall continue by arguing that concepts that are foundational and constitutive necessitate a somewhat different analytical strategy from those in vogue within the study of political thought. Third, since the state concept is inextricably intertwined with modern political discourse and figures in the most diverse theoretical contexts, something has to be said about the possibility of comparison across these contexts.

Analysing the concept of the state

A crucial claim of this book is that the presence of the state is presupposed by the way the concept of the state functions within modern political discourse, and that this function makes important parts of modern political discourse statist. Since this is something that has to be investigated rather than merely taken for granted, we have to elaborate this claim more fully. What does it mean to say that the state is presupposed by the function of the state concept, and that this function renders this discourse statist?

I can think of three different answers, all of them equally valid. First, it means that there is an inferential connection between the concept of the state and other concepts within modern political discourse, and that the concept of the state is more basic in so far as we can make sense of the state concept without the other concepts, but not conversely. Second, it means that this inferential connection is sustained by the function of the state concept within political discourse, in so far as the state is rendered foundational and constitutive through the position of the state concept within that discourse. Third, it means that the state concept conditions the intelligibility of that discourse to such an extent that the conceptual structure of this discourse would suffer from a lack of coherence in the absence of such a concept.

Thus phrased, the question of statism is fully distinct from questions of the state proper and its ontological status, since the former concerns a series of logical relations within discourse while the latter concerns a series of relations between discourse and what might be outside or beneath it.

This distinguishes my way of proceeding from other attempts to make sense of the semantics of statehood, which tend to assume that discourse on the state is somehow necessarily expressive of something else in the social formation. According to Luhmann, for example, the state is nothing but the self-description of the political system, a point of reference for political action in a system whose complexity would otherwise effectively inhibit communication within and between different systems.[8]

As I will argue more fully below, my way of proceeding implies a strong commitment to a logical constructivism, but no commitment as to how the concepts under investigation relate to the domains to which they refer or to what they may happen to be expressive of. For reasons that will become plain later, the relationship between concepts and other things has to remain an open question, something to be investigated rather than assumed. My claim is therefore that an analysis of the presupposed presence of the state in political discourse can, and indeed must, be undertaken while remaining agnostic about the actual claims about the ontological status of the state advanced within a given discourse, since the question of statism concerns the logical relations that hold between concepts within a given discourse, not the relationship between these concepts and their possible referents or the identities underlying them.

Furthermore, if modern political discourse does indeed presuppose the presence of the state, this implies that an analysis of this phenomenon requires at least provisional access to a vocabulary that itself does not presuppose the presence of the state, since what is posited as a presupposition within one discourse cannot by definition be rendered transparent by means of the same discourse. An analysis of the state concept along those lines thus implies that we *can* do what Kant said was both impossible and forbidden, that is, question the foundations of authority. To my mind, this is best done by questioning the existing practices of questioning authority. This is another reason why we have to pay attention to criticism as such, and scrutinize its emancipatory claims.

This brings us to the problem of political order, and to the state as a specific solution to this problem. Phrasing the problem of political order is usually done in terms of the concepts of authority and community, and solving it has been very much a matter of explaining or justifying the presence of the one in terms of the other. Furthermore, such a justification or explanation will necessarily regard authority as either constituting or constituted. This distinction can help us make more sense of the difficulty of questioning authority within modern political discourse.

---

[8] Niklas Luhmann, 'The "State" of the Political System', in *Essays on Self-Reference* (New York: Columbia University Press, 1990), p. 166.

When authority is posited as constituting, authority is seen as without foundation outside itself: it is nothing but an unfounded act which has itself been rendered foundational by the imposition of a certain forgetfulness as to its divine or violent origin.[9] Constituting authority is thus prior to and constitutive of a political community correlated to it in time and space, and also of the specific legal and political expressions of authority within that community. When authority is viewed as constituted, however, its presence is explained and justified by showing how it is based on the imagined will and identity of a given political community, which effectively precedes and constitutes authority by virtue of being itself posited as a constituting force.

While most modern political thought explicitly affirms constituted authority by justifying the authority of the modern state in terms of popular sovereignty and national identity, this book tries to show that the actual place and function of the state concept within crucial parts of modern political discourse indicate that this discourse nevertheless implicitly embraces a notion of authority as being constituting. By presupposing the presence of the state, this discourse tacitly affirms a symbolic authority that structures questionability and conditions the terms of further criticism. Put somewhat differently, a fair share of modern political discourse tacitly implies that the exceptional moment of sovereignty is prior to the rule of law, while the opposite case is defended explicitly by most theories of the state.

As we shall see, the critique of the state amounts to a reproduction of that constituting authority. On the one hand, the fact that constituting authority has no foundation outside itself makes it both tempting and prima facie easy to criticize, since the act that founds it cannot be justified and appears mysterious or illegitimate to the modern and democratically disposed political philosopher. On the other hand, it is difficult, if not impossible, to criticize that same founding act without simultaneously invoking it oneself, since there is no other presumably constituted authority there to validate or justify those acts of criticism.[10]

But to what extent does modern political discourse presuppose the presence of the state, and to what extent is it dependent on this concept for its enunciation? Nothing would be easier than to brand large parts of modern political discourse as statist, yet nothing would be more

---

[9] Jacques Derrida, 'Force of Law: the "Mystical Foundation of Authority"', in D. Cornell, M. Rosenfeld and D. G. Carlson (eds.), *Deconstruction and the Possibility of Justice* (New York and London: Routledge, 1992), p. 14; Agamben, *Homo Sacer*, pp. 39–48. See also Pierre Saint-Amand, *The Laws of Hostility: Politics, Violence and the Enlightenment* (Minneapolis, MN: University of Minnesota Press, 1996), pp. 1–14.

[10] Derrida, 'Force of Law', p. 40.

unfair. Intellectual honesty demands that an analysis of the state concept is directed against those parts of political discourse that themselves have attempted to come to terms with this concept; rather than sampling freely from those parts of political discourse which could be suspected of being most uncritically statist, thus contributing to the paranoia of entrapment, we should analyse those discourses which have evolved in more or less explicit response to the problems of the state during the last century. Hence, we should deal less with those texts which for various reasons have taken the presence of the state for granted, but more with those which have sought to problematicize or even abolish the state concept. To do otherwise would be like putting the devil on trial for being evil.

The modern discourse on the state is above all a critical discourse in so far as it is held together by a common ambition to unmask the state and its authority according to the spirit of criticism referred to above; while being critical of the state in so far as it is invariably portrayed as concealing underlying realities, this discourse is simultaneously conditioned by the state concept in that this concept and its core connotations are both presupposed and reproduced by critical moves within political discourse. Investigating those parts of political discourse that have sought to problematicize the state from different perspectives, I shall focus less on explicit arguments about the state and its ontological status, and more on the modes of enunciation that sustain these arguments. In doing so, I shall pay attention not only to the subject of enunciation but also to the enunciated subject by carefully analysing not only the state concept itself, but also the entire structure of concepts brought into operation by different discourses on the state. Hence, rather than merely analysing statements about the state, I shall ask what makes these statements possible, in terms of what they presuppose or imply, what kind of relations exist between the state concept and other concepts and, finally, how the meaning of these concepts changes as a result of their changing positions across, as well as within, different theoretical contexts.

The claim that the state concept is foundational to and constitutive of modern political discourse is not new. One of the main points of Skinner's seminal *Foundations of Modern Political Thought* (1978) was to show how the discursive preconditions of this concept were established in early modern political discourse in Europe, and how such a modern view of the state gradually came to shape modern political discourse.[11]

---

[11] Quentin Skinner, *Foundations of Modern Political Thought* (Cambridge: Cambridge University Press, 1978), vol. I, pp. x, 349; Quentin Skinner, 'The State', in Terence Ball, Russell L. Hanson and James Farr (eds.), *Political Innovation and Conceptual Change* (Cambridge: Cambridge University Press, 1989), pp. 90–131; Maurizio Viroli, *From Politics to Reason of State: the Acquisition and Transformation of the Language of Politics, 1250–1600* (Cambridge: Cambridge University Press, 1992), pp. 238–80.

But whereas Skinner and other contextualist historians have accounted for the emergence of the modern state concept, they have had very little, if anything, to say about its changing place and function within modern political discourse. Indeed, it could be argued that their accounts of the state concept are themselves inherently statist, since they have posited a modern notion of the state as the end towards which early modern political reflection evolved through a delicate blend of necessity and accident. Given the logic of this account, however, it is difficult to imagine any profound change in the conception of the state beyond the point where political discourse became obsessed by the state and started to define itself in terms of it; it is as if all roads in the past led to Weber but none further beyond.

My perspective is different, as is the thrust of my argument. This book does not attempt to answer the question of how the state concept once emerged within Western political discourse. I have already tried to answer parts of that question in a previous book. What this book attempts to do, rather, is to analyse how the state concept came to fulfil a constitutive function within late modern scientific political discourse – that is, beyond Weber – and how this concept subsequently became an unquestioned part of political reflection despite – and sometimes because of – the numerous efforts to abolish and redefine it. Again, the focus is on its quite remarkable staying power within political discourse.

But before we can analyse the trajectory of the state concept in more detail, we must briefly hypothesize what has made this rather strange trajectory possible. To my mind, the seemingly endless theoretical disputes over the state originate in the ambiguity of the state concept, and this ambiguity is in turn made possible through initial interpretive gestures that have defined the limits of its intelligibility. This ambiguity has been much lamented, and it is common to blame the lack of scientific consensus about the state on the lack of clarity of the state concept.[12] As Hont has argued,

it is hard to find a genuinely historical definition of the 'nation-state' which could be consistently applied in conceptual analysis. Most discussions of the 'nation-state', both in its domestic and international aspects ... are riven by contradiction and inconsistency.[13]

[12] See, for example, David Held, 'Central Perspectives on the Modern State', in G. McLennan, David Held and S. Hall (eds.), *The Idea of the Modern State* (Milton Keynes: Open University Press, 1984), pp. 29–79; B. A. Rockman, 'Minding the State – or a State of Mind?', in J. A. Caporaso (ed.), *The Elusive State: International and Comparative Perspectives* (Newbury Park, CA: Sage, 1989), pp. 173–203; Gabriel A. Almond, 'The Return to the State', in Gabriel A. Almond, *A Discipline Divided: Schools and Sects in Political Science* (Newbury Park, CA: Sage, 1990), pp. 189–218.

[13] István Hont, 'The Permanent Crisis of a Divided Mankind: "Contemporary Crisis of the Nation State" in Historical Perspective', *Political Studies*, vol. 42, 1994, p. 177.

Many of those who have lamented this ambiguity have also suggested an antidote: conceptual analysis. Yet they have never questioned the sources of that ambiguity, or bothered to investigate its limits. Most political scientists simply want to get rid of ambiguity, since to them ambiguity is but an avatar of unreason. Yet it is possible that ambiguity, rather than being just an obstacle to rational inquiry, may possess a certain rationality of its own that could provide clues to how a given concept has become ambiguous and why it has stayed ambiguous despite numerous efforts to clarify it. According to one interpretation, it was the state that brought this quest for clarity, making 'a declaration of war on semantic ambiguity'.[14] Paradoxically, then, while presumably being the source of unequivocal meaning, the state itself is surrounded by the most total ambiguity.

It may therefore prove instructive to analyse the sources of ambiguity, in order to render visible the theoretical space within which the state concept has acquired its identity as an ambiguous concept. To my mind, conceptual ambiguity results both from practices of definition and from the actual position of a given concept within discourse. Standard practices of definition are rituals of purification and, like most such rituals, they help reproduce what they promise to abolish, lest they themselves should become superfluous. Defining a term means making stipulations about its meaning and reference within a given context of employment and according to given criteria; but since both contexts and criteria multiply across time and space, any concept is able to soak up a multitude of different connotations throughout its usage in different contexts and for different purposes, which in turn makes a clear-cut definition seem all the more urgent, provoking yet another attempt at definition that reproduces the initial ambiguity. Hence, ambiguity is an unintended and cumulated consequence of the quest for clarification that has been so dear to the social sciences.

The ambiguity of a concept is also the outcome of its position within discourse. The greater the number of other concepts that are defined in terms of a given concept, the more numerous the inferential and metaphorical connections, and the more numerous these connections between *definiendum* and *definiens* the more central the defining concept. And conversely, the more central a given concept, the easier it is to use as a primitive term when defining other concepts, and the easier it is to use the more ambiguous it will gradually become through frequent employment. Furthermore, the more central a concept becomes within a given discourse, the more likely it is to become implicit in and taken for granted within that very discourse. And the more implicit it is, the more likely

---

[14] Zygmunt Bauman, *Modernity and Ambivalence* (Cambridge: Polity Press, 1991), p. 105.

it is to become foundational to and constitutive of that discourse. Thus, ambiguity and centrality go hand in hand, and concepts which are both central and ambiguous tend to become constitutive and foundational, and conversely.

Taken together, this suggests that one important clue to the tendency to presuppose the presence of the state within political discourse is provided by the mutually reinforcing logic of centrality and ambiguity. In the historical chapters of this book we will see these mechanisms at work, since the state concept provides a good example of a concept which has remained ambiguous precisely by virtue of its centrality, and conversely.

But an analysis of ambiguity should not be confined to its sources and the discursive mechanisms that reproduce it. Behind the semantic disagreements that make ambiguity possible we find those agreements that make it possible to disagree about its meaning, and these agreements together constitute the limits of ambiguity. The best way to render such largely tacit agreements visible is by asking what the state is contrasted with in the standard definitions and most conventional applications. Hence, as a primary step, we should ask how the state concept has been individuated by being defined as categorically distinct from *other* concepts or categories. As a second step, it is necessary to show how these distinctions give rise to theoretical commitments that render the concept internally inconsistent.

If we accept that the state concept is foundational and constitutive of scientific political discourse, we should not be surprised to find that it cannot easily be subjected to the practices of definition referred to above, since the term state itself figures as a positive and primitive term in the definitions of other, equally central, concepts. This is what makes clarification both seem so urgent and yet so difficult to achieve. Hence, and as a consequence of its centrality, the concept of the state cannot be fully determined by the character of its semantic components or by its inferential connections to other concepts, since it is the concept of the state that draws these components together into a unity and gives theoretical significance to other concepts on the basis of their inferential and metaphorical connections to the concept of the state, rather than conversely.[15]

Still, the concept of the state does not organize political discourse from scratch or generate theoretical meaning out of nothing. At the most fundamental level, the modern state concept is individuated by a series of differences which together provide the baseline for further attempts at

[15] A similar point has been made about the concept of nation by Liah Greenfeld, *Nationalism: Five Roads to Modernity* (Cambridge, MA: Harvard University Press, 1992), p. 7.

definition and theorizing, resulting from previous acts of interpretation. These differences manifest themselves as boundaries that condition the possibility of the modern concept of the state in so far as they provide the necessary requirements for its meaningful employment within political discourse, and locate the state concept in a wider system of theoretical and ideological values. As such, these differences together constitute the limits of the modern formulation of the problem of political order, by premising the harmonious convergence between authority and community on two crucial distinctions.[16]

First, the conceptual identity of the state is conditioned by the largely implicit assumption that the political order represented by the state is distinct from the kind of relations that exist between states in an international context. This differentiation affirms the state as a source of authority and community among a multitude of similar units, and construes the state and the international context in which it finds itself as mutually constitutive yet opposed spheres of politics. Whereas the domestic sphere is conventionally associated with the presence of order and peaceful progress, the international sphere is characterized by the absence of these conditions, and instead carries the stigma of war and moral stagnation. Hence, when viewed from the international outside, the state appears as a unified whole, marked by its sovereignty and individuated through reciprocal recognition by other similar entities. Hence state identity appears to be conditioned by the absence of authority and community in the international sphere.[17]

At the heart of this distinction between inside and outside we find the concept of sovereignty. Rather than simply being an attribute of individual states or a rule constitutive of the international sphere, sovereignty is what separates these spheres while simultaneously binding them together. As Agamben has noted, the state of nature thought to prevail in the international realm and the state of exception on which state authority is ultimately based are but two aspects of the same process, 'in which what was presupposed as external . . . now reappears . . . in the inside, and sovereign power is this very possibility of distinguishing between inside and outside'.[18]

Second, state identity is conditioned by the likewise implicit assumption that the state is distinct from the domestic society over which it

---

[16] Gaston Bachelard, *The Poetics of Space* (Boston, MA: Beacon Press, 1994).

[17] Cf. Richard K. Ashley, 'The Powers of Anarchy: Theory, Sovereignty, and the Domestication of Global Life', in James Der Derian (ed.), *International Theory: Critical Investigations* (London: Macmillan, 1995), p. 110; R. B. J. Walker, *Inside/Outside: International Relations as Political Theory* (Cambridge: Cambridge University Press, 1993), ch. 1.

[18] Agamben, *Homo Sacer*, p. 37.

supposedly holds sway.[19] This differentiation inscribes the state as the sole locus of authority within a polity composed of a multitude of other agents, individual or collective, and makes it possible to describe relations between state and society in terms of conflict and harmony. Whereas the state is conventionally associated with the political, society is frequently characterized as either non-political or prepolitical. Hence, when viewed from the domestic inside, the state appears as a locus of authority, indi-viduated through the subjugation or consent of other agents. Thus, state identity appears to be conditioned by the *presence* of authority within a society from which it is thereby rendered distinct.[20]

Today both these distinctions are being questioned with increasing intensity, and with them, the permanence of the modern state as a form of political life. But to those scholars who perform this questioning, the main difficulty arises from their own tendency to presuppose the same conceptual boundaries which they set out to question or dissolve.

In international relations theory it has been fashionable to point out that the boundary between the domestic and the international is becom-ing increasingly blurred thanks to processes of internationalization, and that this profoundly affects the identities and interests of states. But while the state and the international sphere have conventionally been defined in terms of each other, it is enigmatic how the one can really be pro-foundly transformed without equally profoundly affecting the identity of the other. This puzzle automatically spills over into the question of how a discipline devoted to its solution can preserve its identity, since its in-tellectual coherence seems to depend on the givenness of both the state and the international system.[21]

In historical sociology it has been equally fashionable to point out that the boundary between state and society has become blurred thanks to an increasing diffusion of power within societies. Yet it is unclear why the state should be conceptualized as distinct from society within theo-ries that attempt to account for the dissolution of the boundary between

---

[19] Luhmann, 'The "State" of the Political System', p. 165.

[20] Cf. John Keane, 'Despotism and Democracy: the Origins and Development of the Distinction between Civil Society and the State 1750–1850', in John Keane (ed.), *Civil Society and the State: New European Perspectives* (London: Verso, 1988), pp. 35–71; Reinhart Koselleck, *Critique and Crisis: Enlightenment and the Pathogenesis of Modern Society* (Oxford: Berg, 1988).

[21] Cf. James N. Rosenau, 'The State in an Era of Cascading Politics: Wavering Concept, Widening Competence, Withering Colossus, or Weathering Change?', in Caporaso, *The Elusive State*, pp. 17–48; David Held, *Political Theory and the Modern State: Essays on State, Power, and Democracy* (Oxford: Polity Press, 1989), pp. 214–42; David Held, 'Democracy, the Nation-State and the Global System', *Economy and Society*, vol. 20, 1991, no. 2, pp. 138–72; Alexander Wendt, *Social Theory of International Politics* (Cambridge: Cambridge University Press, 1999), pp. 193–245.

them empirically. It seems difficult to uphold an analytical divide between state and society while opening the same divide up to empirical investigation, since what is assumed to be theoretically necessary cannot easily be treated as empirically contingent.[22]

Thus, and as a condition of its identity and as a means of limiting its ambiguity, the modern state has to be conceptualized as essentially distinct from its international and societal contexts, and the only way to make sense of these concepts of the international and the social seems to have been by contrasting them with that of the state. Yet in each of the above cases the concept of the state acquires its theoretical meaning by being placed in an unstable and fluid relation to the concepts from which it has been marked off. The result is that it is difficult to use the state concept without inviting inconsistencies which result when one attempts to problematicize the empirical existence of the state while simultaneously retaining the above distinctions, since they together condition the intelligibility of the state as a distinct species of political life.

But being limits to ambiguity, these distinctions are also the limits of political imagination in the sense that political order would become difficult to make sense of in their absence. The above master distinctions thus condition state discourse in so far as they constitute the very ground for phrasing and answering questions of authority and community within modern political discourse. These distinctions also define the boundaries of political modernity, and condition the interplay of ambiguity and centrality that makes this concept look both foundational to and constitutive of large parts of modern political discourse.

In this section I have hypothesized that crucial parts of modern political discourse indeed presuppose the presence of the state, and that even those parts of political discourse that explicitly problematicize the state are premised upon its presence. Furthermore, I have argued that this phenomenon should be treated as a genuine philosophical and historical problem rather than as a source of political paranoia, and that it should be carefully investigated both philosophically as well as historically. I have also suggested that the discursive habit of presupposing the presence of the state is partly conditioned by the ambiguity of the state concept, and

---

[22] Cf. Held, 'Central Perspectives on the Modern State'; Michael Mann, 'The Autonomous Power of the State: its Origins, Mechanisms and Results', in J. A. Hall (ed.), *States in History* (Oxford: Basil Blackwell, 1986), p. 136; Clyde W. Barrow, *Critical Theories of the State: Marxist, Neo-Marxist, Post-Marxist* (Madison, WI: University of Wisconsin Press, 1993), pp. 109–36; Charles Tilly, *Coercion, Capital and European States AD 990–1992* (Oxford: Basil Blackwell, 1992), pp. 1–37; Bo Stråth and Rolf Torstendahl, 'State Theory and State Development: States as Network Structures in Change in Modern European History', in Rolf Torstendahl (ed.), *State Theory and State History* (London: Sage, 1992), pp. 12–37.

that this ambiguity itself is reproduced through the critical practices that prevail within different theoretical contexts. All this now remains to be substantiated by textual evidence, but before this can be done, we have to make a methodological detour in order to justify the view of political concepts that informs the present study.

Analysing political concepts

The following chapters are intended as a history of the present, both in the sense that they aim to be diagnostic rather than empirically exhaustive, and in the sense that they deal with concepts and theories which are still accepted as viable guides to political reality by a large part of the scholarly community. The historical narrative is also episodic, since the main task is to explain how we got into our current predicament with respect to the state rather than to provide the reader with a full account of the state concept and its historical trajectory within modern political discourse.

This fusion of diagnostic ambition with an attention to concepts not yet perceived as parts of the past gives rise to a peculiar historiographical problem. It is inherently difficult to write histories of twentieth-century discourse simply because the way in which we write such histories is indebted to the historiographical possibilities inherent in that very discourse. Since the twentieth century has not yet been turned into an effective past, but rather constitutes very much of a present, there is a constant risk of short-circuiting topic and resource.[23]

The following account of the state concept also tries to be philosophical, by posing critical questions about its place and function within contemporary political discourse. Subsequent chapters deal with contemporary state theories as if they were addressing different, but commensurable, versions of the problem of political order, and as if their solutions to these problems were commensurate enough to make critical commentary across different theoretical contexts possible, and indeed fruitful. This assumption is crucial, since any analysis of the state concept would be pointless if we did not assume that the problem of political order could at least potentially be reconceptualized in terms that transcended the options structured by the presupposed presence of the state.

If the historical questions of this book have to do with the sources of statism within political discourse, the philosophical questions have more

---

[23] For different versions of histories of the present and their rationale, see Donald R. Kelley, 'What is Happening to the History of Ideas?', *Journal of the History of Ideas*, vol. 51, 1990, no. 1, p. 23. For a classical statement, see Michel Foucault, 'Nietzsche, Genealogy, History', in Donald F. Bouchard (ed.), *Language, Counter-memory, Practice: Selected Essays and Interviews by Michel Foucault* (Ithaca, NY: Cornell University Press, 1977), pp. 139–64.

to do with the limits of statism within the same discourse. Historically, our problem is to describe how modern political discourse has remained statist despite the various efforts to reconceptualize the state. Philosophically, our problem is to explain why these efforts have failed, and how we might possibly reconceptualize the problem of political authority in terms that do not presuppose the presence of the state but instead expose its proper conceptual identity.

But is it reasonable to try to fuse these questions together this way? I imagine that most historians of political concepts and most political philosophers would be sceptical of this suggestion, since the concerns of conceptual history and political philosophy seem far apart: whereas the history of political concepts requires a thorough contextualization of their meaning and function, political philosophy is thought to require a prior stabilization of their meaning by means of stipulative definitions. It is thus common to regard these concerns as mutually exclusive, if not contradictory, since they seem to cancel each other out: while the token historian of political concepts charts conceptual change through time, the token political philosopher reaches out for the timeless by means of unchanging concepts.

To my mind, whether there exist timeless problems, or whether all problems are ultimately circumscribed by the particular context of enunciation, is more a matter of the ways these problems are formulated than a profound philosophical principle. It is always possible to historicize a prima facie perennial problem by demonstrating that it became possible to formulate only against the backdrop of a contingent set of discursive antecedents, as it is possible to reinscribe an already contextualized problem within the domain of philosophy by showing that its antecedents themselves derive from a more abstract philosophical problem. Within this view, the apparent tension between historical and philosophical perspectives results from clashes between questions phrased at different levels of abstraction, rather than from profound differences underlying the possibility of phrasing these questions.

If this is indeed the case, the by now quite tedious dispute between historical and philosophical perspectives in the study of political thought could perhaps be resolved by construing our basic units of inquiry in a way that would allow us to effect a nice compromise between these concerns. In this section, I shall try to justify this claim by arguing that the tension between historical and philosophical concerns is ultimately conditioned by a common understanding of what kind of entities concepts are, and then propose an alternative way of viewing concepts called conceptualism that may help us to handle that tension.

Let us begin by stating the obvious. If we want to understand the changing meaning and function of a given concept within political discourse,
the foremost methodological virtue should be that of historical openness.
This means that the less the semantic content of a concept is determined
in advance through definitions, the more of its meaning is left to historical inquiry to unearth and the more left to inquiry to determine, the
greater the openness of the historical field. The virtue of openness lies
in keeping historiography as free as possible from anachronism and the
projections of present concerns on to the past.[24] Consequently, historical
openness necessitates philosophical minimalism, and being minimalist in
turn requires an agnostic attitude towards those philosophical problems
whose solutions threaten to contaminate our understanding of the past
with untimely content.

But how is such openness best safeguarded? My tentative suggestion
is that historical openness is best served by treating political concepts
as *autonomous* in relation to other entities – discursive or not – but not
necessarily in relation to each other. Yet any talk of conceptual autonomy
is bound to arouse suspicion among those trained to identify conceptual
autonomy as the main source of presentism and finalism within historiography, so such talk has to be carefully distinguished from earlier ways
of defending conceptual autonomy which tended to buy this autonomy
either through reification of concepts into abstract things, or through a
transcendentalist view of concepts as conditions of human subjectivity.[25]
Below I will refer to these views as conceptual realism and conceptual
idealism respectively.

By contrast, a philosophical analysis of political concepts is conventionally thought to require conceptual autonomy of either of the above
kinds, if by philosophical analysis we mean spelling out the conditions of
meaningful and valid usage of concepts. Within this view, by analysing the
semantic content of concepts, we may hope to pass philosophical judge-
ments on the validity of the theories in which they are used. Yet these
requirements are clearly at odds with the historicist ambition to regard
the semantic content of concepts as historically variable, thus preclud-
ing the kind of stable connotations and inferential connections between

---

[24] Dominick La Capra, 'History, Language, and Reading: Waiting for Crillon', *American Historical Review*, vol. 100, 1995, no. 3, pp. 799–828.
[25] The history of the concept of concept remains to be written, but some clues to what such a story would look like can be derived from Steven Collins, 'Categories, Concepts or Predicaments? Remarks on Mauss's use of Philosophical Terminology', in M. Carrithers, Steven Collins and S. Lukes (eds.), *The Category of the Person: Anthropology, Philosophy, History* (Cambridge: Cambridge University Press, 1985), pp. 46–82.

concepts that would make any conventional philosophical analysis possible. Philosophical analysis requires some basic criteria of consistency and coherence, and presupposes that these criteria are sufficiently clear and unchanging to make comparison between different conceptual frameworks possible.[26]

Phrased in this way, the difference between historical and philosophical approaches to the study of political thought becomes a matter of principle. But I believe that the conflict between history and philosophy in the study of political thought has been kept alive by a mutual tendency to ontologize the objects of investigation rather than by any disagreement over the criteria of validity. If concepts are thought of either as abstract things or transcendental ideas with invariable content, this view is, of course, not readily compatible with a view of concepts and their meaning as essentially relative, historically variable, and contextual. When pushed to extremes, these standpoints could well be seen as incommensurable, since they are based upon different views of what kind of stuff concepts are made of, and what shapes their meaning.[27]

Bevir's recent attempt to reconcile historical and philosophical perspectives is a case in point, because it is premised on an irreconcilable tension between the historical and philosophical approaches. Criticizing contextualist historians for neglecting the coherence and consistency of the utterances they investigate, Bevir goes on to assimilate what he takes to be an indispensable presumption of coherence among utterances to a theory of the mind implying coherence among beliefs as a condition of personal identity of the interlocutors.[28] Far from dissolving the tension between historical and philosophical perspectives, the net result of this move is to subject historiography to the kind of universalist concepts of rationality and subjectivity from which it has struggled to escape by taking a linguistic turn. Even a weak commitment to belief coherence as a principle guiding historical reconstruction would impose undesirable

---

[26] This view of philosophical analysis roughly corresponds to that of Wittgenstein, see his *Philosophical Grammar* (Oxford: Basil Blackwell, 1974), and to that held by some analytical philosophers such as Hilary Putnam, *Reason, Truth, and History* (Cambridge: Cambridge University Press, 1981), pp. 18–21; Richard Rorty, *Philosophy and the Mirror of Nature* (Oxford: Basil Blackwell, 1980), pp. 265–73.

[27] For an analysis of the relationship between philosophy and history in more general terms, see Jorge J. E. Gracia, *Philosophy and its History: Issues in Philosophical Historiography* (New York: SUNY, 1992). For important statements of these positions, see J. G. A. Pocock, 'The History of Political Thought: a Methodological Enquiry', in P. Laslett and W. G. Runciman (eds.), *Philosophy, Politics and Society,* 2nd series (Oxford: Blackwell, 1962), pp. 183–202; Leo Strauss, *Natural Right and History* (Chicago, IL: The Free Press, 1953), pp. 3–5.

[28] Mark Bevir, *The Logic of the History of Ideas* (Cambridge: Cambridge University Press, 1999), chs. 2 and 4.

constraints upon our field of historical vision, since this would imply not only that coherent beliefs are indeed necessary to the identity of the interlocutors, but also that the existence of such self-identical subjects is a necessary condition of meaning.[29]

As I shall argue, however, the tension between philosophical and historical viewpoints can be handled better by arguing that conceptual autonomy does not necessitate any commitment to the ontological status of concepts outside the text in which they figure. I take this view to be latent in the way concepts are analysed within much contemporary philosophy, and I shall contend that consistency and coherence concern the relationship between linguistic entities such as concepts and propositions rather than between mentalist entities such as beliefs and, crucially, that the criteria of consistency and coherence do indeed vary across time and context by virtue of the simple fact that they themselves are conceptual in character.

Put differently, provided that we succeed in being consistently constructivist about concepts, it should be perfectly possible to treat them as wholly autonomous yet discursive entitities whose meaning can be seen as both relative and absolute depending on our perspective, that perspective in turn being relative to the questions we pose rather than to the worldviews we subscribe to. Aided by the right questions, it should therefore be possible to describe the historical trajectory of a given concept while analysing it in relation to other concepts, the totality of which composes the terms of the philosophical problem we have singled out for investigation in advance. This is exactly what this book attempts to do.

But apart from philosophical reasons, there are other more pragmatic reasons for arguing in favour of conceptual autonomy, and they also have to do with our topic. If indeed the state concept is an unquestioned foundation of political discourse, this could hardly be expected to be visible in the manifest content of that discourse, since being unquestioned implies being unspoken, and being unspoken means being a condition of speech rather than its object. A denial of conceptual autonomy would hence rule out the concepts being foundational and constitutive by definitional fiat. In this case, conceptual autonomy would allow for the possibility that some concepts might indeed be foundational to and constitutive of political discourse without this implying that they were timeless or necessary. Simply put, granting concepts a certain autonomy can help us to chase the ghosts out of political discourse without ourselves retreating back into the province of *Geistesgeschichte* while doing so.

---

[29] I have dealt with this problem in *A Genealogy of Sovereignty* (Cambridge: Cambridge University Press, 1995), ch. 3.

Unfortunately, today the history of political thought is torn between the methodological principles handed down to us by contextualist history, conceptual history and discourse analysis respectively, each either explicitly or implicitly denying this possibility. Apart from their obvious differences, these approaches share a strong suspicion of concepts as units of investigation: concepts are not autonomous and should not be studied as if they existed independently of other discursive or non-discursive entities.[30] This recommendation is thought of as an important safeguard against anachronism and outright whiggery in historical writing, and disobeying it is thought to lead straight back to the position that concepts indeed contain a hard core of timeless connotations – connotations signalling the presence of perennial problems, immutable institutions or transcendental subjects in history.

My contention is that while the suspicion against the realist or transcendentalist view of concepts as containers of timeless connotations is certainly justified because of the philosophical obligations these options bring with them, subsequent and reductionist attempts to understand conceptual change with reference to other entities themselves bring with them philosophical commitments uncongenial both to historical openness and to philosophical analysis. The existing linguistically oriented study of political thought not only precludes that concepts could or should be autonomous, but also that concepts and their change are best understood by reducing their meaning to changes among other, presumably more basic, entities; whereas contextualism takes conceptual meaning to be epiphenomenal to utterances, conceptual history insists on its dependence on human experience, while discourse analysis finally regards concepts as functions of statements. And whereas contextualism accounts for conceptual change with reference to the interplay between agency and context, conceptual history does so with reference to changing historical experiences, while discourse analysis explains conceptual change with reference to the changing rules of discourse.[31]

---

[30] For an analysis of the affinities between contextualism and conceptual history see Melvin Richter, *The History of Political and Social Concepts: a Critical Introduction* (New York: Oxford University Press, 1995), ch. 6.

[31] For these positions and their evolution, see John Dunn, 'The Identity of the History of Ideas', in P. Laslett, W. G. Runciman and Q. Skinner (eds.), *Philosophy, Politics and Society*, 4th series (Oxford: Blackwell, 1972), pp. 158–73; Quentin Skinner, 'Conventions and the Understanding of Speech-acts', *Philosophical Quarterly*, vol. 20, 1970, no. 79, pp. 118–38; Quentin Skinner, 'On Performing and Explaining Linguistic Actions', *Philosophical Quarterly*, vol. 21, 1971, no. 82, pp. 1–21; Quentin Skinner, 'Meaning and Understanding in the History of Ideas', in James Tully (ed.), *Meaning and Context: Quentin Skinner and his Critics* (Cambridge: Polity Press, 1988), pp. 29–67; Quentin Skinner, 'Some Problems in the Analysis of Political Thought and Action', in Tully, *Meaning and Context*, pp. 97–118; Quentin Skinner, 'Language and Social Change', in Tully, *Meaning*

Now being reductive about concepts is not a vice in itself. Indeed, it may be a sound option, provided the only alternatives are a conceptual realism that reifies concepts into abstract things or a conceptual idealism that turns them into transcendental conditions of human knowledge.[32] Yet it was precisely the perceived necessity of such a dull choice that once brought about the linguistic turn within the history of political thought, and which eventually made it so suspect to talk of conceptual autonomy.[33] But contrary to their promises, each of the above approaches fails to notice that it carries ontological commitments which are detrimental to the same historical openness that constitutes their common rationale, and this for the following reasons.

First, by being reductive, the above approaches simply preclude the possibility that concepts could be seen as constitutive rather than derivative. Being reductive about concepts entails a sharp disjunction between them and what they are supposedly reducible to, such as utterances, experiences or statements. Put into practice, such a disjunction brings historical closure, since it makes it difficult to decipher vocabularies informed by a different understanding of the relationship between concepts and other

and Context, pp. 119–32; Reinhart Koselleck and Hans-Georg Gadamer, Hermeneutik und Historik (Heidelberg: Carl Winter, 1987); Reinhart Koselleck, 'Linguistic Change and the History of Events', Journal of Modern History, vol. 61, 1989, no. 4, pp. 649–68; James Farr, 'Understanding Conceptual Change Politically', in Ball et al., Political Innovation and Conceptual Change, pp. 24–49; Melvin Richter, 'Reconstructing the History of Political Languages: Pocock, Skinner and the Geschichtliche Grundbegriffe', History and Theory, vol. 24, 1990, no. 1, pp. 38–70; see also Melvin Richter, 'Conceptual History (Begriffsgeschichte) and Political Theory', Political Theory, vol. 14, 1986, no. 4, pp. 604–37; Reinhart Koselleck, 'Begriffsgeschichte and Social History', in Futures Past: on the Semantics of Historical Time (Boston, MA: MIT Press, 1985), pp. 73–91; J. G. A. Pocock, 'The State of the Art', in his Virtue, Commerce and History (Cambridge: Cambridge University Press, 1985), pp. 1–33; J. G. A. Pocock, 'The Concept of Language and the Métier d'Historien: some Considerations on Practice', in A. Pagden (ed.), The Languages of Political Theory in Early Modern Europe (Cambridge: Cambridge University Press, 1987), pp. 19–38; Michel Foucault, The Archaeology of Knowledge (New York: Pantheon Books, 1972); Gilles Deleuze, Foucault, trans. S. Hand (Minneapolis, MN: University of Minnesota Press, 1988), pp. 8–22; Hubert L. Dreyfus and Paul Rabinow, Michel Foucault: beyond Structuralism and Hermeneutics (Chicago, IL: University of Chicago Press, 1982); Tom Rockmore, 'Subjectivity and the Ontology of History', The Monist, vol. 74, 1991, no. 2, pp. 187–205; Michael S. Roth, Knowing and History: Appropriations of Hegel in Twentieth-Century France (Ithaca, NY: Cornell University Press, 1988), pp. 189–224; Peter Shöttler, 'Historians and Discourse Analysis', History Workshop, 1989, no. 27, pp. 37–62.

[32] Cf. Jacques Derrida, 'Structure, Sign and Play in the Discourse of the Human Sciences', in Writing and Difference (London: Routledge, 1978), pp. 292–3; Hans-Georg Gadamer, Hegel's Dialectic: Five Hermeneutical Studies (New Haven, CT: Yale University Press, 1976), pp. 75–99.

[33] For an overview, see John E. Toews, 'Intellectual History after the Linguistic Turn: the Autonomy of Meaning and the Irreducibility of Experience', American Historical Review, vol. 92, 1987, no. 4, pp. 879–907.

entities. In other words, being reductive about concepts makes it hard to make unbiased sense of discourses themselves informed by a nonreductive understanding of concepts, and that is another strong reason to view the relationship between concepts and other things as fundamentally open to investigation.

In our present context, a reductionist understanding of concepts is bound to create historiographical problems. I started this section by pointing to the dilemma that arises when we try to write the history of twentieth-century discourse, since this discourse also seems to condition our historiographical possibilities. This dilemma can now be spelled out in more precise terms. Since our current reductionist convictions about concepts evolved out of a polemic against an understanding of concepts as ontologically autonomous, and since that latter understanding has conditioned a fair share of contemporary political discourse, a reductionist history of that discourse would necessarily be but an extension of that polemic, thus, and contrary to what the reductionists promise us, invariably reflecting present concerns while distorting those of the near past. The result will be a historiography that is implicitly debunking of those philosophical positions out of which our present way of doing the history of political ideas evolved in opposition.

Since this book deals with parts of political discourse that are still very much part of our present, it is imperative to avoid this kind of bias. Arguably, the changing meaning and function of the state concept within modern political discourse is to a considerable extent conditioned by underlying changes in the way the relationship between concepts and other entities has been conceptualized throughout the past century, and reconstructing these changes therefore in turn demands that we remain as agnostic as we possibly can about the ontological status of concepts.

Second, what the above approaches tend to overlook is that those entities – utterances, experiences or statements – which are assumed to condition concepts and their meaning are not only nothing but concepts themselves, but are also used as metahistorical concepts whose range of application is constantly extended far beyond the context of *their* invention. Thus, in the final analysis, concepts constitute the horizon of possible intelligibility; without positing concepts as either the topic or resource of analysis, both the history and structure of political discourse would be difficult, if not impossible, to subject to analysis. Therefore, a strong case could be made in favour of the view that concepts are not only autonomous in relation to other things, but that they enjoy a certain primacy as well, since in order to be intelligible, things simply have to be conceptualized.

But how to argue in favour of the autonomy and primacy of concepts while avoiding the twin pitfalls of conceptual realism and conceptual idealism, and how to reconcile our historical and our philosophical viewpoints? If we want to make the case for conceptual autonomy, we have to conceptualize concepts without turning them either into abstract things or into conditions of subjectivity, while simultaneously safeguarding both historical openness and the possibility of philosophical judgement.

A first step towards solving this problem would be to distinguish carefully between two different ways of vindicating conceptual autonomy, one socially constructivist and the other logically constructivist. According to the first way, concepts should be conceptualized as autonomous by virtue of the fact that the world itself ultimately consists of autonomous concepts, or that reality is ultimately reducible to such autonomous concepts. Following this route, concepts can be made to look autonomous because their essence is essential to the way the world really is and to the way we conceive it to be. While this way of reasoning would affirm the autonomy of concepts by affirming their 'reality', it would do so by positing a sharp distinction between the real and the constructed, and then assimilate concepts to the order of the former while analysing them within the order of the latter.

The second, logically constructivist, justification of conceptual autonomy would begin by pointing out that the above distinction between the real and the constructed itself has to be conceptualized in order to become operative within discourse. A consistent logical constructivism would then proceed by arguing that this goes for the rest of the world as well. Whether essentially conceptual or not, the world has to be conceptualized in order to be intelligible, and this is done through the construction of concepts. Questions of being and knowing presuppose conceptualization, and the prior construction of concepts is a necessary condition of answering them. Such a logically constructivist defence of conceptual autonomy does not necessitate any commitment to the ontological primacy of concepts, nor does it entail any commitment as to their possible content. What is of interest to the conceptualist is how concepts are formed and transformed, and their changing place within larger conceptual edifices, but not what kind of stuff they are ultimately composed of.

Unlike other varieties of linguistically oriented study of political thought, this view does not cancel out the possibility of concepts having reference, but regards this possibility as wholly internal to the world of concepts. Whereas contextualism would turn the question of reference into a question of how the criteria for applying a given concept vary across different contexts, and while discourse analysis construes the possibility of reference as a function of discourse and its rules, the kind of conceptualism suggested here makes reference itself a matter of conceptualization. That is, concepts do refer to classes of objects, but since it takes the concept of reference to establish such a relation between what we find in the purely logical domain of conceptual relations and what we find outside that domain by means of concepts, concepts potentially refer outside themselves only by virtue of being internally and ultimately self-referential. Reference is a function of concepts rather than conversely, and the class of objects to which a given concept happens to refer is a class of objects only by virtue of being conceptualized as such.

In order to become accessible to historical and philosophical analysis, concepts must therefore be understood as wholly independent of both signifier and signified. As Deleuze and Guattari have argued, every concept has a finite number of components and is defined by them, and these components come from other concepts. Every concept is a point of coincidence of the components which it shares with other concepts, and overlaps with these other concepts. Thus, concepts have no intrinsic meaning, but draw together multiple components from other concepts and furnish them with meaning. Yet every concept is autonomous, since it renders components from other concepts inseparable within itself; concepts are both heterogeneous and at least potentially consistent. And conversely: a given set of concepts cannot be defined except by a concept that forms part of this set, since concepts posit themselves and their objects at the same time as they are constructed.[34] As Deleuze and Guattari go on to explain,

[t]he concept is therefore both absolute and relative: it is relative to its own components, to other concepts, to the plane on which it is defined, and to the problems it is supposed to resolve; but it is absolute through the condensation it carries out, the site it occupies on the plane, and the conditions it assigns to the problem. As a whole it is absolute, but in so far as it is fragmentary it is relative.[35]

We are now in a position to effect a working compromise between historical and philosophical perspectives within the study of political thought and to dissolve the principal ground of their disagreement. A conceptualist interpretation of concepts along the lines proposed above will permit us to reconcile these viewpoints if we are willing to accept its basic precepts: if concepts posit themselves and their objects at the same time as they are constructed, the historical and philosophical analysis of concepts is necessarily immanent in character. This means that the entities invoked when describing and explaining the formation and transformation of concepts are only instrumental in this respect to the extent that

[34] Gilles Deleuze and Félix Guattari, *What is Philosophy?* (London: Verso, 1994), pp. 17ff.
[35] *Ibid.*, pp. 18, 21.

they have been conceptualized simultaneously with the concepts under investigation, and are situated on the same plane of immanence as these. In the final analysis, this implies that conceptual transformation ought to be explained by itself, that is, with reference to concepts and their changing relations on the same plane of immanence. The requirement of logical immanence thus means that the concepts which we study as well as those we use to describe and explain conceptual change are regarded as part of the same conceptual edifice, and not as arbitrarily compartmentalized into topic and resource.

Accepting this precept means that the history of conceptual formation and transformation is nothing more than the history of their changing relations brought about by the activities of conceptualization and reconceptualization, and that the philosophy of concepts is nothing more than the consistent and coherent ordering of those relations by the same means. Within this view, the historical and the philosophical perspectives look mutually implicating rather than fundamentally opposed: all historicity requires the conceptualization of a hard metahistorical core from which historicization can proceed, and the philosophical conceptualization of that core can only take place by means of concepts, the meaning of which has been shaped through their historical trajectory and intersection with other concepts. We must therefore revise Nietzsche's dictum, because even if only that which has no history can be defined, only that which has already been defined can be turned into history.

But does all this not amount to a reification of concepts? Yes and no. Yes, because a method that grants autonomy and primacy to concepts is susceptible to the same kind of criticism to which it subjects its rivals, namely, that no analytical categories can be ontologically and ethically innocent. No, because concepts are of this world: they are general names of things and ideas, not general things or general ideas to be named. Concepts may structure discourse, but they do not enjoy any existence outside the texts in which they figure any more than the rules of grammar exist outside language; they are ideal without being abstract. In practical terms, this means that concepts – in order to qualify as autonomous objects of investigation – must be present on the surface of the texts brought under investigation, and have their meaning and function enabled and circumscribed by the definitions and their usage in those texts.

Analysing the concept of the state beyond *Sattelzeit*

Now if we assumed that statism was indeed pervasive in modern political discourse, what would that tell us about our present and ourselves? I started this chapter by arguing that the phenomenon of statism is symptomatic of a general ambivalence concerning the question of political authority within modern political discourse, and then went on to argue that the tendency to presuppose the state within political discourse is a way of positing constituting authority prior to any constituted authority. I finally pointed to the role of criticism in sustaining this authority by ritually questioning it, and ended by outlining a few mechanisms that have contributed to its reproduction. Let us now elaborate this set of assumptions by contrasting them with another hypothesis about conceptual change during modernity.

According to this hypothesis, a swift and profound rearrangement took place in political discourse between 1750 and 1850. During that period, political concepts were temporalized, in so far as they ceased to be containers of particular experiences, and instead became carriers of general expectation. They were also democraticized in terms of their usage and reference, so that they came to encompass and describe institutions and practices previously beyond the scope of political discourse. This also made concepts susceptible to ideologization, since they were drawn together, generalized and given more abstract meaning within vocabularies aspiring to universality. But most importantly, political concepts were politicized in the sense that their meaning and reference became increasingly contestable and opened up to divergent and contradictory interpretations by new constellations of interest.[36]

What is striking about this hypothesis is the fact that the concepts used in the characterization of this transformation themselves emerged and took on metahistorical significance simultaneously with the change they were used to portray. Their own historicity is thus subdued in the above account as a consequence of the commitments inherent in the method of *Begriffsgeschichte*; they are treated as historical invariants by means of which history is written, not as potential objects of investigation in themselves.

To the conceptualist, the most fundamental dimension of change in political discourse is change in what counts as political discourse and what is not conceptualized or conceptualizable under that name. The change described above presupposes that the concept of the political has

---

[36] Reinhart Koselleck, 'Einleitung', in O. Brunner, W. Conze and Reinhart Koselleck (eds.), *Geschichtliche Grundbegriffe. Historisches Lexicon zur Politisch-Sozialen Sprache in Deutschland* (Stuttgart: Klett-Cotta, 1972–1997), vol. I, pp. xvi–xvii; Reinhart Koselleck, '"Space of Experience" and "Horizon of Expectation": Two Historical Categories', in *Futures Past*, pp. 267–88; Reinhart Koselleck, '"Neuzeit"': Remarks on the Semantics of the Modern Concepts of Movement', in *Futures Past*, pp. 231–66.; cf. also Paul Ricœur, *Time and Narrative* (Chicago, IL: University of Chicago Press, 1988), vol. III, pp. 208f.; Helga Nowotny, *Time: the Modern and Postmodern Experiences* (Oxford: Polity Press, 1994), ch. 2.

already been reconceptualized to encompass domains of discourse previously excluded from it, and it is likely that this reconceptualization was simultaneous with changes in the structure of epistemic concepts, so that it became increasingly possible to conceptualize the difference between political and scientific discourse in seemingly apolitical terms.[37]

But what happened after 1850? This book does not attempt to contest the validity of the above hypothesis, its main upshot being that what was accomplished by the bright side of the Enlightenment has partly been reversed as a consequence of the broad tendency towards scientification that took place after 1850 within social and political discourse. Using the state concept as an example, I shall argue that the creation of a discourse on politics that aspires to be scientific has contributed to a discursive enforcement of the forbidden impossibility referred to above, and that this in turn is indicative of a reversal of the contestability and openness believed to characterize post-Enlightenment political discourse.

The fate of the state concept aptly illustrates what happens to a political concept when it is removed from contestation in the name of scientific clarity, and what happens to our ability to rephrase our most basic political concerns in the light of new experiences. As I shall contend, the fate of the state concept may help us understand what happens when a genuinely political problem – that of political order understood in terms of authority and community – is dressed up as a scientific one, thus decreasing its 'political' potential. Thus, to my mind, the phenomenon of statism ultimately represents an unintended consequence of the fulfilment of one of the rosiest promises of modernity. Indeed, the attainment of scientific knowledge of the political world has brought with it a depoliticization of the most fundamental political concepts, all while the spirit of criticism pushing this scientification forward has reinforced their constituting authority.

In the previous section, I argued that a conceptualist focus on the state concept will help us understand the phenomenon of statism better. But how should we proceed in actual practice? I have already warned against easy ways out. Given my definition of statism as the presupposed presence of the state, nothing would be easier than to declare large parts of modern political discourse statist and then dismiss them on some ideological ground. This is the way of those of a utopian disposition, who feel imprisoned within the conceptual boundaries of the sovereign state. That the existence of the state has been accepted as a point of departure by many scholars within many subfields of modern political science is hardly

---

[37] Cf. Zygmunt Bauman, *Legislators and Interpreters* (Oxford: Polity Press, 1987), pp. 96–109.

a particularly interesting observation, since all inquiry simply has to start from somewhere in order to get anywhere: it is like accusing chemists of being atomists.

The hard but honest way out would be if we could show that even those who have struggled hard to reconceptualize the state and political order have failed to escape statism themselves, and especially when that has been their aim. Contrary to widespread belief, state criticism and attempts to transcend statist notions of political order are not intellectual practices pioneered by poststructuralists during the last decade, but form an important current in modern political thought in general, and in twentieth-century political science in particular. As I stated above, whereas this current is far from homogeneous in terms of ontological presuppositions and ideological implications, it is nevertheless held together by a common critical spirit that seems to gravitate towards the state just in order to breathe life into it through the unmasking gestures characteristic of that spirit. I imagine that this is what Foucault once refused to deal with, and referred to as the indigestible meal, that is, theories of the state.

Nevertheless, I would like to venture beyond the loose topic that normally organizes textbooks in state theory by suggesting that this discourse has evolved as a fairly systematic response to existing conceptualizations of the state, and that the place and function of the state concept within that discourse have in turn been shaped by these strategies. Simply put, the state concept both conditions and is conditioned by different rhetorical moves within the discourse on the state.

Even if these strategies for unveiling the 'true nature of the state' are perfectly able to coexist and compete within contemporary political discourse, thanks to the ambiguity they together sustain, and even if these strategies were once conceptualized within radically different contexts reflecting radically different concerns, I shall emphasize the logic of unintended implications that has constantly urged reconceptualizations of the state within as well as between these contexts, in a certain chronological order.

In the next chapter, I shall describe how the state concept became constitutive of modern political science in its quest for disciplinary identity, thus arguing that the emergence of statism coincides with the constitution of politics as an autonomous field of scientific knowledge.

Chapter 3 deals with the efforts to excommunicate the state concept from mainstream political science. In line with the state-bashing credo, many of the most celebrated scientific achievements of modern political science became possible only as a consequence of such a successful excommunication. As I shall argue, however, these efforts were largely futile. The superficial conviction that the state concept was redundant to an understanding of politics did not imply that the concept of the state simply vanished from political discourse, only that it was repositioned and came to exert its influence from another and perhaps safer place in a larger conceptual edifice.

Chapter 4 describes the reaction to this marginalization. When the state was brought back into analytical focus, the effort to throw it out was largely interpreted as a way of concealing its capitalist character. What was desired was a concept of the state that could make sense both of its fundamental dependence upon society *and* its capacity for autonomous action. As I shall argue, the attempt to bring the state back in was largely counterproductive, in so far as it left its proponents with an indivisible remainder whose existence could not be explained with reference to the reproductive requirements of capitalist society.

Chapter 5 analyses roughly contemporary attempts to dissolve the state. Whereas both those who wanted to throw the state concept out and those who tried to bring it back in did so without letting the critical spirit touch those distinctions that conditioned its intelligibility, those who struggle to dissolve the state do so precisely by questioning the inherited analytical boundaries between the state and the international system, and between the state and society. As I shall argue, for all its intellectual merits, the attempt to dissolve the state has jeopardized our ability to reconceptualize political authority by turning statism into a self-fulfilling prophecy.

Chapter 6 is devoted to conclusions. While a wholesale reconceptualization of political order might not be within reach, I shall argue that beyond the polemics between different state critiques we find an underlying agreement as to the conceptual identity of the state, and that behind that agreement we find the *proper* identity of the state concept.

2 Unpacking the living museum

It has been common to regard modern political science as a discourse on the state, since politics and the state have frequently been defined in terms of each other. When Weber famously defined the state as a 'human community that . . . claims the monopoly of the legitimate use of physical force within a given territory', he simultaneously defined 'politics' as a 'striving to share power or striving to influence the distribution of power, either among states or among groups within a state'.[1]

Since Weber was interested in 'an empirical science of concrete reality', nothing could be more dangerous than the assumption that 'the essence of historical reality is portrayed in such theoretical constructs'. Hence, the empirical reality of the state is 'an infinity of diffuse and discrete human actions', our state concept being 'naturally always a synthesis which we construct for certain heuristic purposes'.[2] Hence, the institutional realities of the state, being an empirical concept, must not be confused with the abstract idea of the state.

The fact that this definition of the state and its epistemic underpinning seem both so clear cut and indispensable to us testifies to the ease with which it was later incorporated into the lore of mainstream political science. But what is puzzling with this definition is not what it explicitly states about the essence and function of the state, but what it takes for granted in doing so. To Weber, that politics could and should be defined in terms of the state went without saying, as did the presumption that a human community and a given territory are integral to the conceptual identity of the state. Less than self-evident to Weber and his contemporaneity but all

---

[1] Max Weber, 'Politics as a Vocation', in H. H. Gerth and C. Wright Mills (eds.), *From Max Weber: Essays in Sociology* (London: Routledge, 1948), p. 78; for a comment along lines similar to mine, see R. B. J. Walker, 'Violence, Modernity, Silence: from Max Weber to International Relations', in D. Campbell and M. Dillon (eds.), *The Political Subject of Violence* (Manchester: Manchester University Press, 1993), pp. 137–60.

[2] Max Weber, *The Methodology of the Social Sciences*, ed. E. A. Shils and H. A. Finch (New York: Free Press, 1949), pp. 72, 94, 99. For a detailed background account, see Wolfgang Schluchter, *Paradoxes of Modernity* (Stanford, CA: Stanford University Press, 1997), chs. 1–2.

the more to his posterity, however, was the assumption that this entity was knowable only in terms of the actions that constitute it, and that there is supposedly a firm divide between the idea of the state and its institutions.

What we need in order to unpack the unspoken parts of this concept is a brief prehistory that helps us to explain how its component parts were forged together, how their imagined relations were constituted and how the state thus emerged as an object of scientific inquiry. What is further needed is evidence of the claim put forward in chapter 1, namely, that the state concept was once in fact constitutive of political science and its subject matter, and that it subsequently also became an unthought foundation of political inquiry.

In this chapter, I shall analyse the conceptual antecedents of early political science. Hence, it will address itself to the concepts of state, politics and science, arguing that, to the extent to which the state concept was indeed constitutive of early political science, it provided this emergent discipline with a baseline identity, sufficient autonomy in relation to adjacent fields, as well as with scientific authority, assets which I think are indispensable to the constitution of fields of knowledge as distinct and coherent.

In the case of political science and the concept of the state, we may even speak of a double connection. Not only does this discipline gain its identity, autonomy and authority through the ontological importance given to the state concept within this discourse, but partly also through an associative and symbolic identification with the identity, autonomy and authority accorded to the state within and by that very discourse. In its early phase, the state and political science appear to be mutually conditioning through a transference of predicates from the object of knowledge to the field of knowledge constituting the state as an object, thus making the problems of state identity and disciplinary identity rhetorically as well as logically interdependent. This symbolic identification, or so I shall argue, is partly responsible for the later propensity to presuppose the presence of authority within political discourse.

Any comprehensive account of the emergence of political science is clearly beyond the scope of this chapter, however. What is of interest here is to a large extent determined by the concerns of subsequent chapters, rather than by a desire to be exhaustive or any ambition to legitimize any particular version of disciplinary identity.[3] Therefore, the

[3] This ambition is widespread; see, for example, John S. Dryzek, 'The Progress of Political Science', *Journal of Politics*, vol. 48, 1986, no. 2, pp. 301–20; John S. Dryzek and Stephen T. Leonard, 'History and Discipline in Political Science', *American Political Science Review*, vol. 82, 1988, no. 4, pp. 1245–59; James Farr, 'The History of Political Science', *American Journal of Political Science*, vol. 32, 1988, no. 4, pp. 1175–95.

following account attempts to be nothing more than a study of the conceptual birth pangs of modern political science. As such, it tries to analyse the conceptual preconditions of disciplinary identity and disciplinary boundaries, rather than the actual processes of institutionalization and professionalization.[4]

If one of the main arguments of the previous chapter was that concepts should be understood as contingent upon their changing place in relation to other concepts, I want to make an analogous case for disciplinary identity, since within this view, disciplinary identity is wholly dependent upon the concepts that are used to define and demarcate it. Disciplines come into existence as results of conceptualization, and their identity is nothing more than a set of systematic conceptual relations defined by their simultaneity. This implies that some attempts to create a science of politics which have now long been forgotten will be of interest here, while many of those attempts to conceptualize political science that appear important from the viewpoint of present versions of disciplinary identity will be neglected.[5]

Now this chapter is heavily focused on the Anglo-American context, largely because that is where the kind of disciplinary identity that will concern us in subsequent chapters first emerged. It is in this context that we find the first attempts to carve out an autonomous science of politics, aided by self-conscious disciplinary historiography and lofty declarations of independence.[6] This means that continental developments will only be dealt with to the extent that they exercised a measurable influence on these Anglo-American attempts to create such a science of politics.

Another reason for this admittedly narrow perspective is that the Anglo-American context provides us with a crucial example. That the state

---

[4] Ellen Messer-Davidow, David R. Shumway and David J. Sylvan, 'Disciplinary Ways of Knowing', in Ellen Messer-Davidow, David R. Shumway and David J. Sylvan (eds.), *Knowledges: Historical and Critical Studies in Disciplinarity* (Charlottesville, VA: University Press of Virginia, 1993), pp. 1–21.

[5] For a similar approach, see Steve Fuller, 'Disciplinary Boundaries and the Rhetoric of the Social Sciences', in Messer-Davidow *et al.*, *Knowledges*, pp. 125–49.

[6] Cf. Bernard Crick, *The American Science of Politics: its Origins and Conditions* (London: Routledge, 1959), ch. 1; Dorothy Ross, *The Origins of American Social Science* (Cambridge: Cambridge University Press, 1991), pp. 64f.; Peter T. Manicas, *A History and Philosophy of the Social Sciences* (Oxford: Basil Blackwell, 1987), pp. 213–21. This is not to imply that family-resemblant discursive formations were absent elsewhere, only that they did not acquire autonomy until much later. In Germany, the discourse on politics was heavily focused on the concept of the state, yet *Staatswissenschaften* proved incapable of asserting their autonomy in relation to jurisprudence. For an example see Georg Jellinek, *Allgemeine Staatslehre* [1900] (Berlin: O. Häring, 1905), pp. 3–23. In France, *La Science Politique* found it difficult to mark itself off from sociology; see M. Deslandres, *La Crise de la Science Politique et le Problème de la Methode* (Paris: Chevalier-Maresq, 1902).

concept was crucial to continental efforts to create a science of politics is hardly surprising, since in these contexts the experience of statehood had long made itself felt within political and legal theorizing. In America and Great Britain, however, similar experiences were largely lacking, as were distinct traditions of state theorizing, whether legal or political. It thus appears puzzling why the state concept came to occupy such a central yet ambiguous position within Anglo-American political science. Another reason has to do with the great impact American and British political science has had until quite recently on political science in other national contexts.[7] Elsewhere, where political science had difficulties in securing intellectual and institutional independence from adjacent disciplines, the impact and example of Anglo-American political science frequently proved instrumental in its quest for autonomy.

The period singled out for investigation itself poses particular problems of interpretation, since we are easily led astray by the apparent familiarity of nineteenth-century thought. Nineteenth-century texts invite retrospective readings, since the modern practice of finalist and presentist retrospective reading had its point of origin precisely in those texts, texts which habitually conceptualize a past in order to legitimize a present or a desired future. Above all, since we still owe so much to late nineteenth-century knowledge, it is constantly tempting to superimpose what in fact are outcomes of its reception upon its sources, thus overlooking or marginalizing the largely alien parts of its conceptual world.

Hence, arguably, the relationship between political science and its conceptual antecedents is much more complex than we have been led to believe by those accounts that take the identity of these antecedent concepts for granted. First, whereas there seems to be a wide agreement that the modern science of politics originates in the study of history, the fact that the concept of history itself underwent important and roughly simultaneous mutations seems to have escaped notice.[8] Second, to the extent that existing historiography speaks of the concept of the state and its role in the formation of early political science, it does so by tacitly assuming that this concept was already available as a generic category of political reflection, seemingly oblivious of how this concept was turned into a generic

---

[7] See for example Björn Wittrock, 'Discourse and Discipline: Political Science as Project and Profession', in M. Dierkes and B. Biervert, *European Social Science in Transition: Assessment and Outlook* (Boulder, CO: Westview, 1992), pp. 268–308; Björn Wittrock, 'Political Science', in UNESCO, *The Scientific and Cultural Development of Humanity*. Vol. VII: *The Social Sciences* (London: Routledge, 1997).

[8] Cf. C. Antoni, *From History to Sociology: the Transition in German Historical Thinking* (Detroit, MI: Wayne State University Press, 1959); W. G. Runciman, *Social Science and Political Theory* (Cambridge: Cambridge University Press, 1969), pp. 22ff.

concept by early political science.[9] Third, to the extent that the concept of politics figures in existing accounts, it does so as if it denoted a preexisting domain of knowledge which was entered by the founding fathers of the discipline, rather than as something laboriously conceptualized into existence by them and their immediate predecessors.[10] Fourth, to the extent that existing accounts have paid attention to the concept of science, there is a tendency to reduce the attempts to construe a science of politics to a choice between epistemic options that have come to appear as ready made and fixed to us. The epistemic change that largely attended and justified the efforts to create a science of politics has been overlooked.[11]

The state and its doubles

In chapter 1 I said that one important clue to the phenomenon of statism was to be found in the double status of the concept of the state within political knowledge. On the one hand, the state is inscribed within discourse as a potential object of knowledge whose true nature and function that discourse has as its objective to reveal. On the other hand, or so I hypothesized, the same state is inscribed as a condition of political knowledge, in so far as this concept is integral to the definition of the domain of politics and to the possibility of attaining knowledge of that domain. In this section, my task is to show how the concept of the state attained this double status as both empirical and transcendental.

As has been argued, what distinguishes the modern concept of the state from its medieval and Renaissance antecedents is the fact that it is conceptualized not in terms of rulers and ruled, but as an entity independent of both. What characterizes the modern concept of the state, writes Skinner, is

that the power of the State, not that of the ruler, came to be envisaged as the basis of government. And this in turn enabled the State to be conceptualized in distinctly modern terms – as the sole source of law and legitimate force within its own territory, and as the sole appropriate object of its citizens' allegiances.[12]

Thus, taken in its modern sense, the state is abstract, since being divorced from rulers as well as ruled, it is both a subject capable of acting

---

[9] See for example John G. Gunnell, *The Descent of Political Theory: a Genealogy of an American Vocation* (Chicago, IL: University of Chicago Press, 1993), chs. 1–2; Ross, *The Origins of American Social Science*, pp. 64f.

[10] Crick, *American Science of Politics, passim.*

[11] Manicas, *History and Philosophy*, ch. 1.

[12] Quentin Skinner, *The Foundations of Modern Political Thought* (Cambridge: Cambridge University Press, 1978), vol. I, p. x.

and an object of political action.[13] Fair enough. But as I shall argue, three important things happened to the state concept after it became abstracted from rulers and ruled; taken together, these transformations endowed the state concept with the duality necessary to its constitutive function within early political science.

First, the state concept came to internalize a certain historicity of its own, in so far as it became possible, and indeed necessary, to comprehend the state not only in terms of its history, but as nothing more than the sum of its history as reconstructed from the vantage point of that very same state. Second, and largely simultaneous with its historicization, the state concept became fused with the concept of the nation, thus establishing a firm logical and rhetorical connection between political authority and political community. Thus, whereas historicization made it possible to analyse the state as a historical phenomenon and to use the state concept generically, the fusion with the concept of nation made it possible to differentiate the state from the international system according to a dialectic between outside and inside referred to in chapter 1. Both these features would have been totally unfamiliar to a Bodin or a Hobbes, to whom the state primarily signified sovereign authority removed from the corrosiveness of historical time and in no need of either any collective identity or a demarcation between such identities and a larger system as the very basis of its existence or legitimacy.[14] Third, and as a result of the above mutations, the state could also be differentiated from civil society, conceptualized as a prima facie apolitical and autonomous sphere of human activity, yet conceived of as interdependent with the state.

Let us start with historicization. As Foucault has argued and others suggested, towards the end of the eighteenth century entire fields of knowledge and their constituent concepts were rapidly historicized, and objects became knowable only by virtue of being defined as profoundly historical beings, historical time from now on being internal to their very self-identity. Furthermore, and largely parallel to this epistemic change, human subjectivity is rendered both an object of knowledge as well as its condition of possibility.[15] The core concepts of political thought are no

[13] Skinner, *Foundations*, vol. II, pp. 350ff.; Quentin Skinner, 'The State', in Terence Ball, Russell L. Hanson and James Farr (eds.), *Political Innovation and Conceptual Change* (Cambridge: Cambridge University Press, 1989), pp. 90–131; cf. also Quentin Skinner, *Liberty before Liberalism* (Cambridge: Cambridge University Press, 1998), pp. 3–7.

[14] Cf. Gigliola Rossini, 'The Criticism of Rhetorical Historiography and the Ideal of Scientific Method: History, Nature, and Science in the Political Language of Thomas Hobbes', in A. Pagden (ed.), *The Languages of Political Theory in Early Modern Europe* (Cambridge: Cambridge University Press, 1987), pp. 303–24.

[15] Michel Foucault, *The Order of Things: an Archaeology of the Human Sciences* (London: Routledge, 1989), pp. 217ff., 312ff.; cf. Maurice Mandelbaum, *History, Man, and Reason* (Baltimore, MD: Johns Hopkins, 1974), pp. 51ff.

exception, even if their historicization obeys a slightly different chronology; I believe Koselleck to be right in arguing that previously static concepts were temporalized and connected to metahistorical assumptions about evolution and progress.[16]

Historicization has many faces. In its most general form, it breathes life into the *aporia* between being and becoming. On the one hand, that which is historicized can be thought to retain its essence through time as a condition of its intelligibility. On the other, that which is historicized may find its identity suspended in thin air, since that which was previously thought of as given and unchanging is set in historical motion, and perhaps ultimately reduced to nothing but the sum of its history.[17]

To the nineteenth century, therefore, historicization represented both a promise and a threat. It represented a promise in so far as it opened new vistas of thought and inquiry and a relentless quest for the origins of things; a threat in so far as it deprived beings of their seeming stability and simplicity. To take three statements indicative of the unfolding of this truly modern ambivalence:

Everything upon the earth is in continual flux. Nothing in it retains a form that is constant and fixed, and our affections, attached to external things, necessarily pass and change like things themselves. Always, ahead of or behind us, they recall the past which no longer exists, or they anticipate a future which often will never come to pass: there is nothing there solid enough for the heart to attach itself to.[18]

When, in former times, our ancestors thought of an antiquarian, they described him as occupied with coins, and medals, and Druid's stones; these were then the characteristic records of the decipherable past, and it was with these that decipherers busied themselves. But now there are other relics; indeed, all matter has become such.[19]

It is undeniable that in every department of thought either the objects of our present thought or our thoughts about them, or both, are conceived by us as a present that has had a past different from it.[20]

---

[16] Reinhart Koselleck, 'Einleitung', in O. Brunner, W. Conze and R. Koselleck (eds.), *Geschichtliche Grundbegriffe. Historisches Lexikon zur Politisch-Sozialen Sprache in Deutschland* (Stuttgart: Klett-Cotta, 1972–1997), vol. I, pp. xvi–xvii, and 'Staat und Souveränität', in vol. VI, p. 3.

[17] Cf. Friedrich Nietzsche, *The Will to Power* (New York: Vintage, 1968), §§ 520, 552, 574.

[18] Jean-Jacques Rousseau, *Rêveries* (Paris: Larousse, 1993): 'Tout est dans un flux continuel sur la terre: rien n'y garde une forme constante et arrêtée, et nos affections qui s'attachent aux choses extérieures passent et changent nécessairement comme elles. Toujours en avant ou en arrière de nous, elles rappellent le passé qui n'est plus ou préviennent l'avenir qui souvent ne doit point être: il n'y a rien là de solide à quoi le coeur se puisse attacher', p. 5.

[19] Walter Bagehot, *Physics and Politics: Or Thoughts on the Application of the Principles of 'Natural Selection' and 'Inheritance' to Political Society*, 3rd edn (London: Henry S. King, 1875), p. 2.

[20] Henry Sidgwick, 'The Historical Method', *Mind*, vol. 11, 1886, p. 204.

To a certain extent, the order of these statements reflects the chronological order of historicization itself, if it is indeed possible to speak of
such an order without inviting a vicious game of self-reference: what begins as a vague attitude towards the world ends up as doctrine of Being
and the conditions of knowing it. Natural history, the study of language
and the analysis of labour and wealth were all subjected to historicization,
their respective objects of investigation being conceptualized as historical
objects, with a past distinct from their present.[21]

Yet historicization was not easily accomplished in areas where the concepts of time and history had formerly been most closely associated with
otherness. Before the modern age, the concepts of political order and
history were not the good companions they later became, since historical
change constituted a threat to political order as much as the creation of
political order was a way of coping with the threats posed by such change.
While clearly beyond the scope of the present analysis, it may suffice to
briefly comment upon this relationship.

While in crucial respects interpreting the concept of time differently,
both Aristotle and Augustine understood time – and therefore also historical change – as inherently destructive, as something that undermines
both the stability of political authority and the identity of political communities. If time means change, and change brings decay to political
authority and dissolution to communities, then time is a condition that
somehow must be escaped in order to create a home for man in the world.
As Aristotle stated in his *Physics*,

A thing, then, will be affected by time, just as we are accustomed to say that time
wastes things away, and that all things grow old through time, and that there is
oblivion owing to the lapse of time ... [f]or time is by its nature the cause rather
of decay, since it is the number of change, and change removes what is.[22]

With time denied as the Other of order, the maintenance of authority and the creation of community were essentially ways of reclaiming
eternity by safeguarding authority and community against the destruc-
tion that time would ultimately bring. From Polybius and Machiavelli
to proponents of the *ius naturale* such as Grotius and Hobbes, solving
the problem of political order was therefore tantamount to finding the
proper means of escaping the inherent corrosiveness of time. Without a

---

[21] Foucault, *Order of Things*, pp. 250–302; cf. also Dietrich von Engelhardt, 'Historical Consciousness in the German Romantic *Naturforschung*', in Andrew Cunningham
and Nicholas Jardine (eds.), *Romanticism and the Sciences* (Cambridge: Cambridge
University Press, 1990), pp. 55–68; Jacques Roger, 'The Living World', in G. S.
Rousseau and Roy Porter (eds.), *The Ferment of Knowledge: Studies in the Historiography of Eighteenth-Century Science* (Cambridge: Cambridge University Press, 1980),
pp. 255–83.
[22] Aristotle, *Physics* (Bloomington, IN: Indiana University Press, 1969), 222[b].

firm foothold in the cosmos or any recourse to timeless principles, individual political communities would inevitably rise and fall according to a preestablished pattern of growth and decay, every instance of which could be explained and justified with reference to the historical inevitability and immutability of such a pattern. Thus, the creation of political order was a way of coping with human finitude in general, and, as it were, a way of achieving immortality at the level of community.[23]

Beginning in the eighteenth century, the relationship between history and political order underwent a profound transformation: from having been the very antitheses of order, the concepts of time and history become sources of sameness, or at least of promises of its perpetual return. Historical time is now tied to expectations of a new and different future, but of a future in which the most cherished traits of present identities are also conserved or refined. All that was solid certainly melted into air in this process, yet everything previously considered fluid simultaneously became petrified, since time itself took on the quality of a thing. As we shall see, there remains a strong tension between the demands of political order and the recognition of its inherent temporality; yet early political science derived much of its scientific authority from its attempt to reconcile these demands by means of the concepts of order and progress.

Using Pocock's terminology, one could perhaps characterize the period after the French Revolution as a period when concepts of authority were removed from the dimension of contingency and reinscribed within the dimension of continuity.[24] As we shall see below, the net result of this change was that the concepts of state and history became closely intertwined. Not only was the state turned into a historical being and history interpreted as the successive unfolding of the state in time, but also, and more intriguingly, the presence of the state became a condition of possible history, in so far as its existence became integral to the possibility of historical knowledge as much as it was an object of the same knowledge. Thus, and already by virtue of being historicized, the state concept becomes a dual one: it signifies a condition of knowledge as well as an object of inquiry.

This historical understanding of the state and state-centric understanding of history are closely related to another major change in the structure

---

[23] Cf. John G. Gunnell, *Political Philosophy and Time: Plato and the Origins of Political Vision* (Chicago, IL: University of Chicago Press, 1987), pp. 225f.; J. G. A. Pocock, *The Machiavellian Moment: Florentine Political Thought and the Atlantic Republican Tradition* (Princeton, NJ: Princeton University Press, 1975), pp. 75ff., 150ff.

[24] J. G. A. Pocock, 'Modes of Political and Historical Time in Early Eighteenth-Century England', in *Virtue, Commerce, and History: Essays on Political Thought and History, Chiefly in the Eighteenth Century* (Cambridge: Cambridge University Press, 1985), pp. 92–3.

of sociopolitical concepts: the fusion of the concepts of state and nation. Yet much of what had happened to the state concept in terms of
historicization had already happened to earlier notions of political community, even if it took some time before these mutations were taken up
and brought to bear upon discourses on authority. For example, it is
well known that from Vico to Herder, the concept of nation gradually
emerges as a profoundly historical identity, nationhood being expressed
in linguistic traits and popular customs evolving from a common ancestry,
and reflecting manifest and irreducible differences between peoples.[25]

By outlining a comprehensive general narrative of human community,
Vico was able to describe the evolution of specific political communities
as if their individual histories conformed to a general pattern underlying
their actual diversity. Each community has an individual trajectory within
this universal history, since 'the nature of institutions is nothing but their
coming into being at certain times and in certain guises'.[26] Yet simultaneously, all human communities traverse the same ideal and universal
pattern in time, so that '[o]ur science therefore comes to describe at the
same time an ideal eternal history traversed in time by the history of every
nation'.[27]

Thus, by arranging political communities in a parallel series reflecting
a totality of human experience, and inscribing this totality within a universal history, historical time becomes a principle of identity rather than
the antithesis of political order. But while contributing to a rephrasing
of the problem of community, the resulting historicization of communities did not bring it closer to any stable solution. Rather the contrary: if
concepts of political community are grafted on to a plane of historicity,
this implies that such a historicized notion of community can hardly be
used to *justify* particular forms of authority, since any such move exposes
that authority to the same profound historicity, thereby depriving it of
timelessness and thus of any transhistorical legitimacy. If mores vary and
laws necessarily with them, it is difficult to see how and why a certain
arrangement of authority and community could be expected to retain its
essential sameness through time; if the ultimate conditions of political

---

[25] See for example Giambattista Vico, *The New Science* [1725] (Ithaca, NY: Cornell Uni-
versity Press, 1968), § 915; Johann Gottfried Herder, 'Yet Another Philosophy of
History', in F. M. Barnard (ed.), *J. G. Herder on Social and Political Culture*
(Cambridge: Cambridge University Press, 1969). Cf. also Isaiah Berlin, *Vico and Herder:
Two Studies in the History of Ideas* (London: Hogarth Press, 1976), pp. 145f.; F. M.
Barnard, 'National Culture and Political Legitimacy: Herder and Rousseau', *Journal of
the History of Ideas*, vol. 44, 1983, no. 2, pp. 231–53; also Georg G. Iggers, *The German
Conception of History: the National Tradition of Historical Thought from Herder to the Present*
(Middletown, NJ: Wesleyan University Press, 1968), pp. 29–43.
[26] Vico, *New Science*, § 147.
[27] *Ibid.*, § 349.

order vary across history, any such order becomes difficult to legitimize in other than strictly temporal and therefore also contingent terms.

The fictitious reconciliation of historicized communities with equally timely and profanized authority had to await the French Revolution for its realization. As Hont has described the final discursive enactment of the nation state, it was the outcome of deliberate efforts on behalf of Sieyès and others to make sense of popular sovereignty, and to justify it by means of a particular account of popular representation within the state. Whereas Rousseau had tried and ultimately failed to account for the possibility of popular sovereignty by locating it directly in the laws of the state, the project of Sieyès was to redefine the identity of the community in such a way that it could serve as the ultimate source and locus of sovereignty. But rather than focusing on the nature of the representer, Sieyès struggled to reconceptualize the Third Estate as the very totality of citizens, together constituting a nation to be represented.[28]

To Sieyès, the nation is a genuinely political community. It is nothing more than 'a fairly considerable number of isolated individuals who wish to unite', but who have become unable to 'exercise their common will easily by themselves', since they are 'now too numerous and occupy too large an area'.[29] Their will thus has to be represented by a representative body, which 'must partake of the same *nature*, the same *proportions* and the same *rules*'.[30] As Wokler has remarked on this fusion of state and nation,

[i]n addition to superimposing undivided rule upon its subjects, the genuinely modern state further requires that those who fall under its authority be united themselves – that they form one people, one nation, morally bound together by a common identity... the modern state generally requires that the represented be a moral person as well, national unity going hand in hand with the political unity of the state.[31]

Yet there is more to this fusion than a mere successful rhetorical performance, since this reconceptualization posed a particular problem that

---

[28] István Hont, 'The Permanent Crisis of a Divided Mankind: "Contemporary Crisis of the Nation State" in Historical Perspective', *Political Studies*, vol. 42, special issue, 1994, pp. 184, 188–90, 202–4; cf. also Pasquale Pasquino, 'Emmanuel Sieyès, Benjamin Constant et le "Gouvernement de Modernes"', *Revue Française de Science Politique*, vol. 37, 1987, pp. 214–28.

[29] Emmanuel Joseph Sieyès, *What is the Third Estate?*, trans. M. Blondel (London: Pall Mall Press, 1963), pp. 121–2.

[30] *Ibid.*, p. 137.

[31] Robert Wokler, 'The Enlightenment and the French Revolutionary Birth Pangs of Modernity', in Johan Heilbron, Lars Magnusson and Björn Wittrock (eds.), *The Rise of the Social Sciences and the Formation of Modernity* (Dordrecht: Kluwer, 1998); see also Robert Wokler, 'Contextualizing Hegel's Phenomenology of the French Revolution and the Terror', *Political Theory*, vol. 26, 1998, no. 1, pp. 33–55.

was as much logical as it was rhetorical in character. Even if the identity of the nation could not be treated as a given, it had to be presupposed in order to become operative as a source of authority and persuasive as its locus. As such, this problem is analogous to that of legitimizing author- ity *ex nihilo*, since the nation in this case has to be the source of its own identity before it can be the source of any authority. As Sieyès himself ex- plains, '[t]he nation is prior to everything. It is the source of everything. Its will is always legal; indeed, it is the law itself.'[32]

Yet if the identity of the nation is explained with reference to itself, its authority to demarcate and actualize itself is not. To Sieyès, the concept of nation is profoundly dual. On the one hand, it figures as the ultimate source of all authority, thus conditioning the possibility of the political order. On the other, the nation is supposed to be the outcome of the revolutionary recognition game that constitutes the nation in time by an exclusion of the privileged orders from it. What we have here is thus the logical antecedent of the forbidden impossibility that characterizes modern political discourse in its relationship to authority; the *demos* of modern representative democracy is instituted through an act of inter- pretive violence that renders its origin logically opaque.

Consequently, the solution proposed by Sieyès is circular: the nation is capable of realizing itself in time only by virtue of being something more than a multitude of particular wills together composing the Third Estate, yet the only warrant of this assumption lies in the expectation of its realization in time. Following the logic of this solution, the sovereign authority of the state becomes premised upon the identity of the nation as much as the identity of the nation becomes derivative of the sovereign au- thority of the state, so that the concept of a nation state comes to express nothing more than a vaguely tautological relationship between two enti- ties which are merely numerically distinct from each other. Thus, while Skinner is certainly right to characterize the modern state as an entity conceptually divorced from both rulers and ruled, this conceptualization paved the way for the post-revolutionary symbolic identification of rulers and ruled within it, brought about by the fusion of state and nation.

Once conceptualized as a fusion of identity and authority in time, the state was to become the chief object of early political science in its quest for identity. But in order to become such an object, the state had to be marked off from what was outside it on its inside: civil society.

Here Hegel appears as the vanishing mediator. Having left his im- print on modernity and its conception of political order, his reinterpre- tation of the state became self-evident to the extent that its status as an

---

[32] Sieyès, *What is the Third Estate?*, p. 124.

interpretation was soon forgotten. As he famously stated in the preface to his *Philosophy of Right* (1821), its task was 'to comprehend and portray the state as an inherently rational entity'.[33] What is of interest here is not the internal validity of the result of this attempt, but its discursive implications and hence its effective truth; in this and subsequent chapters, we will constantly be reminded of how much the spectres of Hegel still haunt us, and how much Hegel's solution to the problem of political order came to be constitutive of subsequent reformulations of it. In this restricted sense, we are all heirs to Hegel by virtue of being moderns, if being modern means something as simple yet strange as being citizens of states.

The basics of Hegel's conceptualization of the modern state are well known. As a first step, the state is first separated from and then elevated above civil society as an independent source of both authority and community. The state is more real than any of its components or their sum total, since it is 'an external necessity and the higher power to whose nature their laws and interests are subordinate and on which they depend'.[34] This ontological subordination of civil society to the state simultaneously furnishes 'the scientific proof of the concept of the state'.[35] As a second step, the state and the nation are identified as two sides of the same coin within the context of world history, so that 'the being-for-itself of the actual spirit has its existence in this independence, the latter is the primary freedom and supreme dignity of a nation'.[36] Within this view, the state is not only a concrete political institution, but also the proper *telos* of world history. In the history of the world, writes Hegel, 'the *Individuals* we have to do with are *Peoples*; Totalities that are States'.[37] Thus, 'only those peoples can come under our notice which form a state. For it must be understood that this latter is the realization of Freedom, *i.e.* of the absolute final aim, and that it exists for its own sake.'[38]

To Hegel, the state is an individual totality, its institutional reality coinciding perfectly with its idea by virtue of being its fulfilment. This conception implies that the state cannot be grasped by analysing its particular institutional components in isolation, since the state is something more than the sum of its components. Rather, it is the state that draws these components together and organizes them into a coherent whole. Its fundamental nature is moral: by virtue of being a synthesis between freedom and necessity, the state represents a viewpoint made necessary

---

[33] G. W. F. Hegel, *The Philosophy of Right* (Cambridge: Cambridge University Press, 1991), preface, p. 21.

[34] *Ibid.*, § 261, italics deleted.

[35] *Ibid.*, § 256.

[36] *Ibid.*, § 322, italics deleted.

[37] G. W. F. Hegel, *The Philosophy of History* (Buffalo, NY: Prometheus, 1991), p. 14.

[38] *Ibid.*, p. 39.

by and indispensable to reason itself. The Hegelian concept of the state is thus simultaneously historical and generic. It is immanent and historical in so far as it refers to an institution which has supposedly evolved out of successive historical stages, if only to reach completion and perfection during modernity. It is transcendental and generic in so far as it is a principle of identity and the ultimate goal of history, and thus the point from which history can be narrated as a march towards rational freedom.[39]

To Hegel, therefore, the state indeed is and ought to be second nature to us as truly ethical beings precisely because it bridges the lacuna between is and ought. This second nature is an inescapable condition of modernity: during modernity, man cannot attain self-identity except within the state, and the state can attain its universality only by virtue of being instantiated in the individual.[40] So instead of being an individual person writ large as in Hobbes, the state now furnishes the very principle of personal identity and individual autonomy: the individual becomes the state writ small. As Schiller expressed this connection between man and state:

Every individual human being, one may say, carries within him, potentially and prescriptively, an ideal man, the archetype of a human being, and it is his life's task to be, through all his changing manifestations, in harmony with the unchanging unity of this ideal. This archetype, which is to be discerned more or less clearly in every individual, is represented by the State, the objective and, as it were, canonical form in which all the diversity of individual subjects strive to unite. One can, however, imagine two different ways in which man existing in time can coincide with man as an Idea, and, in consequence, just as many ways in which the State can assert itself in individuals: either by the ideal man suppressing empirical man, and the State annulling individuals; or else by the individual himself becoming the State, and man in time being ennobled to the stature of man as Idea.[41]

So if history is understood as the gradual realization of reason in the guise of the modern nation state, then this history takes on meaning and intelligibility only from the vantage point of the state, and if our present is only intelligible in the light of that history, that present also signifies that statehood has become an inescapable part of the modern condition and the sole source of its intelligibility.[42] Thus, implicit in this concept of the

---

[39] See for example Shlomo Avineri, *Hegel's Theory of the Modern State* (Cambridge: Cambridge University Press, 1979); Fred R. Dallamayr, *G. W. F. Hegel: Modernity and Politics* (London: Sage, 1993), pp. 135ff.

[40] Hegel, *Philosophy of History*, pp. 40, 52.

[41] Friedrich Schiller, *On the Aesthetic Education of Man*, ed. E. Wilkinson and L. Willoughby (Oxford, 1967), pp. 17–19, quoted in Laurence Dickey, *Hegel: Religion, Economics, and the Politics of Spirit 1770–1807* (Cambridge: Cambridge University Press, 1987), p. 258.

[42] Hegel, *Philosophy of History*, pp. 46–7.

state is an assumption not only of the profound historicity of the state as a form of political life, but also that political history is ultimately nothing but a history of statehood, and that the state is integral to modernity and the self-descriptions it makes possible and privileges. The state is now not only doubly abstract, but also stands in a double relation to historical time, at once being an outcome of the past and the condition of possibility of both that past and the present. And, most important, from Hegel on, transcending the state becomes tantamount to transcending modernity itself, and transcending modernity tantamount to transcending ourselves, since the state is now a condition of our reasoned reflexivity as citizens of states. In sum, after passing through the hands of Sieyès and Hegel, the modern concept of the state emerged as a historicized fusion of authority and community, ontologically demarcated from an international outside composed of similar entities and from a domestic inside composed of a multitude of prima facie apolitical forces.

What then happened to this concept is perhaps best understood against the backdrop of the changes the conception of history underwent at the hands of the founders of modern historiography.[43] Whereas historians such as Ranke and his disciples self-consciously sought to distance themselves from Hegel's philosophy of history and what to them appeared as unfounded speculation, they nevertheless remained indebted to him in so far as they retained basic features of his state concept while gradually filling it with empirical content.[44] This resulted in a mode of historical writing focused upon concrete singularities of experience, yet governed by suprahistorical principles of validity such as those provided by emergent source criticism.[45]

One source of controversy among early historians – and later, between them and Weber – concerned the ontological status of the state, and how the state could and should be rendered accessible to empirical inquiry. What was needed and provided was an ontology of statehood that could be reconciled with contemporary criteria of epistemic validity. In the way that this problem was most commonly phrased, the objective reality of the state was never in doubt, nor was the soundness of its transcendentalist and monistic underpinnings. What was questioned, however, was the

---

[43] For accounts of the attendant change in the conception of history, see for example Richard Ashcraft, 'German Historicism and the History of Political Theory', *History of Political Thought*, vol. 8, 1987, no. 2, pp. 289–324; H. Stuart Hughes, *Consciousness and Society: the Reorientation of European Social Thought 1890–1930* (New York: Vintage, 1977), pp. 185ff.; Iggers, *German Conception*, pp. 78–80.

[44] Iggers, *German Conception*, pp. 63–89.

[45] Hayden White, *Metahistory: the Historical Imagination in Nineteenth-Century Europe* (London and Baltimore, MD: Johns Hopkins, 1973), chs. 2, 4; Donald R. Kelley, 'Mythistory in the Age of Ranke', in Georg G. Iggers and J. M. Powell (eds.), *Leopold von Ranke and the Shaping of the Historical Discipline* (Syracuse, NY: Syracuse University Press, 1990), pp. 3–20.

exact terms of the existence of the state as the expression of the political consciousness and culture of a given nation. That the state was an individual whole was abundantly clear; what was desired was a way to explain this whole in terms of its constituent parts and the constituent parts in terms of that whole, taking into account both its coherence and the diversity of its component parts.

Much as a response to this need, the state concept was interpreted – or, better, if some anachronism is permitted, operationalized – in line with the then prevalent pre-darwinian conception of living beings. This was not merely a matter of restating old analogies – such analogies had animated much medieval thought, and also had been a dominant theme in post-Enlightenment political speculation[46] – but a matter of inscribing the state within a fairly coherent epistemic framework that made it possible to explain the origin and historical trajectory of individual political communities in the same terms as those used to account for the history of living beings, that is, in terms of their organization and structural coherence.[47] As a consequence, to the same extent that the concept of the state was filled with empirical content, it was also conceptualized as a natural species.[48]

Thus, from von Humboldt and von Ranke on, we can observe how history is carved out as a domain of empirical rather than merely philosophical knowledge, and how the ideally convergent concepts of nation and state are sedimented into one uniform object of inquiry – the nation state – which constituted the obvious point of departure for historical narratives that aspired to both empiricity and objectivity. Even within this proto-scientific historiography, the nation state and the category of history appear to be mutually constitutive.[49] As Lenz could confidently put it,

The *Reich* had to be founded first before a sense of reality, and likewise a proper appreciation of reality regarding past events could reemerge... [a]s long as the

---

[46] Cf. R. H. Bowen, *German Theories of the Corporate State* (New York: McGraw-Hill, 1947), pp. 13f., 212f.; Andrew Vincent, *Theories of the State* (Oxford: Basil Blackwell, 1987); Friedrich Meinecke, *Machiavellism: the Doctrine of Raison d'Etat and its Place in Modern History*, trans. D. Scott (Boulder, CO and London: Westview, 1984).

[47] Cf. P. H. Reill, 'History and the Life Sciences in the Early Nineteenth Century', in Iggers and Powell, *Leopold von Ranke*, pp. 21–35.

[48] Some remnants of this view were to survive even in the twentieth century; see John S. Dryzek and David Schlosberg, 'Disciplining Darwin: Biology in the History of Political Science', in James Farr, John S. Dryzek and S. T. Leonard (eds.), *Political Science in History: Research Programs and Political Traditions* (Cambridge: Cambridge University Press, 1995), pp. 123–44.

[49] Cf. Wilhelm von Humboldt, 'On the Historian's Task', *History and Theory*, vol. 6, 1967, no. 1, pp. 57–71; Leopold von Ranke, 'The Great Powers', trans. H. Hunt-von Laue, in T. H. von Laue, *Leopold Ranke: the Formative Years*, Princeton Studies in History, vol. IV, (Princeton, NJ: Princeton University Press, 1950); Wolfgang J. Mommsen, 'Ranke and the Neo-Rankean School in Imperial Germany', in Iggers and Powell, *Leopold von Ranke*, pp. 124–40.

nation had to fight for its highest objectives, there was no room for objective historiography; after victory had been achieved it rose to predominance by itself. The passions have subsided; hence we can practice justice once again.[50]

So much for the conceptual and discursive antecedents of modern political science. We have noted a series of cumulative mutations in the state concept that rendered the state a profoundly historical being; we have also noted how this grafting was parallel to its logical and rhetorical association with the concept of the nation as a paradigmatic form of political community; we further noticed how the resulting fusion was rendered distinct from both the international system and civil society yet ontologically intertwined with them. This was the kind of state concept that was inscribed as a condition of possible history and as a condition of modern identity at large. We finally noted how this transcendental concept was used to define an entire domain of historical objectivity while simultaneously signifying its main empirical object of inquiry. The time has now come to describe how early political science was able to emerge and acquire an identity of its own by means of this nebulous concept.

The state and the quest for disciplinary identity

That modern political science emerged out of and remained methodologically indebted to historiography is one of the commonplaces of disciplinary history, as is the awareness that it owed much of its philosophical debt to German idealist philosophy. As Ross has argued, the discourses on history and politics remained fused together into what she has labelled 'historico-politics' for several decades until political science finally succeeded in acquiring an identity of its own.[51]

But while this happy marriage curiously failed to give rise to an autonomous science of politics in the German context where it had first taken place, it spurred numerous efforts to constitute such a discipline in Great Britain and America.[52] The strange result was that a statist

---

[50] M. Lenz, *Die Großen Mächte. Ein Rückblick auf unser Jahrhundert* (Berlin: Paetel, 1900), p. 26, quoted in Mommsen, 'Ranke and the Neo-Rankean School', p. 129.

[51] Ross, *Origins of American Social Science*, pp. 64f.

[52] Stull W. Holt, 'The Idea of Scientific History in America', *Journal of the History of Ideas*, vol. 1, 1940, no. 3, pp. 352–62; Jürgen Herbst, *The German Historical School in American Scholarship* (Ithaca, NY: Cornell University Press, 1965), pp. 99–128; D. S. Goldstein, 'History at Oxford and Cambridge: Professionalization and the Influence of Ranke', in Iggers and Powell, *Leopold von Ranke*, pp. 141–53; Dorothy Ross, 'On the Misunderstandings of Ranke and the Origins of the Historical Profession in America', in Iggers and Powell, *Leopold von Ranke*, pp. 154–69.

discipline emerged in societies that would appear relatively stateless both to us and to some contemporaries – to one American scholar, the state was indeed a very Prussian invention. It was

the living personification of the fatherland, the instrument of its strength at home and abroad, the author and enforcer of the law, the supreme arbiter of interests, judge of peace and war, the protector of the weak, the representative of all that is general in the wants of society, the organ of the common reason and the collective force of society: such is the state in all its power and majesty.[53]

Thus, in this section, I shall attempt to show how the concept of the state, together with the statist conception of history it brought with it, became crucial to the identity of the emergent science of politics. Since the rhetorical function of the state concept in the efforts to create a discipline of politics has been documented by Farr and Gunnell, I shall first discuss some of their findings.[54] What these authors seem to have neglected, however, is that the state concept was not only instrumental to attempts to legitimize the institutionalization of political science, but also a source of theoretical coherence and discursive identity. I shall therefore focus more on these latter functions.

Beginning with Lieber's *Manual of Political Ethics* (1838), most attempts to create a science of politics in America remained firmly focused on the state, both as an object of empirical inquiry and a source of moral values. As Lieber had stated three years earlier in the *Encyclopedia Americana*,

[a]s the idea of *politics* depends on that of the *state*, a definition of the latter will easily mark out the whole province of the political sciences ... This idea of the state is the basis of a class of sciences, and gives them a distinct character as belongs to the various classes of ... sciences.[55]

Similarly, Woolsey could confidently claim that '*state* is the only scientific term proper for a treatise on politics'.[56]

[53] J. F. Lalor, *Cycloedaedia of Political Science, Political Economy, and the Political History of the United States* (New York: Charles E. Merrill, 1888), pp. 257, 800.
[54] Cf. James Farr, 'Political Science and the State', in J. Brown and D. K. van Keuren (eds.), *The Estate of Social Knowledge* (Baltimore, MD: Johns Hopkins, 1991), pp. 1–21; John G. Gunnell, 'In Search of the State: Political Science as an Emerging Discipline in the US', in P. Wagner, B. Wittrock and R. Whitley (eds.), *Discourses on Society* (Dordrecht: Kluwer, 1990), pp. 123–61.
[55] Francis Lieber, ed., *Encyclopedia Americana* (Philadelphia, PA: Thomas Desilver, 1835), vol. X, quoted in Gunnell, *Descent of Political Theory*, p. 27. See also James Farr, 'Francis Lieber and the Interpretation of American Political Science', *Journal of Politics*, vol. 52, 1990, no. 4, pp. 1027–49.
[56] Theodore W. Woolsey, *Political Science or the State Theoretically and Practically Considered* (London: Sampson Low, Marston, Searly & Rivington, 1877), p. 142.

According to Gunnell, no one did more to make the state the primary object of political science than Burgess, who turned it into 'a historical science focusing on the evolution of the state and the development of liberty and sovereignty, from classical democracy through modern representative governments and projected toward an eventual world state wherein politics and political science would be complete'.[57]

Half a century later, when political science eventually began to assert its presence in university curricula, it was to encompass the 'history of institutions, the origin and development of the State through its several phases of political organization down to the modern constitutional form... and seek finally through comprehensive comparison to generalize the ultimate principles of our political philosophy'.[58] And when the first issue of *Political Science Quarterly* appeared in 1886, it defined its subject matter as the historical and comparative study of the state.[59]

This focus on the state as the prime object of investigation and the insistence on a close relationship between history and the science of politics was visible even in the less successful efforts at institutionalization in Great Britain. Thus, according to Freeman, what distinguishes the modern conception of the state from the ancient one is that while the latter departed from the city, the former is conditioned by the existence of the nation, 'a considerable and continuous part of the earth's surface inhabited by men who at once speak the same language and are united under the same government',[60] and 'such a nation forms the ideal of a State... which forms the ground of all modern political speculation'.[61] To Seeley, the science of politics is 'a field of speculation almost boundless, for it includes almost all that is memorable in the history of mankind, and yet it is all directly produced by the fact that human beings almost everywhere belong to states'.[62] To Sidgwick, it is possible to conceive of a distinct science of politics since the 'development of... the State is one

[57] Gunnell, *Descent of Political Theory*, p. 55; cf. John W. Burgess, *Political Science and Comparative Constitutional Law* (Boston, MA: Ginn & Co, 1890–1); John W. Burgess, 'Political Science and History', *American Historical Review*, vol. 2, 1897, pp. 403–4.

[58] John W. Burgess, 'The Study of the Political Sciences in Columbia College', *International Review*, vol. 1, 1882, p. 348, quoted in Gunnell, *Descent of Political Theory*, p. 52.

[59] Munroe Smith, 'Introduction: the Domain of Political Science', *Political Science Quarterly*, vol. 1, 1886, no. 1, quoted in Gunnell, *Descent of Political Theory*, p. 56.

[60] E. A. Freeman, *Comparative Politics: Six Lectures Read Before the Royal Institution in January and February, 1873* (London: Macmillan, 1873), p. 81.

[61] Freeman, *Comparative Politics*, p. 83.

[62] John R. Seeley, *Introduction to Political Science* [1885] (London: Macmillan, 1911), p. 17; cf. S. Collini, D. Winch and J. Burrow, *That Noble Science of Politics: a Study in Nineteenth-Century Intellectual History* (Cambridge: Cambridge University Press, 1983), pp. 225ff.; D. Wormell, *Sir John Seeley and the Uses of History* (Cambridge: Cambridge University Press, 1980).

thread or strand of human history which may be usefully separated from other components of the complex fact of social development'.[63]

The fact that those who struggled to create a science of politics did so by a constant appeal to the concept of the state does not tell us much about how this concept did in fact function within the emergent discourse, and to what extent it furnished it with the coherence and sense of direction necessary to constitute disciplinary identity. Behind the above proclamations of independence in inaugural addresses lurks the reality of conceptual relations, forces much less easily domesticated by speech than the wealthy and benevolent targets of the fundraisers.

Thus, when we bother to move beyond the performative level in the exemplary texts of early political science, we are once more reminded of how much the centrality of this concept depends on ambiguity, and how much its ambiguity is conditioned by its centrality. The concept of the state was able to soak up meanings from a wide spectrum of philosophical ideas and to contain elements from prima facie incompatible ideological positions. To the late nineteenth century, the concept of the state offered a convenient point of convergence, which could be employed to defuse philosophical and political controversies by removing them from overt dispute, thus effectively cancelling any remaining *Sattelzeit* hopes of politicization.

So what were the early political scientists tacitly agreeing on when they put the concept of the state to use in their discourse? Indeed, answering this question is crucial if we ever are to understand the role played by the concept of the state in the formation of disciplinary identity, and why it later lost so much of its attraction and organizing power.

First, and fully consonant with the inherited historicist connotations of the state concept, there was wide agreement that the state, by analogy with all other living beings, was the outcome of growth from the embryonic to the mature, and that this pattern of growth was the natural and perhaps inevitable trajectory of all human collectivities. This way of conceiving the historical importance of the state was formed in explicit opposition both to theories of contract and to attempts to deduce the proper nature of authority from ideas of human nature, but fully consonant with the way the state had earlier been conceptualized by German historicists. What we reject by using abstractions such as those handed down to us by contractarians and proponents of the *ius naturale*, writes Maine, 'is the entire history of each community', since '[t]he most nearly universal fact that can be asserted respecting the origin of the political communities called states is that they were formed by the coalescence

---

[63] Henry Sidgwick, *The Elements of Politics* (London: Macmillan, 1891), p. 5.

of groups, the original group having been in no case smaller than the patriarchal family'.[64]

This theory had first emerged within the study of primitive law, but was then transposed more or less wholesale to the political domain, with the result that the state was regarded as the ultimate expression of a long and gradual evolutionary sequence. Thus, to Burgess, that the state was a product of history meant that 'it is the gradual continuous development of human society, out of a grossly imperfect beginning, through crude but improving forms of manifestation, towards a perfect and universal organization of mankind'.[65] To Woolsey,

[t]here is no highly civilized society, if its history is traced back, [that] does not contain some vestiges of a type of polity, which may fairly be supposed to be connected with, and have grown out from, the first institution of mankind. There is no savage or uncivilized race, which cannot in its institutions be referred back, on the supposition of degeneration or of natural departure, to social forms that grew out of the family state or out of something like it.[66]

Thus, the origin of the state is to be found in the family, from which it has evolved in a slow sequence, ranging from tribal associations to city states to the modern nation state. While the exact pace of this process, its detailed chronology and the precise trajectory of each individual political community through time were subject to substantial scholarly debate, that this process had a common origin was largely beyond dispute, as was its ultimate goal. To the extent that there was any disagreement, it concerned the ultimate source of statehood in time. To some, this was buried in the depths of history, in the mysterious origin of the Teutonic peoples, tracing their common descent to a primordial Aryan community on the Indus, which later spread in a western direction, and was always ready to erect its most ancient institutions in still more advanced forms.[67] To others, this point of origin was instead located in the dawn of Platonic Christian civilization, and gradually rendered visible during its march towards perfection, eventually to become manifested in popular sovereignty and liberal institutions.[68] Thus, on this point early political science was torn between what would later become an ideological polarity: that between culture and civilization.

---

[64] Henry S. Maine, *Lectures on the Early History of Institutions* (London: John Murray, 1875), pp. 359, 386.

[65] John W. Burgess, *The Foundations of Political Science* [1892] (New York: Columbia University Press, 1933), p. 63.

[66] Woolsey, *Political Science*, vol. II, p. 434.

[67] Freeman, *Comparative Politics*, pp. 11f.; cf. Collini *et al.*, *That Noble Science of Politics*, pp. 209–46.

[68] Seeley, *Introduction to Political Science*, pp. 30ff.; Woodrow Wilson, *The State: Elements of Historical and Practical Politics* (London: Heath, 1899), pp. 17ff.

This way of applying the state concept was closely intertwined with the inductive and historicizing tenets of early political science, and was later to become a crucial resource in subsequent attempts to rescue this emergent science from the threat posed by deductive and nomothetic ambitions, and more surprisingly, from the monist state concept itself.[69] The state, no matter how much it happened to resemble other forms of political life, was the outcome of a highly specific, necessary and desirable course of development: it was the mark of both culture and civilization, and once completed, the state was here to stay. This understanding of the state was also supplemented by a mode of reconstructing the history of political thought in finalist terms, itself understood as evolving from a primitive and unreflected grasp of political life to the full consciousness of statehood.[70]

Second, and in precarious coexistence with the above uses, it was widely assumed that the state was and always had been present everywhere in some form or another, and that it was a more or less universal feature of all mankind. This assumption permitted a generic and sometimes totally indiscriminate application of the concept across different contexts. When the concept was used in this way, it was commonly imported from those philosophical and legal theories of the state which dealt with it from a juristic and ethical point of view, and sought to justify particular notions of state authority with reference to its timeless and universal presence, but without acknowledging the historical plurality of state forms.[71]

When transposed to empirical inquiry, this transcendental and generic state concept was filled with empirical content by stretching its range of application far beyond what was warranted by the historicist and evolutionist usages exemplified above. Simply put, when applied this way, the empirical and historicist face of the state was made subordinate to its transcendentalist one. Thus, to Seeley, the use of the term state is warranted wherever human beings are found, and if you 'compare the most

---

[69] Cf. Frederic W. Maitland, translator's introduction to Otto Gierke, *Political Theories of the Middle Age* (Cambridge: Cambridge University Press, 1900), p. ix; Frederic W. Maitland, 'The Body Politic', in H. D. Hazeltine, G. Lapsley and P. H. Winfield (eds.), *Maitland: Selected Essays* [1899] (Cambridge: Cambridge University Press, 1936), pp. 240–56.

[70] See, for example, Raymond G. Gettell, *History of Political Thought* (London: Allen & Unwin, 1924); Westel W. Willoughby, *Political Theories of the Ancient World* [1903] (Freeport, NY: Books for Libraries Press, 1969). For a discussion, see Ashcraft, 'German Historicism', pp. 297–99.

[71] For all their differences, the obvious sources of inspiration were Bernard Bosanquet, *The Philosophical Theory of the State* [1899] (London: Macmillan, 1951), p. 3 and *passim*; John Austin, *The Province of Jurisprudence Determined* [1832] (Cambridge: Cambridge University Press, 1995). For a discussion, see David Runciman, *Pluralism and the Personality of the State* (Cambridge: Cambridge University Press, 1997), pp. 76–83.

advanced state with the most primitive tribe . . . you will see the same features, though the proportions are different'.[72] Indeed, once the reference of the concept was made wide enough, the absence of the state seemed close to impossible, since 'the need of such an institution as the state [and] the fact that it has appeared everywhere in the world . . . show that it is in a manner necessary, and if necessary, natural, and if natural, divine'.[73]

This transhistorical use of the concept was closely connected to the deductive and nomothetic aspirations of the new science, and became foundational to most further attempts to theorize the state independently of its history, that is, as a universal response to a timeless problem. According to the logic governing this usage, the state was and would always remain identical with itself, no matter how different it appeared across time and space. Furthermore, the logic of transhistorical usage not only made it possible to investigate the past as if states had always been present, but also as if political science itself – to the extent it was defined in terms of its preoccupation with the state – were wholly identical with statehood. Also, and wholly consonant with this conception, the foundation was created for the kind of presentist historiography that has since been used to reinforce the identity of political science by depicting its history as a succession of responses to the same timeless 'problem of the state'.[74]

Thus, while focusing on the state as an object of investigation, late nineteenth-century theorists were able to speak of the state both as an outcome of evolution (and hence something that must have arisen at a certain time and in a certain place) and as a transhistorically present medium of such political evolution (and hence as something that exists always and everywhere) all at once, and with no profound contradiction between these usages being felt, but rather a difference in emphasis. Yet behind this rather superficial disagreement, and as its condition of possibility, there was an agreement to the effect that the institutional reality of the state was wholly coincident with the idea of it as expressed by its concept, that is, that the state and its concept were ontologically and historically inseparable.

As ideas and institutions were rendered inseparable across the entire field of the social sciences, the above duality of the state was shared by other objects of contemporary intellectual obsession, each of which

---

[72] Seeley, *Introduction to Political Science*, p. 24.

[73] Woolsey, *Political Science*, p. 198.

[74] For an overview of such historiography, see Farr, 'The History of Political Science'. For early examples, see Frederick Pollock, *An Introduction to the History of the Science of Politics* (London, 1890). For a criticism, see John G. Gunnell, 'The Myth of the Tradition', *American Political Science Review*, vol. 72, 1978, no. 11, pp. 122–34.

figured preeminently both as objects of empirical analysis and as conditions of the very same empirical field in which they were situated. The most widespread way of handling what to us would appear as a categorical clash between the concerns of history and those of a generalizing social science, was the comparative method.

Thus, the fact that each particular state had a historical trajectory of its own was generally assumed to permit historical comparison across time and space, much as had already happened in geology and natural history.[75] Yet since comparison always presupposes an element of classification, the categories used when classifying historically variable phenomena must themselves be assumed to be invariable in order for comparison to be distinct from mere historical description of singular cases; the possibility of change must be compartmentalized into unchanging categories in order for comparison to be possible. Thus, when that which was classified was the state in all its historically and culturally specific guises, the procedure of classification permitted the dovetailing of historical and generic connotations within the same analytic grid. By treating each state as an individual whole with a specific past while subjecting its institutional features to analysis according to transhistorical categories, the difference could tentatively be split between the two conflicting concerns that were fed by an indiscriminate usage of the ambiguous state concept.

But what you will find through comparison depends on how deep you venture into the bottomless well of identity and difference. All comparison, by virtue of the very kind of questions it asks, is conditioned by what you expect to find. If one poses questions of similarity, one presupposes that the objects of comparison are sufficiently different in order for the expected results to be non-trivial. Conversely, if one poses questions of difference, one tacitly presupposes that the objects of comparison are sufficiently similar to permit comparison in the first place. In both cases, however, the results of the comparison depend on what you initially took for granted and what you expected to find.

Now the kind of questions asked by the early political scientists were predominantly of the first kind. Whereas a mixture of religious and national sentiment predisposed them to accept the difference of communities and cultures as a baseline fact of the political world which they inhabited, their questions made them go searching for points of resemblance and identity across historical and cultural divides, especially since most of them were anxious to demonstrate the common origin of Western culture and civilization. Thus, to Freeman, the 'most profitable analogies,

---

[75] Cf. Kelley, 'Mythistory in the Age of Ranke'; also Charles C. Gillespie, *Genesis and Geology: the Impact of Scientific Discoveries upon Religious Belief in the Decades Before Darwin* (New York: Harper & Row, 1959).

the most striking cases of direct derivation are not those which are most obvious at first sight... it is in truth the points of superficial unlikeness which often give us the surest proof of essential likeness'.[76] Consequently, the big theoretical challenge was how to explain how the detectable similarities between states had originated: by direct imitation, like circumstances, or with reference to a common origin.[77]

Here the concept of progress was a great helper since it held out the hope of reconciling these explanations – and ultimately, of making the questions underlying them redundant in the light of its universality. But to early state theorists, however, unlike late modern subscribers, the concept of progress and its semantic equivalents initially brought with them a shift in focus from the resemblance and convergence of political orders to the profound differences that existed between them:

The polity of a country, if foreign conquest has not interfered with its orderly developments, is as truly indigenous as the growth of local causes, as the animals and flowers. At first, if we conceive of regular progress, all parts of the world ought to agree; afterwards special causes will give the same variety to human institutions that we observe in race and language, only the diversity will be somewhat less.[78]

Granted that the evolution of political communities follows an ideal and uniform but not necessarily universal sequence, historical comparison could create a chronology of its own on the basis of the degree of advancement of each particular unit, as indicated by its relative positions in the same classificatory scheme that had made comparison possible. Again Freeman was most explicit on this point:

if we read history as chronology requires us to read it... we are, for many purposes of this inquiry, reading history backwards... The notion of the State as a city is, as we have seen and *as it must be in the nature of things*, a later notion than the state as tribe... the lower unit is not a division of the greater, but... the greater is an aggregate of the smaller.[79]

Now what looks like a blunt submission of chronology to classification was no empty gesture of a whig mind, but in fact an effective way of handling the essential ambiguity of the state as it had been handed down to the early political scientists from Hegel and the historicists. It was a way of resolving the essential tensions between the empirical and the transcendental, between the historical and the generic, between the inductive and the deductive, that became obvious whenever the state concept was put to use.

[76] Freeman, *Comparative Politics*, p. 20.
[77] *Ibid.*, pp. 24f.
[78] Woolsey, *Political Science*, p. 432.
[79] Freeman, *Comparative Politics*, pp. 100, 119, my italics.

The result of this juxtaposition was that early political science came
to view the world as one big living museum of all that was contained in
its classificatory schemes, since these were supposed not only to aid the
classification of existing political orders into neat and mutually exclusive
categories, but also to be exhaustive of the historical possibilities of political order by representing them as contained in the present. Ranging
from the most primitive to the most advanced, these orders were marked
by their essential stateness, yet they could be said to coexist as *exempla*
dispersed in the present, across space and across cultures. This resembles
the way some contextually oriented archaeologists handle their findings
even today. And as such, this move was integral to the *fin de siècle* worldview conveyed by the early science of politics:

As fragments of primitive animals have been kept sealed up in the earth's rocks,
so fragments of primitive institutions have been preserved, embedded in the rocks
of surviving law and custom, mixed up with the rubbish of accumulated tradition, crystallized in the organization of still savage tribes, or kept curiously in the
museum of fact and rumour swept together by some ancient historian.[80]

As has been pointed out by Mandelbaum, and contrary to what was
the case in the other comparative sciences of the age such as geology
and natural history, the social and political sciences could not furnish
independent evidence concerning the chronological order of their objects
in the same way as geology could point to different strata, and natural
history to its fossils.[81] In the absence of such independent sources of
evidence, a chronological sequence between different forms of political
order could only be established by transferring an assumption of uniform
evolution on to the realm of political institutions and arranging them
in due sequence from the primitive to the more advanced. And in the
course of such tabulation, the essential sameness of the political orders
thus represented was established and preserved by means of the state
concept.

Making the chronology of political orders subservient to the principles
that governed their classification implies not only that the state is posited
as the ideal origin and ultimate horizon of political order – thus being a
presupposition not only of these orders and their identity – but also that
the state is constitutive of their chronology as well. Thus, by virtue of itself
being historicized, the state becomes foundational in relation to the same
historical time within which it is inscribed as a paradigmatic form of political order. Consequently, it would be quite pointless to criticize the above

[80] Wilson, *The State: Elements of Practical Politics*, p. 1.
[81] Mandelbaum, *History, Man and Reason*, pp. 99–109.

practice of reducing chronology to classification on the grounds that it invents an artificial time and posits fictitious origins, since this is exactly the way all temporality is constituted, that is, by placing beings along an *a priori* constructed trajectory as defined by a series of metahistorical concepts.[82]

Hence, the superimposition of classification upon chronology veils the fact that chronology itself depends on a simultaneous conceptualization of time as an axis upon which things can be situated and ordered according to their qualitative differences, a conceptualization that in turn presupposes access to a whole series of metahistorical concepts that can be used to define these differences between preconstituted identities. The nineteenth century had invented for itself a whole series of such concepts – growth, evolution, development and progress – and used them to define time itself and create sociopolitical temporality. And it is precisely this concept of time and the mode of historical understanding it brings with it that make philosophies of development and progress look at once so problematic and so inescapable, since it makes us quite unable to understand time and historical change except in terms of principles and laws themselves thought to be situated outside time.

Therefore, comparison across time was equally a means of constructing a new time into which political institutions such as the state could be inscribed and rendered intelligible, thus overcoming the potentially corrosive effects unrestricted historicity would have upon the happy fusion of authority and community within the modern nation state.[83] But since the state could only become the prime vehicle of human progress by virtue of being understood as gradually unfolding in time, that time and its progressive unfolding were only measurable with reference to the degree of statehood – in its turn understood as the relative intensity and scope of political authority attained within each political community when dispersed in temporal sequence.

Through this temporal understanding of the state, geopolitical space could be neatly compartmentalized and subjected to empirical inquiry. The separation between the state and the international system that had been conceptualized in ontological terms by the German historicists could now be understood as different *aspects* of statehood, each containing its own viewpoint and corresponding to distinct but related subspecies

---

[82] Cf. Cornelius Castoriadis, 'Time and Creation', in J. Bender and D. Wellberry (eds.), *Chronotypes: the Construction of Time* (Stanford, CA: Stanford University Press, 1991), pp. 38–64; Foucault, *Order of Things*, pp. 332–4.

[83] Cf. D. Gross, 'The Temporality of the Modern State', *Theory and Society*, vol. 14, 1985, no. 2, pp. 53–82.

of political knowledge:

> We may separate the relations of states one to another – the international rela-
> tions – from the national. We may divide the national relations into questions of
> state organization and state action. We may distinguish between the various func-
> tions of the state. But there is no good reason for erecting these various groups
> of questions into distinct political sciences. The connection of each with all is too
> intimate.[84]

From this brief analysis we might conclude that the concept of the
state, while being a salient part in the rhetoric and self-description of early
political science, was also the centrepiece in a web of conceptual relations
that together constituted its disciplinary identity, and this in at least three
different ways. First, by both constituting its object of inquiry and by
being the tacit condition for attaining knowledge of that object – in the
past as well as in the present. Second, by ultimately being integral to the
possibility of historical time. Finally, and throughout its early scientific
employment, that state concept was defined in strict disjunction from
what was outside it – the international system – but in an equally strict
conjunction to what was contained within it: the nation.

As we have also seen, the efforts to create a science of politics were
largely simultaneous with the efforts to provide scientific legitimacy for
the study of history, an emergent discipline which also shared this concern with the state. Yet this disciplinary identity did not automatically
spill over into disciplinary autonomy. Rather, during this period, when
disciplinary boundaries were fluid and intellectual territories unsettled,
intellectual autonomy was both highly desirable and profoundly problematic. Political science, like most of the emergent social sciences, faced
severe problems of demarcation, since it was far from obvious that the
political itself was autonomous in relation to other domains of human
activity and knowledge. As I shall argue in the next section, the concept of the state was instrumental in the attempts to conceptualize an
autonomous territory for political science since this concept furnished it
with a way to make sense of politics as a distinct category of thought and
action. Furthermore, and as I shall try to show, this struggle for independence from adjacent disciplines favoured the transhistorical and generic
interpretation of the state concept over the historicist one.

The quest for autonomy and reflexive politics

If the identity of early political science was strongly conditioned by the
concept of the state, its autonomy was dependent on the possibility of

---

[84] Smith, 'Introduction', pp. 2–3.

conceptualizing politics as an autonomous sphere of knowledge and action. As we shall see in this section, the concept of the state furnished the early science of politics with such a possibility, but also circumscribed this autonomy by making the concept of politics more or less semantically coextensive with that of the state. Thus, in this section, I shall focus on the concept of politics and the difficulties confronted by those who tried to carve out politics as a distinct domain of knowledge.

As has been pointed out frequently enough, the concept of politics was virtually unknown in medieval Europe before the translation of Aristotle's *Politica* began to penetrate (and gradually subvert) the theological and legal discourse of the scholastics.[85] When the term politics was brought back in, so were its ancient connotations: in classical Greece, the concept of politics had been directly related to the activity of free and equal men within the civil community – the *polis* – this activity being regulated by a constitution. Acting politically was to act in the general interest of that community and in accordance with its constitution.[86] Within this view there was no room for a modern concept of the state, since this conception of politics effectively rules out precisely what the modern concept of the state presupposes, namely, that the state is something categorically distinct from both rulers and ruled. Indeed, the late medieval concept of politics presupposed a positive and institutionally mediated identity of rulers and ruled.

As Viroli has argued, what distinguishes the modern concept of politics from its ancient and medieval antecedents is the fact that the former has been closely associated with and defined in terms of the concept of the state. In its medieval and early Renaissance connotations, the concept of politics was used to discourse upon the relationship between political institutions and civic virtue, and through the logic of its usage ruled out the possibility of that kind of monopolized power which we have come to regard as a defining property of statehood and an indispensable point of departure for most varieties of modern political discourse.[87] This point

---

[85] Walter Ullmann, *A History of Political Thought: the Middle Ages* (Harmondsworth: Penguin, 1965), pp. 15–20; Walter Ullmann, *Principles of Government and Politics in the Middle Ages* (London: Methuen, 1974); Nicolai Rubinstein, 'A History of the Word "*Politicus*" in Early Modern Europe', in Pagden, *The Languages of Political Theory in Early Modern Europe*, pp. 41–56; Cary J. Nederman, 'Aristotelianism and the Origin of "Political Science" in the Twelfth Century', *Journal of the History of Ideas*, vol. 52, 1991, no. 2. pp. 179–94.

[86] Cf. Christian Meier, *The Greek Discovery of Politics*, trans. D. McLintock (Cambridge, MA: Harvard University Press, 1990), pp. 13–19.

[87] Maurizio Viroli, *From Politics to Reason of State: the Acquisition and Transformation of the Language of Politics, 1250–1600* (Cambridge: Cambridge University Press, 1992); Maurizio Viroli, 'The Revolution in the Concept of Politics', *Political Theory*, vol. 20, 1992, no. 3. pp. 473–95.

has also been touched upon by Skinner, to whom 'the acceptance of the modern idea of the State presupposes that political society is held to exist solely for political purposes'.[88]

For all their merits, these contextualist accounts of the history of the concept of politics have missed one further dimension of change, however. To my mind, what characterizes the modern concept of politics is its reflexive and limitless character. In theory and practice alike, what politics is and what the concept of politics ought to signify and refer to are ultimately themselves political questions. Politics is boundless to the extent that the drawing of boundaries separating the political domain from other domains is itself a political activity, performed in and mediated by a discourse that is political by virtue of being self-demarcating.[89] As Pizzorno has pointed out, reflexivity and absoluteness are crucial and lasting premises of modern political discourse which distinguish it from earlier periods when the demarcation of the political domain was subject to intense struggles between different kinds of authority, spiritual as well as worldly.[90]

In the context of modern political philosophy, the reflexivity and absoluteness of the concept of politics make it susceptible to a variety of interpretations, but pose a dilemma for any kind of discourse that aspires to be at once political and autonomous, since in order to demarcate itself from other domains of activity and knowledge, it must already have acquired an identity of its own: an identity as political. Put somewhat differently, in order for political discourse to constitute itself as autonomous and potentially boundless, it must be able to demarcate itself by itself. As I shall argue below, the concept of the state has indeed been an indispensable resource in this respect, since it functions both as a silent presupposition and a crucial limit to the modern attempts to demarcate politics from what is not politics.

Interpreted in this way, it is difficult to speak of a fully distinct concept of politics and a truly autonomous political discourse until quite late during the modern period. Typically, those modes of discourse which we retrospectively feel tempted to subsume under this label were themselves wrestling, often unsuccessfully, with the dilemma posed by the reflexivity of the concept of politics. Perhaps the most edifying example of the difficulties involved in creating an autonomous discourse on politics from a vast and diversified domain of sociopolitical reflection are the close to

---

[88] Skinner, *Foundations*, vol. II, p. 352.

[89] Jens Bartelson, 'Making Exceptions: some Remarks on the Concept of Coup d'État and its History', *Political Theory*, vol. 25, 1997, no. 3, pp. 323–46.

[90] Alessandro Pizzorno, 'Politics Unbound', in C. S. Maier (ed.), *Changing Boundaries of the Political* (Cambridge: Cambridge University Press, 1987), pp. 27–62.

ceaseless disputes over the relationship between economics and politics in the history of political economy – disputes which culminated in their split into two distinct discourses.

In this regard, the trajectory of the concept of politics in the writings of Hegel and Mill is crucial to our understanding of early political science and its relationship to political economy, since the problems confronted by the former gave rise to solutions adopted by the latter. In their early works, the concept of politics does not occupy a very prominent place: politics is not conceptualized as an autonomous realm, but rather subsumed under other quasi-transcendental concepts such as universal history and human nature.

Much in the same way as authority was sometimes considered expressive of identity in eighteenth- and early nineteenth-century thought, politics and the political sphere were not regarded as things *sui generis*, but rather assumed to be subordinate to and dependent on the presumably objective forces reigning in civil society, or reducible to immutable traits of human nature. Politics and the political were the offspring of more profound identities, and what took place in the political realm was viewed as wholly contingent upon these. Thus, the early Hegel, much like Rousseau and Ferguson before him, was much more concerned with the problems of sociocultural improvement of men than with the creation of political institutions such as the state as a means of attaining their final perfection.[91] In his *System of Logic* (1843), Mill explicitly denied the possibility of an autonomous science of politics, since there is a 'necessary correlation between the form of government existing in any society and the contemporaneous state of civilization; a natural law which stamps out the endless discussions and innumerable theories respecting forms of government in the abstract'.[92]

But despite profound differences in philosophical outlook, both Hegel and Mill had to confront the same basic problem stemming from their reception of the doctrines of early political economy: that of differentiating between the economic and political spheres of human activity in order to be able to account systematically for their interrelation. Thus, in their later works, the concept of politics is gradually carved out and detached from the entire series of other concepts that had been used to determine man as a labouring being in a societal context of production, and was now used to subsume these social relations under common signs and principles such as those provided by classical sovereignty. In the case

[91] Cf. Dickey, *Hegel*, p. 284.
[92] John Stuart Mill, *A System of Logic Ratiocinative and Inductive. Being a Connected View of the Principles of Evidence and the Methods of Scientific Investigation*, vol. II, 8th edn (London: Longmans, Green, Reader and Dyer, 1872), pp. 502, 518.

of Hegel, this has been described as a process of conversion, through which the inorganic and prepolitical aspects of social existence are dialectically translated into political consciousness and agency embodied in the state.[93] In Mill, this shift in conceptual focus has been described as an adjustment undertaken to resolve the inherited conflict between the historicist and transcendentalist foundations of earlier liberal thought, culminating in an increasing autonomy of the political sphere in relation to that of economy.[94] In both cases, however, the *a priori* autonomy of politics was secured through a set of internal transitions leading from a concern with social ethics and civic virtues to a concern with political institutions supposedly congenial to their cultivation, such as the modern state. This transition not only affected the relationship of political discourse to adjacent domains of knowledge, but also that between Hegel and Mill on the one hand and their predecessors on the other; it is no coincidence that they both felt obliged to rewrite their respective lines of intellectual descent in the process.[95]

But if both Hegel and Mill did carve out a concept of politics and give it a sufficiently autonomous standing to warrant a divorce between political discourse proper and that of political economy, this did not mean that the domain to which this concept had been made to refer was accessible to empirical inquiry at the moment of its birth. As we saw above, at least some of the salience of the concept of the state in early political science could be explained by the fact that this concept, largely thanks to its fruitful ambiguity, could soak up conflicting pressures within nineteenth-century ontology and epistemology, and tentatively reconcile them in the comparative method. Much of the same goes for the very domain to which the concept of politics was made to refer in the course of the above mutations.

Again Ross's term 'historico-politics' aptly captures the essential fluidity of this emergent domain, since the notion of politics was both conditioned by a particular mode of historical being and writing, and yet contained a vague promise of full disciplinary autonomy, to be realized through a conclusive subjection of historical inquiry into the state to the demands of deductive science. As one of the first but decisive steps in translating this conceptual mutation into intellectual practice, Mill changed his mind and started to celebrate the scientific potential of the

---

[93] Dickey, *Hegel*, pp. 273ff.

[94] Robert D. Cumming, *Human Nature and History: a Study of the Development of Liberal Political Thought*, vol. I (Chicago, IL: University of Chicago Press, 1969), pp. 21–75.

[95] Dickey, *Hegel*, pp. 183f.; Cumming, *Human Nature and History*, pp. 51–68; Collini *et al.*, *That Noble Science of Politics*, pp. 127–59.

new domain of knowledge:

All true political science is ... being deduced from the tendencies of things, tendencies known either through our general experience of human nature, or as the result of an analysis of the course of history, considered as a progressive evolution.[96]

That politics and history were conceptual twins became a commonplace soon after, and an indisputable starting point for those who asserted the autonomy of political science while admitting their indebtedness to the historical method. Thus, the interdependence between the categories of history and politics was reflected in Freeman's famous dictum that 'history is past politics and politics is present history'.

But behind such easy formulæ lurk the concepts of universal history and reflexive politics, both potentially boundless yet sufficiently distinct to make their interdependence open to theoretical and empirical elaboration. To Seeley, such cross-fertilization between the two domains was essential if both the studies of history and politics were to realize their inherent potential. Whereas the study of history could merely supply an unorganized body of facts, a study of politics unaided by history would have to remain content with abstract principles and assumptions. When brought together, however, history would furnish politics with facts while politics would furnish the principles for their classification and ordering. Not surprisingly, the point of convergence of these concerns was the state:

All that perplexity about the object of their labours which besets historians, all that perplexity about their method which hampers those who would form a political science, disappear together if we regard history as a mass of facts ... out of which an inductive science of states is to be constructed.[97]

This supplementarity of politics and history formed part of the background understanding of early attempts to construe a science of politics focused on the state. At the same time, however, history proved to be both enabling and constraining in the quest for disciplinary autonomy. While it had certainly furnished political science with an object of inquiry necessary to its identity, it posed a constant threat to its autonomy, since this object as well as the methods for investigating it also fell within the legitimate province of historical scholarship.[98] This is best exemplified in the American context, where the Rankean influences were

---

[96] John Stuart Mill, *An Inaugural Address to the University of St Andrew's*, 1867, quoted in Collini *et al.*, *That Noble Science of Politics*, p. 127.

[97] Seeley, *Introduction to Political Science*, p. 24.

[98] For the relationship between early political science and history, see Herbst, *German Historical School*, pp. 18, 112ff., 203ff.; Dorothy Ross, 'The Liberal Tradition Revisited and the Republican Tradition Addressed', in J. Higham and P. K. Conkin, *New Directions in American Intellectual History* (Baltimore, MD: Johns Hopkins, 1979).

strongly felt and the sense of complementarity sometimes gave way to identification:

The bands which unite history and politics cannot be broken. History reaches its goal in politics and politics are always the resultant of history. The two subjects are related like our own past and present. The living man preserves in memory and his own constitution all that has gone before. No tendency in politics can be called good which does not take into account the historical development of a given people. Whoever will understand the political situation of any State must study its past history.[99]

Such an insistence on the close ties between history and politics was, of course, open to the objection that the closer the ties, the less the autonomy of the science of politics. Any further intimacy was likely to backfire: if political science indeed was as close to history as it was sometimes claimed, why should it deserve any autonomous standing from the discipline of history, intellectually, institutionally or financially? Indeed, it seems as if the separation from the increasingly deductive field of political economy and the orientation towards inductive historical methods made the study of politics increasingly vulnerable to total absorption.[100]

But as we saw above, one possible escape route out of this dilemma went through the comparative method, which made it possible to reconcile the inductive and the deductive sensibilities of nineteenth-century knowledge. Another possible way to secure relative autonomy from history was to adapt political science methodologically to the exemplars of political economy while insisting on the *sui generis* character of politics, by arguing that politics ought to be studied in isolation, unimpeded by excessive concerns with the past.[101] Now both these strategies to gain and preserve disciplinary autonomy privileged the generic usage of the state concept over its historicist applications, either by making the transhistorical presence of the state an assumption integral to the classificatory schemes governing comparison or, as was the case in the more orthodox deductive approaches, by turning the presence of the state into an axiom of political inquiry. From this latter vantage point, politics and statehood were coextensive, so that in the absence of the state, no politics could possibly exist at all.

Thus the conceptual world of history in the late nineteenth-century mode we are discussing here constituted an enabling element behind the

---

[99] Henry B. Adams, 'Is History Past Politics?', *Johns Hopkins University Studies in Historical and Political Science*, series 7, vols. III–IV (Baltimore, MD: Johns Hopkins, 1895), p. 78.

[100] This was one of the major difficulties encountered by attempts to establish a discipline of politics in the British context; see Collini *et al.*, *That Noble Science of Politics*, chs. 10–11.

[101] Sidgwick, *The Elements of Politics*, pp. 2–8.

emergence of a science of politics, since it provided the science of politics with both an empirical object and a set of methods that privileged a historicist conception of that object. And this object of investigation – the state – became crucial to the possibility of defining political knowledge as distinct from other disciplines, since there was no apparent way to define politics as an autonomous sphere of thought and action except in terms of the state, understood either as a subject which acts or as an object which is acted upon.

But if the concept of the state supplied a point of convergence within historico-political discourse, it also constituted a crucial limit to the efforts of political science to emancipate itself fully from historical scholarship. This problem of gaining and preserving autonomy in relation to historical discourse was further complicated by the methodological affinity of the two disciplines. The methodological concerns of the emergent historical discipline hovered between the gathering of objective facts and the construction of philosophical principles thought to subsume and explain these facts, but with no deeply felt tension between these preoccupations.[102] A similar tension was visible within early political science as well, but was gradually aggravated through the quest for autonomy. With some simplification, one could perhaps say that it was the deductive tendency within early political science that came to be the most promising route to autonomy, while the gathering of facts rendered objective by a rigorous application of source criticism came to constitute the disciplinary core of later historical scholarship. Hence, in the war of independence fought by early political science, it constantly but often unwittingly borrowed its resources from the deranged family home of history while trying to resist the temptations of going wholly deductive, thereby becoming but an incoherent younger sibling of political economy. In all instances, however, the state concept proved to be an indispensable strategic resource.

But the more real and lasting difficulty lies in the modern concept of politics itself. If modern politics is indeed a reflexive and absolute category, it is also potentially boundless in time and space. By comparison, then, the concept of the state appears much easier to dispose of, a fact that was to be capitalized on by state-bashers of the coming generations. Thus, it is not very difficult for a political scientist to speak of a time and place when and where the state did not exist – all he has to do is to shake off the habit of employing that concept transhistorically or axiomatically. But it is all the more difficult to speak of a time and place when and where politics itself does not exist, since politics must be assumed to be present

---

[102] Holt, 'The Idea of Scientific History', pp. 356–60.

in some guise in order for the political scientist to have something to speak of in the first place. And in its absence, the political scientist had better shut up: being aware of this necessary truth consequently makes him or her unwilling or unable to forget politics, thereby unwittingly becoming an accomplice in its reflexive reproduction.

Yet if politics is boundless by virtue of being bounded only by itself, everything human can at least hypothetically be subsumed under this concept; all that is needed is a political perspective that is encompassing enough, a resource kindly handed down to us by our democratic self-understanding. But such attempts inevitably lapse into paradox: if politics potentially encompasses everything, it can itself be but nothing. Thus, as long as a science of politics has its subject matter exclusively defined by a reflexive and absolute concept of politics, it is likely to be both imperialist in outlook and self-defeating in its endeavour to politicize new phenomena in order to remain alive.

In this respect, the concept of the state did function as a limit and source of coherence, but with the obvious consequence that the domain of political science became coextensive with what could possibly be signified by the concept of the state. This, as we shall see in subsequent chapters, posed a dilemma later confronted by those who wished to banish the state concept from scientific discourse.

The quest for authority and legislative science

As Manicas has argued, the epistemic concerns of the early social sciences were based on a perverted reception of Newtonian principles, a misunderstanding which prohibited inferences from the observable to the unobservable and therefore condemned the social sciences to a lasting scientific inferiority in the name of mock empiricism.[103]

It should, however, be clear from the above sections that the early efforts to create a science of politics were not undertaken in conformity with any singular or ready-made epistemic option. Early political science was torn between a multitude of epistemic concerns and drew upon a variety of disparate philosophical resources in order to validate itself. This implies that many of the categories commonly used to characterize what to posterity appear as the major tensions within nineteenth-century epistemology are particularly unfit in this case, since some of these tensions were not as intensely felt, while others were effectively produced by the quests for scientification and disciplinarity.

Hence, rather than reconstructing the range of epistemic concepts that informed the early attempts to create a science of politics on the basis of

---

[103] Manicas, *History and Philosophy*, ch. 1.

distinctions that have come to make sense only to a victorious positivist posterity, I shall try to do this in terms of those concepts which were contemporary with its emergence. Before venturing into nineteenth-century epistemology, however, we might as well pose the question of the relationship between authority and knowledge, since authority was the main benefit expected to ensue from going scientific.

Authority is a necessary supplement to disciplinary identity in so far as it reinforces and confers indisputability upon it. Authority makes the objects of investigation within a given field look given and immutable, and makes them appear independent of the practices of knowing. Furthermore, authority makes the disciplinary demarcations that separate this field from others appear natural, as if they corresponded to divisions inherent in the order of things themselves. Finally, authority is an essential asset in the production and dissemination of knowledge, since the authority of a particular way of knowing comes with the authority to mark it off from the other kinds of knowledge as well as from other possible ways of knowing. Simply stated, scientific authority presupposes that science can be more or less rigorously demarcated from non-science, and this demarcation in its turn presupposes access to an authority of an extra-scientific kind.[104] That is, in order for science to be constituted as authoritative, it must first be able to successfully claim constituting authority.

As I shall argue in this section, to early political science, such constituting authority was provided by a largely unarticulated but nevertheless crucial identification of the quest for scientific authority with the authority symbolized by the state itself. Thus, the concept of the state fulfils an important mediating function in the constitution of disciplinarity, since scientific and political authority were not yet conceived of as distinct, but were brought together to coincide in the concept of law, and this concept was metaphorically as well as inferentially connected to that of the state.

Living in an age which has witnessed many attempts to demarcate science from non-science by means of overarching principles, we are still in the habit of thinking of this demarcation in epistemic and philosophical terms rather than in political and pragmatic terms. We tend to conceive of scientific reason as founded on itself, forgetful of the fact that the class of statements which are used to demarcate cannot be a member of any of the classes of statements constituted as separate by the act of demarcation. But before the turn of the century, no big difference was felt between claiming scientific authority and claiming authority as such, most probably because science had not yet acquired sufficient authority to uphold and assert the possibility of drawing and legitimizing such a

---

[104] Steve Fuller, 'Disciplinary Boundaries'.

distinction from within its own territory. Put somewhat differently, there were no elaborate attempts to justify the practice of demarcating science from non-science by demarcating this very practice of demarcation from other possible practices of demarcation; this task had to await the age of Russell and Popper, and the set-theoretical taboos of self-reference so dear to that age.

The crucial difference between different attempts to demarcate knowledge from other domains consists in the means used for the purpose of demarcation as well as what is excluded from the domain of knowledge in the process. Hence each age has its own enemy: whereas the early claims of scientific authority were targeted against rhetoric, passion and superstition, the early social sciences had chosen opinion and ideology as their chief enemies.[105] What is characteristic of the concepts of opinion and ideology is not only that they are self-referential – all concepts are – but that they are constituted through self-reference: the constitutive feature of opinion and ideology is the ability to define themselves *in contrast* to mere 'opinion' and mere 'ideology'.[106]

As it turned out, the concept of opinion was able to soak up and contain all those verbalized forces that were released in a society beset by swift social transformation and which could not yet be reconciled through a democratic procedure, and had not been moderated through popular education. As Bauman has characterized the task of the early social sciences, 'it consists of making authoritative statements which arbitrate in controversies of opinions and select those opinions which, having been selected, become authoritative and binding'.[107]

Perhaps one could add that this necessarily involves the capacity to define what is opinion and what is not. But far from the late modern luxury of a supposedly apolitical and value-free terra firma to be freely enjoyed by political scientists, this legislative role was essentially contested in the nineteenth century, and claims to scientific authority were often met by political suspicion as well as by rivalling and incompatible claims to the same authority from 'scientific' positions long since forgotten or marginalized by disciplinary historiography. To early political science, claims to authority were especially problematic, since the very term politics carried a host of negative connotations far removed from the positive connotations conventionally attached to the concept of science. Whereas politics made people think of corrupt practices of politicking and bribery, science signified one of the most noble of human pursuits,

---

[105] James Farr, 'Political Science and the Enlightenment of Enthusiasm', *American Political Science Review*, vol. 82, 1988, no. 1, pp. 51–69.

[106] See Slavoj Zizek, *The Plague of Fantasies* (London: Verso, 1997).

[107] Zygmunt Bauman, *Legislators and Interpreters* (Oxford: Polity Press, 1987), p. 4.

so to fuse these concepts into a label with some selling power was not altogether easy. Thus, one of the greatest challenges of the early science of politics was how to acquire the necessary scientific authority by insisting that political science was a science *in* politics, without simultaneously being confined on the messy inside of politics, and yet being able to use this authority in order to exercise influence *over* politics.[108]

That is, taken in a wide metapolitical sense, the legislative potential of political science resided in its ability to translate its internally constituted demarcation from politics proper into a political authority of its own. Such successful claims to authority not only necessitated a simultaneous demarcation from opinion, but also required that politics was indeed conceived of as autonomous in relation to other domains of knowledge and activity; yet the ensuing claims to authority were tailored to reinforce such an autonomy. Hence, political science legislates not only over itself when defining itself as at once concerned with the political and yet soberly detached from it, but also indirectly over the content of those domains of human activity and knowledge from which it detached itself in order to become scientific. As I shall argue below, there were two basic yet interrelated ways through which early political science asserted this kind of authority, the first through the concept of virtue and the second through the concept of law. Crucially, both of these presupposed the state concept as their condition of possibility.

The first way to back authority claims was through an emulation of the Baconian virtues; through an explicit affirmation and celebration of the beneficial effects of knowledge upon state and society.[109] One such desired benefit was political order: by pouring cold water on disruptive outbursts of opinion, early political science could claim to fulfil old Hobbesian promises about the political use of science in the creation and maintenance of sovereign authority.[110] Thus, a proper scientific method, when applied to the study of politics, will not only

make all the difference to the science itself but it will have a vast effect on the course of affairs by changing the whole character of public opinion, for public opinion will gradually conform itself to scientific opinion. That political fanaticism which is so rife on the continent... is nothing but a public opinion dominated by bad method. Socialism, communism, everything of the kind, are simply bastard political science divorced from history.[111]

---

[108] Cf. Gunnell, *Descent of Political Theory*, ch. 2.
[109] Cf. Steve Fuller, *Social Epistemology* (Bloomington, IN: Indiana University Press, 1988), ch. 7.
[110] Cf. S. Shapin and S. Shaffer, *Leviathan and the Air-Pump* (Princeton, NJ: Princeton University Press, 1985).
[111] Quoted in Wormell, *Sir John Seeley*, pp. 128–9.

But to the extent that political science could provide a welcome antidote against threats of political disorder, this science itself demanded
a certain politics of discourse; as Bagehot explained, 'in the interest of
sound knowledge, it is essential to narrow to the utmost the debatable
territory'.[112] Thus, in order to be instrumental to the maintenance of
political order, political science had to duplicate the conditions of that
order within itself by gradually eliminating the seeds of debate from
within. What ultimately separated *episteme* from *doxa* was not a set of
higher principles themselves subject to universal consent, but a fine and
flexible line between agreement and disagreement, where the former was
cherished as the basis of sound political discourse, and the latter condemned as a source of discord. Thus, in order to render itself instrumental to the maintenance of political order within the state, the discipline
of politics had to demonstrate an exemplary ability to maintain discursive discipline within itself. This endeavour chimes well with one of the
main promises of all early social science, namely to combat opinion and
rhetoric by continuously expanding the territory of agreement outside
the realm of scientific inquiry.[113]

Another major benefit that it was hoped would ensue from scientific
knowledge of man's political condition was progress, which was not in-
frequently interpreted by early political science as the gradual advance
towards mature statehood. Like Hegel, both Comte and Mill had placed
their concepts of knowledge in a circular relation to the notion of progress.
To them, knowledge was understood as both the medium and outcome
of progress in history: it was a medium to the extent that it permitted prediction and control, and an outcome to the extent that progress would
inevitably give rise to a constant increase in human knowledge, which
would spill over into further progress, and so forth.

Yet such a circularity was possible to uphold only if knowledge itself was
governed by the same general laws of development as the various domains
and objects with which it dealt. As we learn from the *Cours de Philosophie
Positive I* (1830), 'in order to explain purposefully the true nature and
character of positive philosophy, we must take a brief and general glance
at the progressive march of the human mind... each of our principal
conceptions, each branch of our knowledge passes successively through
three different theoretical stages'.[114] To Mill, knowledge is the predomi-
nant element of progress in all stages, being determined by 'the state of
the speculative faculties of mankind; including the nature of the beliefs

---

[112] Bagehot, *Physics and Politics*, p. 119.
[113] Cf. Farr, 'Political Science'.
[114] Auguste Comte, *Cours de Philosophie Positive*, vol. I (Paris: Bachelier, 1830), p. 2.

which by any means they have arrived at, concerning themselves and the world by which they are surrounded'.[115]

Within this view, knowledge and progress were both historically simultaneous and logically interdependent. In the context of early political science, this virtuous circle manifested itself in expectations about the utility of the emergent discipline in the constitution and consolidation of the modern state, as well as in its accounts of the development of modern states out of more primitive forms – a process that was supposed to be propelled by gradual advances in knowledge. Sometimes these two functions could be brought to coincide neatly in intradisciplinary rhetoric. As Woolsey argued,

[i]n earlier times the progress was not so much voluntary and caused by reflection as the result of the laws of man's condition and of the accidents that might befall him. Now he becomes in a greater degree the master of his own condition, he criticizes and analyses, he seeks a better constitution, he shapes his own governments in a degree, he resists grievances and plans changes.[116]

But if the concepts of order and progress were used to express the chief virtues cultivated and worshipped by early political science, and if they also constituted the main rhetorical resources when backing claims to scientific authority and political influence, these concepts were not always easy to reconcile at a deeper philosophical level. Even scientific opinion remained divided as to whether these two sacred concepts were compatible or not, and they were frequently portrayed as contradictory goals of the modern state by the opinionated forces of the day; whereas conservatives tended to place their bet on the former, liberals put their confidence in the latter.

Yet great intellectual and political gains were thought to ensue from their ultimate reconciliation. The most potent strategy in this regard was to point to the crucial role played by scientific knowledge in maintaining a harmony between the forces of order and progress in society, and it was considered a challenge by early political science to demonstrate the mutually reinforcing character of their relationship, all the while emphasizing its own importance in presiding over such a union. In this respect, Comte provided the foundation for most subsequent attempts to reconcile order and progress by reducing both to manifestations of the same underlying law, accessible to positive knowledge alone:

Order and progress, which antiquity regarded as essentially irreconcilable, constitute through the nature of modern civilization two equally intractable conditions,

---

[115] Mill, *A System of Logic*, vol. II, p. 525.
[116] Woolsey, *Political Science*, vol. II, p. 466.

whose intimate and indissoluble combination hereinafter characterize the fundamental difficulty and principal resource of all truly political systems ... order and progress will appear [within a positive science of politics] as two necessarily inseparable aspects of one and the same principle.[117]

Still, the symbiotic relationship between the concept of knowledge on the one hand and the concepts of order and progress on the other also implied a certain undecidability between these concepts, especially since the post-Kantian difference between explaining how knowledge was possible on the one hand, and justifying knowledge on the other had now become common stock. To return to the circle: if knowledge is a condition of order and order a requisite of knowledge, and if progress is a condition of knowledge and knowledge a requisite of progress, then there is no way to explain, let alone justify, knowledge except by recourse to the underlying principles of order and progress, principles which are knowable only within the very same mode of knowledge engendered by progress.

Now one way to handle this circularity – that is, to keep it virtuous – was through a direct appeal to the concept of law itself, which by virtue of a certain ambiguity of its own could sustain claims to scientific authority by associating these with legitimate political authority. While any comprehensive analysis of the concept of law is beyond the scope of the present chapter, the concept needs some elucidation.

Let us start by noting that until quite recently the concept of scientific law has been a rather unproblematic one, since all but a few social scientists still subscribe to some version of basic empiricism to the effect that what is held to exist is a function of what is knowable. According to this background understanding, scientific laws are supposed to be fundamentally different from the laws instituted by some legislative authority, whether human or divine. Whereas the latter are invariably assumed to reflect some will or intention, however cryptic or hidden, the former only express regularities and correlations themselves inherently meaningless and devoid of intentional content. Whereas the latter can be understood as forces influencing the course of phenomena and therefore as existing in their own right, the former are understood as mere constructs in the mind of the scientist, which at best permit prediction and control of phenomena within a universe of chance.[118]

Now this background understanding was not accessible to nineteenth-century science, but is the outcome of a later and logical empiricist

---

[117] Auguste Comte, *Cours de Philosophie Positive*, vol. IV (Paris: Bachelier, 1839), pp. 9–10; cf. also J. B. Bury, *The Idea of Progress: an Inquiry into its Origin and Growth* (New York: Dover Publications, 1955), pp. 291–312.

[118] Cf. I. C. Lieb, 'The Ontological Status of the Laws of Nature', *Review of Metaphysics*, vol. 29, 1985, no. 2, pp. 227–41; Manicas, *History and Philosophy*, chs. 12–13.

attempt to separate the wheat from the chaff in that body of knowledge. To the late nineteenth century, the concept of law was nearly as ambiguous as it had been all the way from the Renaissance on, and it was close to impossible to rigorously discriminate between the above senses of the concept without simultaneously undermining its seeming coherence and general applicability. The fact that we today intuitively discriminate between these senses merely bears witness to the speed with which some concepts die when assisted with a fair amount of philosophical propaganda. Thus, in order to make sense of the nineteenth-century usage of the concept of law, we have to be aware of both its basic ambiguity and its theological ancestry.[119]

What is peculiar to the nineteenth-century interpretation of the concept of law is that even on those occasions when the concept seems to be taken in a purely descriptive sense, particular laws were supposed to have the capacity to act by themselves, yet not necessarily by virtue of being of human or divine origin. Whereas these laws and their workings themselves were unobservable, they nevertheless conditioned phenomena and their interconnections as if they enjoyed independent existence and possessed an authority of their own, since when one spoke of phenomena obeying laws or being governed by them, one did so in quite literal terms.[120]

However, it was not any doctrine of divine implantation that made it seem necessary to impute such mysterious forces to the laws of nature, but a premise which even in our own days conditions some modes of explanation within the social and political sciences, namely, that of the essential uniformity and wholeness of the order of things. Within such a coherent and uniform order, laws are by no means only theoretical expressions of observable regularities between phenomena, but are supposed to be productive of those surface phenomena in much the same way as an authoritative command supposedly gives rise to compliance among those subject to it.

In this respect, and precisely because of his supposedly post-Humean sobriety on this score, Mill stands out as a better example than the more obvious ones of Comte and Spencer.[121] Even if he explicitly denied interest in things in themselves, the very assumption that there is a given

---

[119] J. E. Ruby, 'The Origins of Scientific "Law"', *Journal of the History of Ideas*, vol. 47, 1986, no. 3, pp. 341–59; E. Zilsel, 'The Genesis of the Concept of Scientific Law', *The Philosophical Review*, vol. 51, 1941, pp. 245–67; Louis Dupré, *Passage to Modernity: an Essay in the Hermeneutics of Nature* (New Haven, CT: Yale University Press, 1993), pp. 68f., 126f.

[120] Cf. Mandelbaum, *History, Man, and Reason*, pp. 87f.

[121] Cf. Herbert Spencer, *Essays: Scientific, Political and Speculative* (New York: Appleton, 1892); cf. Comte, *Cours de Philosophie Positive*, vol. IV, *passim*.

order of things, and that this order is readily accessible to investigation made it possible, and indeed inevitable, for Mill to explain the observable by recourse to the unobservable:

[T]he expression law of nature has generally been employed with a sort of tacit reference to the original sense of the word law, namely, the expression of the will of a superior. When, therefore, it appeared that any of the uniformities which were observed in nature would result spontaneously from certain other uniformities, no separate act of creative will being necessary for the production of the derivative uniformities . . . [122]

This notion of productive uniformities had originally found wide acceptance within the natural sciences,[123] and it was very easy to transpose to the sociopolitical domain, since within this context the concept of law already carried a more unequivocal connotation of authoritative command. Within political discourse, the prime source and locus of such an authority to command was the state, which, by means of force and moral persuasion, had the capacity to create and sustain the regularities in the social body deemed essential for the maintenance of political order. Thus, by virtue of its ambiguity, the concept of law not only permitted easy leaps from the natural to the sociopolitical sphere, but made it possible to associate observed regularities in the one sphere with observable regularities in the other, since both were thought to reflect an underlying and stable order, whether celestial or political. Such an interpretation of the concept of law was to remain essentially intact until the natural and cultural domains were finally separated, and the attendant fusion of prescriptive and descriptive connotations broken up.

Thus, it is no coincidence that the late nineteenth century is sometimes described as a period of crisis for determinism.[124] On the one hand, the ambiguity of the concept of law made it less difficult to accept that laws could exist in the political domain, which until then had been widely understood as an oasis of free will in the desert of a wholly determined nature. On the other hand, while those laws holding in the natural domain precluded explicit reference to a lawgiver of any kind, they were not yet open to probabilistic interpretation.[125] Thus, in an age when scientific discourse had been painfully purged of the concept of *causa finalis* but not of *causa efficiens*, the then not-so-enigmatic presumptions of wholeness

[122] Mill, *Science of Logic*, vol. I, p. 366.
[123] Perhaps the best example from the natural sciences is J. Herschel, *Preliminary Study of Natural Philosophy* (1831), part I, ch. III.
[124] Ian Hacking, 'Nineteenth-Century Cracks in the Concept of Determinism', *Journal of the History of Ideas*, vol. 44, 1983, no. 3, pp. 455–75.
[125] Cf. Ian Hacking, *The Taming of Chance* (Cambridge: Cambridge University Press, 1990), pp. 11–15, 125–32, 180–8.

and uniformity could be invoked in order to explain observable facts:

> When states of society, and the causes which produce them, are spoken of as a subject of science, it is implied that there exists a natural correlation among these different elements; that not every variety of combination of these general social facts is possible, but only certain combinations; that, in short, there exist Uniformities and Coexistence between the states of the various social phenomena. And such is the truth; as is indeed a necessary consequence of the influence exercised by every one of those phenomena over every other.[126]

The worldview conveyed by the manuals that provided early political science with its most cherished methodological precepts leaves us with the impression of a well-ordered and predictable universe, but one which God had abandoned in haste, leaving it vibrating with his presence. It was alive, and it was as orderly as a museum in so far as its laws were thought to be as uniform and immutable as those prevailing in the natural world, but with one important difference: whereas the sociopolitical world was also supposed to be inherently progressive, this did not apply to the natural world, whose phenomena were recurrent and whose laws were static.

As I have already mentioned, this left the social and political sciences with the challenge of reconciling the concepts of order and progress by finding the most basic law that conditioned both. The hope of finding such a law carried a great promise with potentially vast political implications since it would permit manipulation of all the lesser laws that governed the course of everyday events, thereby making it possible to attain both order and progress in political practice by carefully reforming society into conformity with its most basic laws; that this hope was paradoxical rarely occurred to early political scientists. Also, and interwoven with this latter expectation, solving this problem was crucial to the possibility of justifying knowledge, and thereby crucial also to the authority of early political science, which was to be instrumental in the process of rational reform.

The search for the ultimate laws of the political world presented the science of politics with another paradox, since the ultimate law of progress must be identical to the inner law of knowledge itself. The ultimate law of progress was reason in its purest and most uncorrupted form, and knowing this law was therefore equivalent to knowing the conditions of possible knowledge. Hence, if knowledge presupposes progress and progress knowledge, progress cannot be known if knowledge is not inherently progressive. But how do we then know that this is the case? As Mill put it, anxiously trying to step out of this circle, progress is 'not a question of the method of the social science, but a theorem of the science itself'.[127]

---

[126] Mill, *Science of Logic*, vol. II, p. 509.
[127] *Ibid.*, p. 511.

Hence, if the ultimate law of the sociopolitical world is that one knows because one progresses and one progresses because one knows, ultimate authority resides firmly in the claim to epistemic authority. Thus, to have access to the laws of the political world was to share in an authority of a different kind from that which came from a mere experience of their surface manifestations. This modern *arcanum imperii* made it possible for early political scientists to bestow their role as legislators with a pre-Enlightenment splendour, since epistemic access to those laws that determined the course of the political world was restricted to them. Furthermore, since the fusion of prescriptive and descriptive connotations in the concept of law made it difficult to distinguish sharply between issuing and discovering laws, the latter activity could easily be seen as equivalent to the former, thus enhancing the legislative role and political legitimacy of political science.

Thus, to the scientification of a province of speculation formerly restricted to divinity and princes corresponded a certain divinization of the new science, and to this divinization of political science corresponded in turn new ways in which political scientists could authorize themselves and their activity, not only by focusing upon the state as an object of inquiry, but also by associating themselves with its authority. Furthermore, in this process, the concept of the state took on an even more transhistorical ring, since being conceived as the sole source and locus of authority, the state was assumed to be an immutable presence behind and ultimate condition of those laws reigning unobstructed in the sociopolitical world.

In this chapter, we have seen how the concept of the state became constitutive of modern political science, but also how the concept of the state was transformed in the process of disciplinary constitution. First, as I have tried to show, the concept of the state furnished early political science with identity. By virtue of its ambiguity, this concept provided early political science with a point of convergence necessary to its coherence. Second, the concept of the state provided early political science with autonomy, by being inferentially connected to the concept of politics in such a way that the latter could be understood as signifying an autonomous domain of knowledge within which the state was given as an object of investigation. Third, this concept was also crucial to the efforts to bestow early political science with scientific and political authority by associating and sometimes identifying these claims to authority with the authority of the state.

To fulfil these constitutive functions, the state concept figured as an empirical and transcendental doublet in both historical and political discourse. It was as much an object of knowledge as a condition of knowledge, its status as object constantly being reinforced by its status as condition, as well as conversely. This double status was further sustained by what to us would look like an outright confusion of concept and reality; by signifying both the institutional reality of the state as an empirical object and the idea of the state as a coherent and abstract whole, the state concept was able to soak up, contain and reconcile an array of conceptual tensions that animated late nineteenth-century political discourse, and which posed a constant threat to efforts at scientification. Simply put, the state concept enabled political discourse to cross the threshold of scientificity.

Yet this concept was modified in the process. Having been conceptualized as doubly abstract with both empirical and transcendental connotations, the state concept was put to use within early political science both as a historical and as a generic category. Gradually, however, and largely as an unintended consequence of the quests for autonomy and authority, the concept came to be interpreted in more squarely transhistorical terms, that is, as signifying the permanent or even axiomatic presence of the state as *the* source of political order in the world. It is this conception rather than a historicized one that accounts for the easy reception that Weber's famous definition enjoyed among political scientists a few decades later.

This conceptual change might well provide clues to the later fate of the state concept within modern political science. The emergence of a more unequivocal transhistorical conception of the state can then be interpreted as indicative of an implicit conviction that the state, once in place, had come to stay for ever, open to progressive modification but closed to total transcendence. Furthermore, by being firmly inscribed within a discourse aspiring to scientific status, the concept of the state was deprived of some of its rhetorical potential, since its proper meaning was now subjected to the authority of political science. Thus, from the viewpoint of *Sattelzeit* expectations, the triumph of the state in political science marks the postponement of political Enlightenment.

Finally, and as we shall see in subsequent chapters, it was the transhistorical concept of the state that at once constituted the obvious target of later attempts to marginalize this concept within scientific discourse. Yet it was precisely its transhistorical connotations that made these attempts futile, since even if one sucessfully got rid of the state as an object of investigation, its presupposed presence as a condition of political knowledge remained a powerful source of coherence and identity. So by the turn of the century, this concept had, fully consonant with Hegel's prophecy, become second nature to us.

3   Throwing the state out

In the previous chapter, I tried to show that the concept of the state was constitutive of modern political science during its formative phase. By providing this emergent discipline with identity, autonomy and authority, the state concept became indispensable to the first efforts to achieve a scientific understanding of politics in tune with contemporary criteria of validity.

What then happened to the concept of the state is well known, but nevertheless somewhat surprising given this legacy. From having been the centrepiece of early political science, during the first decades of the twentieth century the state becomes a target of criticism, until we find the state topic completely marginalized within mainstream political science towards the middle of the century. To take a typical remark from the heyday of state-bashing, the word 'state'

commonly denotes no class of objects that can be identified exactly, and for the same reason it signifies no list of attributes which bears the sanction of common usage. The word must be defined more or less arbitrarily to meet the exigencies of the system of jurisprudence or political philosophy in which it occurs.[1]

Much as a result of this bashing, few political scientists today would argue that the concept of the state has been of any importance to their discipline during the last decades, and many of them would certainly be very happy with this: it is part of the contemporary lore of the discipline that many of its intellectual achievements became possible only after the concept of the state had lost its influence over political theorizing and been excommunicated from scientific vocabulary. When the study of politics did its best to become scientific by a new set of standards, the concept of the state was thrown out from mainstream political science and replaced by substitutes such as 'governmental process' or 'political system'.[2]

---

[1] George Sabine, 'The State', *Encyclopedia of the Social Sciences* (New York: Macmillan, 1934).
[2] Not surprisingly, theories of the state are marked by their absence in a recent survey of postwar political science by L. Tivey, 'Introduction: Philosophy, Science, Ideology', in

In this chapter I shall deal with this attempt to throw the state concept out from the vocabulary of political science, arguing that such attempts have largely been futile. As I shall try to show, the spectres of Hegel have continued to haunt us: arguments to the effect that the state concept ought to be excommunicated from political science abound in the literature, but however persuasive such arguments may have been, they have invariably led to a quest for conceptual substitutes.

These substitutes have left the basic conceptual identity of the state untouched by the spirit of criticism, however. As I shall argue, whenever the concept of the state has been thrown out, some other semantically equivalent concept has been brought in through the back door in order to explain and justify the presence of political order, thus merely restoring the initial problem which state-bashers were trying to avoid or circumvent. By a semantically equivalent concept, I mean a concept which does nothing to change the inferential connections in the larger system of concepts into which it is introduced.

The objective of this chapter is not primarily to recapitulate arguments against the state, since most of them are already too well known to deserve reiteration. Rather, what is of interest is to analyse what these arguments presuppose in order to make sense and persuade, and what they in turn have done to the state concept in terms of its place and function within political discourse. Doing this requires attention to how the underlying ontological and epistemological foundations of political science have changed, and how these changes have affected the semantics of the state concept in terms of its meaning and reference.

Now what makes attempts to excommunicate the concept of the state puzzling is the fact that they took place against the backdrop of another development that would intuitively lead us to expect the reverse. The estrangement of the concept of the state within scientific discourse occurred during a period and in national contexts which most sociologists, political scientists and historians agree to be marked by the final triumph of the state, now in its welfare guise, and this quite regardless of their disagreement over what the state is and why this happened.

This poses a peculiar methodological problem since we have to account for the relative silence surrounding the state concept within a

L. Tivey and A. Wright (eds.), *Political Thought since 1945: Philosophy, Science, Ideology* (Aldershot: Edward Elgar, 1992), pp. 1–71. This neglect has been subject to lamentary remarks; see Jean Blondel, *The Discipline of Politics* (London: Butterworths, 1981), pp. 134–61; Kenneth H. F. Dyson, *The State Tradition in Western Europe: a Study of an Idea and an Institution* (Oxford: Martin Robertson, 1980); John Keane, introduction, in J. Keane (ed.), *Civil Society and the State: New European Perspectives* (London: Verso, 1988).

discourse that has arguably remained animated by its presence, and been instrumental in its consolidation.

But how to deal with discursive silences without explaining them in terms of intentional concealment? I think we have to make silence speak for itself. Since people speak most of what they do not have, speech is sometimes the best evidence of the absence of those objects which men desire or fear most. Conversely, since people rarely speak of that which goes without saying, silence is sometimes the best evidence that some objects have become all too present to qualify as objects of desire or fear. Perhaps the discourse on the state is another example of this human propensity, since it seems to culminate at times when and in places where its object is but a dream, and recedes into the background when and where the dream seems within reach and desire or fear fades away.

This requires us to investigate changes in the semantics of the state. As I argued in the previous chapter, the living museum of political forms created by early political science had its inner order defined by a posited convergence between concept and reality in which the state concept functioned as an indispensable nexus. In the living museum, concept and reality were inseparable within this particular way of analysing political order, since concept and reality had not been logically divorced. Ideas and institutions were supposed to coincide within a given concept, and political reality was nothing more and nothing less than the fusion of ideas and institutions as signified by such a concept. In the domain of objectivity created by early political science, political concepts were real by virtue of political reality being essentially conceptual.

But the possibility and persuasiveness of state-bashing is conditioned by a dramatic change in this relationship between political concepts and political reality. First and most important, the fusion of concept and reality described above is broken up, and political reality becomes conceptualized as classes of phenomena represented by concepts, these concepts themselves being defined and structured according to the demands of a theoretical logic, divorced from actual political practices by means of new epistemic criteria of validity. Second and corollary, an *aporia* between descriptive and prescriptive statements is brought to bear on political reflection as its primary instrument of self-criticism. While this distinction had been around before, it was now given a new twist: is and ought are not now merely regarded as distinct, but there is a growing paradoxical insistence that they ought to be held distinct for reasons of scientific clarity and political legitimacy. Third and finally, the concept of law described in the previous chapter becomes bifurcated, and a firm logical distinction between positive law and mere regularities reinforces the split between positive political theorizing, normative concerns and political practice. Taken together, these tendencies condition a major change in the structure and content of political knowledge; as has been pointed out by Gunnell, the history of modern political science is in part a history of how a science *in* politics is gradually transformed into a science about politics.[3]

The rest of this chapter is subdivided as follows. In the first section I shall describe how state-bashers identified their target in terms of a tradition of state theorizing. Second, I shall describe some of the main arguments directed against the state concept. Third, I shall discuss the proposed replacements, trying to demonstrate that they merely serve to reintroduce the concept of the state in forever new semantic guises.

Reconstructing monism

When state-bashing first gained momentum within political science, it was targeted at a conceptual edifice that was considerably larger than the state concept we have been discussing in the previous chapter. What was criticized was neither the state concept in isolation, nor early political science, but an entire tradition of state theorizing and state practice. Before we can direct our attention to the critique of the state concept proper, a few words need to be said about this tradition, and how it was construed and redefined to fit these critical projects.

Within academic disciplines traditions are usually invented in order to reinforce or undermine some present version of disciplinary identity. Telling a good story fulfils an important function in the constitution of disciplinarity, and talk of traditions provides explanations of how a given disciplinary identity has emerged that are either supportive or debunking of that identity.[4]

By the way they are defined, traditions also sometimes presuppose what is explicitly denied by those inventing them for their critical or legitimating purposes. As I shall try to show in this section, the construction of a state tradition was made possible by granting a significance to the state concept which it had lacked before it was inscribed within the context of early political science. Consequently, by granting such significance to the state, its critics came to share assumptions of the tradition which they had construed in order to oppose, a fact which explains some of the ultimate futility of the state-bashing enterprise.

[3] John G. Gunnell, *Between Philosophy and Politics: the Alienation of Political Theory* (Amherst, MA: University of Massachusetts Press, 1986), pp. 2, 152.

[4] Jens Bartelson, 'Short Circuits: Society and Tradition in International Relations Theory', *Review of International Studies*, vol. 22, 1996, no. 4, pp. 339–60.

The construction of this state tradition rested upon a set of implicit assumptions. First, state-bashers were inclined to regard the concept of the state as the centrepiece of the Western political tradition, and this tradition was held to be sufficiently coherent and lasting to merit critical attention. Second, the state concept was held to be redundant, either when taken as an embodiment of the ideas and institutions of modern politics or when taken as a purely lexical entity, wholly external to those ideas and institutions. Taken together, these assumptions created a dilemma for state-bashers. The greater the constitutive role attributed to the concept of the state when defining the state tradition, the more difficult the case for discursive marginalization would seem to be at first glance. And conversely: the more persuasive the arguments in favour of excommunication, the more difficult it would seem to be to explain why this tradition had been able to prevail for so long. The rhetorical success of state-bashing depended on the ability to handle this dilemma, by asserting the historical importance of the state concept while denying its significance in the present. This was a delicate rhetorical strategy which in turn made it necessary to posit a sharp discontinuity between past and present in political theory and practice alike, most visible in the claims to newness attending the efforts at excommunication.

But as these efforts continued, the way of constructing the state tradition underwent significant changes. It is to these that we now must turn our attention. What the early critics of the concept of the state opposed were not primarily the legal and political theories of their immediate predecessors, but what they took to be *the* traditional concept of the state. What was criticized was not a singular concept embodied in singular works but rather, since the critics had inherited their understanding of the relationship between concept and reality from their idealist predecessors, a tradition embodying the total experience of statehood. To early state-bashers, this was a fruitful confusion which permitted them to blend political engagement with pleas for scientific rigour, thus reinforcing their political arguments with epistemological ones, and conversely.[5]

In order to construct this tradition, the state concept was superimposed upon a past which stretched far beyond the origins of this discipline, and whose scope sometimes even extended far beyond its transhistorical application during that period. The state concept was still commonly

[5] Cf. Stephan Collini, Donald Winch and John Burrow, *That Noble Science of Politics: a Study in Nineteenth-Century Intellectual History* (Cambridge: Cambridge University Press, 1983); James Farr, 'Political Science and the Enlightenment of Enthusiasm', *American Political Science Review*, vol. 82, 1988, no. 1, pp. 51–69; see also R. Seidelman and E. J. Harpham, *Disenchanted Realists: Political Science and the American Crisis 1884–1984* (New York: SUNY, 1985:), esp. ch. 5.

thought to connote a unified political organization within a fixed territory, endowed with indivisible, limitless and morally supreme authority, but now it became equally common to interpret it as both expressive and constitutive of a distinct and coherent tradition, being embodied in the state and its institutions.[6]

In order to provide the raw material out of which alternative notions of political order could be conceptualized and legitimized, a rival tradition of pluralist political thought was simultaneously constructed. The rudiments of such a tradition were already present in the historiography of Gierke, Maitland and Figgis, so much of the work was a matter of articulating it and spelling out its political implications in the present.[7] These authors, and Gierke in particular, had narrated the history of political thought as if the state – however embryonic – had been present from the beginning, while lamenting this presence with a nostalgic glance at that which it had gradually cancelled out during its march forward: the real personality of corporations and groups, as opposed to the fictitious personality granted to them by the state.[8]

When it came to the exact origins of the state tradition, there was no agreement among state-bashers. According to Laski, the traditional theory of the state 'was born in an age of crisis and . . . its revivification has synchronized with some momentous event which has signalized a change in the distribution of political power'.[9] In this process, the 'medieval worship of unity . . . is inherited by the modern state; and what changes in the four centuries of its modern history is simply the place in which the controlling factor of unity is to be found'.[10] Likewise Cole, another fierce

[6] For some contemporary statements see Ellen Deborah Ellis, 'The Pluralistic State', *American Political Science Review*, vol. 14, 1920, no. 3, pp. 395–7; Francis W. Coker, 'The Technique of the Pluralist State', *American Political Science Review*, vol. 15, 1921, no. 2, pp. 186–213; George H. Sabine, 'Pluralism: a Point of View', *American Political Science Review*, vol. 17, 1923, no. 1, pp. 34–9. To take a few examples from contemporary historiography, C. H. McIlwain, *The Growth of Political Thought in the West* (New York: Macmillan, 1932); Raymond G. Gettell, *History of Political Thought* (New York: Century, 1925); A. R. Lord, *The Principles of Politics: an Introduction to the Study of the Evolution of Political Ideas* (Oxford: Clarendon, 1921); C. E. Vaughn, *Studies in the History of Political Philosophy before and after Rousseau* (Manchester: Manchester University Press, 1925).

[7] See for example Otto Gierke, *Political Theories of the Middle Age*, trans. Frederic W. Maitland (Cambridge: Cambridge University Press, 1900); Frederic W. Maitland, translator's introduction to Gierke, *Political Theories of the Middle Age* (Cambridge: Cambridge University Press, 1900); John N. Figgis, *Churches in the Modern State* (London, 1913).

[8] For an analysis, see David Runciman, *Pluralism and the Personality of the State* (Cambridge: Cambridge University Press, 1997), chs. 2–3; Andrew Vincent, *Theories of the State* (Oxford: Basil Blackwell, 1987), ch. 6.

[9] Harold J. Laski, *Foundations of Sovereignty and Other Essays* (New Haven, CT: Yale University Press, 1921), p. 233.

[10] Harold J. Laski, *Authority in the Modern State* (New Haven, CT: Yale University Press, 1919), p. 22.

critic of the state, saw the origin of this tradition in the battles between the Church and emergent secular powers during the Middle Ages.[11] But while Laski and Cole traced the origin of the traditional theory of the state to the dissolution of medieval Christendom, Duguit identified such a tradition as a more recent and specifically modern phenomenon, an offspring of political modernity and its rationalism. Thus, to him

[t]he theory of the state under which most civilized peoples of the world over have lived was based on principles which many people served with almost religious intensity. They were, so it was contended, entitled to the final loyalty of men. They were a political hinterland won for science. It was a system with an honourable history.[12]

Another example is provided by Friedrich, who saw the rise of the modern state tradition as the result of a gradual corruption of Aristotelian ideals:

[u]nderlying all the many arguments and disagreements between these modern thinkers we find a common core of worship for the secular political community and its organization – a deification of the state.[13]

Even those who were less radical in their criticism of the state nevertheless started out from the undisputed assumption of a state tradition organizing political thought and action into a coherent and continuous whole. For example, Sabine and MacIver, both of whom were trying to strike a balance between the traditional theory of the state and the rival pluralist conception, assumed not only that there was such a thing as a lasting state tradition, but that this tradition had also been constitutive of the institutional realities of the modern state.[14] Sabine was most explicit on this point:

The sovereign state is a specifically modern phenomenon and its appearance was the epoch-making event of the early-modern period. It was born of century-long contests, and political theory, then as now, was largely an attempt to state the general drift of events and to bring the newer tendencies to successful birth.[15]

For critical purposes, the state and the concept of a distinct state tradition were associated in three different ways. First, since the state tradition was defined in terms of the state concept and vice versa, the target of criticism was inherently ambiguous right from the start; yet in this way the

[11] G. D. H. Cole, *Essays in Social Theory* (London: Macmillan, 1950), p. 14.
[12] Leon Duguit, *Law in the Modern State* (New York: Huebsch, 1919), p. xxxvii.
[13] C. J. Friedrich, 'The Deification of the State', *Review of Politics*, vol. 1, 1939, p. 29.
[14] Sabine, 'Pluralism: a Point of View', pp. 34–50; MacIver, R. M., *The Modern State* (London: Oxford University Press, 1926), pp. 426ff.
[15] George H. Sabine, 'The Concept of the State as Power', *Philosophical Review*, vol. 29, 1920, no. 4, pp. 30–3.

leverage of criticism could be maximized, since critics could move back and forth between the state concept and the state tradition with considerable ease. Second, by targeting a state tradition thus constructed, its critics implicitly accepted its existence as a historical fact. What was doubted was the value of such a tradition, not its existence. Third, by assuming that this tradition had been constitutive of modern political life, state critics elevated it to imperial proportions, the net consequence being but a further reification of the state.

Taken together, these elements of critical practice had perverse effects, since the importance of the tradition thus invented increased with the leverage of the criticism directed against it. The more past political theory and practice that could be declared parts of a state tradition, the more urgent their demise would seem. But the more of the past that could be subsumed under that tradition, the more organizing power was thereby invested in the concept of the state. This concept was now used to reconstruct a past from which its early critics eagerly wished to emancipate modern political knowledge, but with that concept still functioning as a principle of identity of the discipline, criticism could not but simultaneously affirm its discursive centrality.

But all this was to change with the second wave of criticism of the state. If the early ways of conceptualizing a state tradition assumed that the state concept was both constitutive and expressive of that tradition, later ways of doing this started by assuming that the state concept should ideally represent a given institutional reality, and then went on to construct a tradition consisting of a succession of failures in this respect. The state tradition was now conceptualized as a tradition of state theorizing within political science, a tradition tied together by its systematic inability to make sense of political reality as a result of its obsession with the state.

As we shall see below, legal positivism and logical empiricism provided political science with the conceptual resources necessary for this redefinition of the state tradition. This change in the way the state tradition was conceived enabled a new set of rhetorical strategies in the debate over the state. On the one hand, those who sought to defend what they believed to be a traditional conception of the state could now confidently argue that pluralists and guild socialists had merely engaged in beating a straw man, since if subjected to careful analysis, the kind of tradition which they opposed did not exist outside the realm of legal fiction.[16] On the other, state-bashers had to confront a crude awareness of the difference

---

[16] Ellis, 'The Pluralistic State'; W. Y. Elliot, 'The Pragmatic Politics of Mr H. J. Laski', *American Political Science Review*, vol. 18, 1924, no. 2, pp. 251–75; W. Y. Elliot, 'Sovereign State or Sovereign Group?', *American Political Science Review*, vol. 19, 1925, no. 3, pp. 475–97.

between ought and is in political reasoning, and a perceived difference between a tradition of normative theorizing and a tradition of empirical theorizing about the state. The obvious challenge here was how to turn these rather freshly felt distinctions to a rhetorical advantage in the battle over the state.

Gradually, the state tradition becomes reconceptualized into an intradisciplinary concern, however. What is targeted is no longer the imagined referent of the state concept, or any imagined state tradition responsible for its permanence in political reality, but the prevalence of the singular term 'state', and its lamentable spell upon empirical theorizing. Thus Bentley, in a work that retrospectively came to be celebrated as the 'beginning of the modern political behaviour approach',[17] declared the concept of the state to be at once redundant, yet as having been quite indispensable as a rhetorical resource:

The 'idea of the state' has been very prominent, no doubt, among the intellectual amusements of the past, and at particular places and times it has served to help give coherent and pretentious expression to some particular group's activity ... I may add here that 'sovereignty' is of no more interest to us than the state. Sovereignty has its very important place in arguments in defense of an existing government, or in verbal assaults on a government in the name of the populace or of some other pretender, or in fine-spun legal expositions of what is about to be done. But as soon as it gets out of the pages of the lawbook or the political pamphlet, it is a piteous, threadbare joke.[18]

Likewise, even to Merriam, who had earlier put the state concept to analytical use, theories of the state were now seen as being of dubious value to empirical political science, and instead being 'large measure justifications and rationalizations of groups in power or seeking power – the special pleading of races, religions, classes, in behalf of their special situation'.[19]

Gradually, however, the presence of the concept of the state was not exclusively interpreted as expressive of group interests, but rather associated with disciplinary accidents that had given this concept undue prominence within the discipline of political science. What appeared as increasingly problematic was no longer the salience of the state concept in prescientific political theorizing, but rather those scientific theories which had invested it with explanatory power. Thus, if there was any state tradition

[17] Heinz Eulau, Samuel J. Eldersveld and Morris Janowitz (eds.), *Political Behaviour: a Reader in Theory and Research* (Glencoe, IL: The Free Press, 1956), p. 7.

[18] Arthur F. Bentley, *The Process of Government: a Study of Social Pressures* [1908] (Bloomington, IN: Principia Press, 1935), pp. 263–4.

[19] Charles E. Merriam, *New Aspects of Politics* (Chicago, IL: University of Chicago Press, 1931), p. xiv; cf. Charles E. Merriam, 'The Present State of the Study of Politics', *American Political Science Review*, vol. 15, 1921, no. 2, pp. 173–85.

to oppose, it was to be found within political science, not in the legacy of Western political thought and practice. According to Catlin,

> To the nature of the subject-matter of Politics far too little attention has been given. It has been assumed off-hand that the subject-matter of Politics is the State or states, regardless of the fact that the State, in the modern sense, did not exist in the Middle Ages, and that the *Polis* which formed the centre of Aristotle's thoughts on τα Πολιτικα could more appropriately be described as 'the city-community' than as the State... [t]his is one great *petitio principii* inherited from an age which wished, for polemical reasons, to regard the State and not the Church as the paramount organization, and as synonymous with the community and with organized society. The assumption is unwarranted, unscientific, and obstructive.[20]

Later, when a discursive hegemony had been established within mainstream political science to the effect that the state concept was redundant, the temptation to beat the dead horse remained strong, even if such beating was now a strictly intradisciplinary affair with no obvious political implications outside academia. With the state concept being constitutive of prescientific political theorizing, rather than constitutive of its main object of inquiry, state-bashing became seemingly depoliticized: it was perfectly possible for one and the same scholar to deny the importance of the analytical value of the state concept to political theorizing, while being in favour of, say, the expansion of the welfare state. Obviously, the study of politics and and politics proper were now further apart.

This is nowhere more visible than in the behaviouralist manifestos, in which credit was claimed for having banished the concept of the state from scientific discourse, on grounds that this concept was to blame for the inability of political science to attain scientific credibility. 'If we are to understand what has given political science its minimal coherence over the centuries', writes Easton, 'we must reconstruct prevailing conceptions of the subject matter of political science.' According to him, the 'opinion is broadly held that what draws the various divisions of political science together is the fact that they all deal with the state'.[21]

The critique of the concept of the state had now become wholly divorced from a political critique of the institutional realities of the state. The behavioural reconstruction of the state tradition presupposed a sharp divide between concept and reality: if we cannot attain knowledge of the state because of the opacity and ambiguity of the state concept, that

---

[20] G. E. G. Catlin, *The Science and Method of Politics* (New York: Knopf, 1927), pp. 139–40.

[21] David Easton, *The Political System: an Inquiry into the State of Political Science* (New York: Knopf, 1953), p. 107.

means that the state itself does not exist, and what does not exist cannot be criticized. As a consequence of the attempt to assimilate the core concepts of political philosophy to the new standards of scientific inquiry, the critique of the concept of the state became as crucial to behavioural self-consciousness as the concept of the state itself had been to the founders of modern political science:

[b]earing in mind the actual history of the political use of the concept, it is difficult to understand how it ever could prove to be fruitful for empirical work; its importance lies largely in the field of practical politics as an instrument to achieve national cohesion rather than in the area of thoughtful analysis.[22]

When the behaviouralists later celebrated their successes, almost all talk of the concept of the state and a corresponding tradition had given way to a reconstruction of the history of political science in other terms, preferably in such terms that also were used to describe and analyse present political conditions; even accounts of what Plato and Aristotle had written and possibly meant could now be phrased in terms of political systems and processes, without the slightest anachronism being felt.[23] Hence, the fact that modern political science had been logically and historically conditioned by the concept of the state was effectively denied through the imposition of a silence, as was the importance of the earlier pluralist critique of the state concept that had cleared the space for the behavioural revolution.[24]

Eventually the identity of modern political science was conditioned by a historiography that not only implicitly denied the importance of the state concept during the formation of the discipline, but which also implicitly denied the importance of the state concept as a target of intradisciplinary criticism. It was this double denial of its traditional status that made the silence surrounding it so difficult to ponder, and its previous presence so enigmatic to a discipline for which '[p]olitical behavior is not and should not be a speciality, for it represents rather an orientation or a point of view which aims at stating all the phenomena of government in terms of the observed and observable behavior of men'.[25]

[22] *Ibid.*, p. 112.
[23] Cf. Gabriel A. Almond, 'The Return to the State', in Gabriel A. Almond, *A Discipline Divided: Schools and Sects in Political Science* (Newbury Park, CA: Sage, 1990), pp. 189–218.
[24] See Robert Dahl, 'The Behavioral Approach in Political Science: Epitaph for a Monument of a Successful Protest', *American Political Science Review*, vol. 55, 1961, no. 4, pp. 763–72.
[25] David Truman, 'The Implications of Political Behavior Research', Social Science Research Council, *Items*, December 1951, p. 39.

In this section, we have seen how the efforts to excommunicate the state concept necessitated the construction of a tradition against which criticism could be directed, and how the ways of constructing and identifying such a tradition changed in the course of the bashing. Whereas the early pluralist critics identified this tradition as a coherent and lasting fusion of the ideas and institutions of statehood, their behaviouralist successors considerably narrowed the target of criticism, by identifying the presence of such a tradition as an intradisciplinary problem. But if one defined the state tradition on the basis of the concept of the state, one also defined the content of this concept on the basis of its perceived place in this tradition. It is to this aspect of the state-bashing enterprise we now must pay attention.

Making the case against monism

Turning now to the arguments why the concept of the state ought to be excommunicated from the domain of political science, we will be able to see how these are conditioned by a reconceptualization of the relation between concepts and political reality. From having been essentially constitutive and expressive of the state, the state concept was gradually disentangled from its institutional realities and turned into a means of representing these realities, and then criticized for its inability to represent these realities accurately.

Yet this kind of semantic criticism would hardly have been possible or intelligible without a prior criticism of the state concept as a fusion of ideas of institutions. Criticizing the state concept for its inability to accurately represent a class of phenomena came close to presupposing that this class was in fact empty. As I will try to show, the behaviouralist critique of the state was conditioned by the failure of early pluralists to account for the presence of political order without invoking the state concept or any semantically equivalent concept. Their way of doubting the reality of the state without doubting the inherited way to phrase the problem of political order seems to be an important condition of all later tendencies to doubt the analytical value of the state concept.

The trouble with most early attempts to criticize the state was the fact that they were phrased within the same vocabulary out of which the modern state concept had once emerged and acquired its double status as both empirical and transcendental as described in chapter 2. Thus the efforts to reconceptualize the state in other terms made the presence of political order difficult to explain, let alone justify, as long as the latter problem remained phrased in the idiom of idealist philosophy.

As Barker stated in an article that came to define the terms of much of the subsequent debate on the state,

[a]dmitting for the moment that the State is the broader and wider synthesis, it may, just because of its breadth, be an imperfect synthesis, which only achieves success by neglecting factors for which it should find room. It may be a bare and forced universal, purchased at the cost of many individuals. The very attempt of factors which conceive themselves neglected to push themselves forward as absolute wholes on their own account may serve as an incentive to a truer synthesis.[26]

Or, as John Dewey had it:

Every institution ... has its sovereignty, or authority, and its laws and rights. It is only a false abstraction which makes us conceive of sovereignty, or authority, and of law and rights as inhering only in some supreme organization, as the national state.[27]

Articulated in this way, criticism of the state was bound to be much of an away game. Since the monist underpinnings of the traditional theory of the state were beyond the reach of criticism, rather constituting its very foundation, early state-bashers had to confront a problem of political order which was cast in monist terms. Questioning the state concept then implied that the actual presence of political order became difficult to account for coherently. Since early attempts to dispose of the state concept were caught in a field of tension between monist and pluralist doctrines, any argument to the effect that sovereignty is or ought to be divisible merely begged the question of how order and relative harmony was possible among a plurality of institutions and values, themselves nominally or relationally sovereign, in the absence of any universally sovereign institution or value. To question the state concept was therefore to invite a conceptual zero-sum game, and early attempts to diminish the importance of or to excommunicate the state concept within political theorizing were frequently trapped within a problematic that was defined as *a priori* insoluble. Since the terms of this problematic were accepted by state-bashers themselves, they had considerable difficulties in remaining consistent in their critique, let alone in their more practical recommendations.

Yet simultaneously the above statements also indicate what was becoming the main upshot of the early critics, namely, that political reality

---

[26] Ernest Barker, 'The Discredited State: Thoughts on Politics Before the War', *The Political Quarterly*, vol. 7, 1915, no. 5, p. 116; cf. also Ernest Barker, 'The Superstition of the State', *Times Literary Supplement*, July 1918.

[27] John Dewey, *Outlines of a Critical Theory of Ethics* [1891] (New York: Hilary House, 1957), p. 172.

had changed dramatically, and that the traditional concept of the state was now unable to make sense of what was going on on its outside. As Hobhouse argued in his *The Metaphysical Theory of the State* (1918),

[t]he idealistic habit of talking of 'the state' as though there were only one type that is real, while all existing instances may be regarded as merely casual and secondary aberrations, bars the way to a frank exposition of the contrast of which in experience we are painfully aware between that which might be and that which is.[28]

Or as Sabine put it, '[t]he traditional notion of the state is out of accord with present political conditions; in a word, we have here a case in which the political evolution has outstripped the theoretical statement of political relations'.[29] Hence, a strong case for conceptual scepticism was articulated against the backdrop of a perceived mismatch between the conceptual world of political science and its way of conceptualizing political reality. It is to the nature of this perceived mismatch that we now must turn.

Four aspects of the concept of the state were singled out for criticism by the early pluralist critics. First, it was asserted that this concept had carried with it the assumption of a unified political whole in which the interests, loyalties and moral allegiances of the citizen subjects converged, but that this ideal was now about to wither away in the face of present tendencies such as the intensified polarization of interest between labour and capital. The state was no longer a unity but a multiplicity that happened to be stuck within a given territory.[30]

Second, it was asserted that the same set of developments that had dissolved the sociocultural unity of the state was also incompatible with the notion of indivisible sovereignty, itself one of the defining characteristics of the traditional concept of the state. Authority was no longer indivisible, but ought to be understood as profoundly and irreversibly divided between groups and institutions in society.

Third, and largely corollary, the authority wielded by the state over the social body could no longer be understood as comprehensive and unlimited, since democratization and enlarged franchise had effectively bridled any such claims. Authority was no longer centralized and absolute, but ought to be understood as diluted and dispersed in the social body.[31]

---

[28] L. T. Hobhouse, *The Metaphysical Theory of the State* (London: Allen & Unwin, 1918), p. 96.

[29] Sabine, 'Concept of the State', p. 301.

[30] That the emergence of organized labour necessitated a reconceptualization of the state was a widespread conviction during this period, but was perhaps most explicitly argued by G. D. H. Cole. See Cole, *Essays*.

[31] For a contemporary list of the factors which had contributed to their reaction against the state, see M. P. Follett, *The New State: Group Organization – the Solution of Popular Government* (London: Longmans, Green, 1918), p. 9.

Fourth, it was generally held among the critics of the state that the state should no longer be understood as having moral superiority in relation to competing sources of value within society. Instead, the virtues of statehood ought to be judged in more pragmatic terms, on the basis of their instrumental value for the needs and goals of the community at large. The state was no longer an end in itself, but ought to be understood as a means to different and sometimes competing ends. In moral terms, society contained a plurality of values and norms to be reckoned with.

Thus, and according to the way in which early twentieth-century political experience was now conceptualized, the traditional concept of the state appeared to be hopelessly outdated, since it failed to make sense of the emergent plurality of institutions and values within what until then had appeared as a unified whole. Taken together, however, these critical claims amounted to a wholesale questioning of the very foundations of political order, since the state had been identified as *the* source and locus of such an order. This becomes evident if we turn to the arguments directed against these aspects of the state.

As indicated above, even if the notion of the state as a unity which transcends all particularity was attacked primarily because it was out of tune with the way political realities of the day were conceptualized, arguments against this *a priori* unity tended to accept the ontological presuppositions which had made it possible to conceive of the state as a unity in the first place. Thus, according to Laski, on the one hand, '[w]e cannot avoid the temptation that bids us make our State a unity. It is to be all-absorptive. All groups within itself are to be but ministrants to its life; their reality is the outcome of its sovereignty, since without it they could have no existence.'[32] But, on the other, and now drawing on the theory of real personality of groups, 'we do not proceed from the State to the parts of the State on the ground that the State is more fundamentally unified than its parts, but we, on the contrary, admit that the parts are as real and as self-sufficient as the whole'.[33] But all critics of the state did not have to assert the real personality of groups and associations within the state in order to do away with its *a priori* unity. According to Barker, we are at liberty to eliminate

transcendent personality and transcendent will from associations; we may be content to speak of associations as schemes in which real and individual persons and wills are related to one another by means of a common and organizing idea. We may conceive of the state as such a scheme based on the political idea of law

[32] Harold J. Laski, *Studies in the Problem of Sovereignty* (New Haven, CT: Yale University Press, 1917), p. 1.
[33] *Ibid.*, p. 9.

and order; we may conceive it as containing, or at any rate coexisting with, a rich variety of schemes based on a rich variety of ideas.[34]

Similarly, Duguit, also vehemently arguing against the presumption of a unitary will embodied in the state, held that 'all we have is the will of some individuals and that will, even if it be unanimous, is still only a will of a sum of individuals, that is to say, an individual will with no right to impose itself on anyone who resists it'.[35] And again, a similar point was made by Friedrich, according to whom

[w]e may go so far as to assert that *the state does not exist*. There are governments, peoples, countries, there are kings, parliaments, dictators, parties and concentration camps, but there is no evidence in support of the idea that some sort of holy unity, some mystical transcendence need be attributed to them, that they indeed should be seen as a whole.[36]

Now this kind of criticism was echoed not only by those who shared the pluralist and guild socialist suspicion against the state, but also by those who sought to rescue the concept of the state from total demise, while granting that it stood in need of reinterpretation in order to make sense of new realities. To MacIver, 'it is a logical error to seek to interpret the unity of a whole as though it were exactly correspondent to the unity of its members or components',[37] yet the state itself 'has the essential character of a corporation'.[38] Likewise Sabine, to whom the 'unity imputed to the state is of a purely formal, or even nominal, kind', the 'hypothesis of a unified state power, wholly abstracted from any agency of government, must be examined in the light of some salient features of political organization'.[39]

Since this kind of criticism aimed at bringing the concept of the state closer to reality by reducing it to more tangible components and then granting these components a life of their own, the chief manifestation of the problem of political order that had to be confronted was what constituted the most fundamental parts of the state, and how the relationship between these parts ought to be understood in the absence of a higher unity or principle to which they could be referred. After all, in order to be conceived of as parts, they had to be conceived of as parts of something that was not a part of itself. As we shall see in the third section, by accepting the ontological terms in which this problem had originally been cast, critics of the state found it increasingly difficult to provide a

[34] Barker, 'The Discredited State', p. 113.
[35] Duguit, *Law in the Modern State*, p. xli.
[36] Friedrich, 'Deification of the State', p. 29.
[37] MacIver, *The Modern State*, p. 452.
[38] *Ibid.*, p. 479.
[39] Sabine, 'The Concept of the State', p. 311.

solution to the problem of political order without bringing the concept of the state, or some semantically equivalent notion, back in.

The second line of criticism was directed against another central aspect of the traditional concept of the state, namely the idea that the sovereignty of the state is or ought to be indivisible. In most accounts of the traditional concept indivisibility of state authority was interpreted as a necessary condition of state unity, and state unity interpreted as a corollary of indivisibility. Consequently, the same set of arguments that was used to demonstrate that this *a priori* unity was but a legal and philosophical fiction could easily be twisted into arguments to the effect that the idea of indivisible sovereignty was also fictitious, since it failed to do justice to the actual distribution of power in the social body and was incompatible with the ideals of pluralist democracy. Again according to Laski, '[w]e are told that sovereignty is indivisible; yet, unless again we wish merely to play upon words, the fact of its broad partition is on every hand obvious'.[40] Therefore, in order to make sense of the facts of modern political life, we have to realize that

[p]ower is . . . the right to will acts of general reference, and the suggestion is made that it should be conferred where it is probable that it can be most usefully exerted. In this aspect it becomes not unlikely that we have in the past, over-emphasised the necessity for its concentration at a single point in the social structure. We have been so concerned, particularly as lawyers, in demonstrating the paramountcy of the state, that we have taken too little regard of the life outside its categories.[41]

Similarly, to Duguit

national sovereignty is by definition one and indivisible; it implies the suppression in the national territory of all groups exercising independent control. It is however obvious that where there is decentralization or federalism such groups maintain a vigorous existence.[42]

Due to the inherent logic of their arguments, these critics were predisposed to discern an outright contradiction between the idea of indivisibility and the way they conceived of modern politics; but instead of dissolving this contradiction by appealing to the distinction between legal fiction and empirical reality, as some of their contemporaries did, they wanted to accommodate the theory of the state to the new 'facts' by insisting on the theoretical *cum* practical divisibility of sovereignty. As we shall see below, this meant that they sought to retain some notion of sovereign authority while dovetailing it with the actual independence and autonomy of other institutions in the social body, which of course begged the

---

[40] Laski, *Authority in the Modern State*, pp. 119–20.
[41] *Ibid.*, p. 74.
[42] Duguit, *Law in the Modern State*, pp. 18, 19–25.

question of how one could possibly justify the exercise of state authority over those institutions. This leads us over to the next line of criticism.

As said above, there was a widespread suspicion among state-bashers that the imagined unity of the state and the indivisibility of its authority also licensed an unlimited exercise of that authority over the social body, and that this was a tendency that must be safeguarded against in modern societies. Again, Laski was among the first to reformulate this old whig suspicion in functionalist and organizational terms. To him, 'it is a sheer illusion to imagine that the authority of the state has any other safeguard than the will of its members'.[43] Yet the sovereignty of the state

no longer commands anything more than a partial and spasmodic acceptance. For it is clearly understood that it in practice means governmental sovereignty; and the need for the limitation of governmental powers is perceived by men of every shade of opinion.[44]

The proper antidote to the expansive tendencies of the state was to insist that the state in fact is nothing but a 'society of governors and governed' and that 'its superiority can have logical reference only to the sphere that it has marked out for its own and then only to the extent to which that sphere is not successfully challenged'.[45] Since

it is obvious that there are realms over which its authority ought not to be exerted. That is to foreshadow a division, not of powers, but of power upon the basis of functions. It is to picture a society in which authority is not hierarchical but coordinate.[46]

Of course, very little was new about this strongly felt need to subject state power to limits. What was new, however, was the idea that this problem was a matter of social organization rather than a matter of constitutional checks and balances. Even a jurist such as Duguit, having stripped the rights of the state of philosophical validity, goes on to recast the problem of state authority in terms of its organization and proper functions in relation to other constellations of interests and need in the social body.[47]

But the need to limit state power was felt even outside the circle of the most zealous state-bashers. Other less radical proposals on how to conceptualize the proper limits of state authority came from Lindsay: '[t]he power of the state over its members depends upon the will of the members themselves ... [t]he state, therefore, can have control over the corporations within it only if, and so far as the citizens are prepared to

---

[43] Laski, *Studies in the Problem of Sovereignty*, p. 14.
[44] Laski, *Authority in the Modern State*, p. 119.
[45] *Ibid.*, p. 66.
[46] *Ibid.*, p. 74.
[47] Duguit, *Law in the Modern State*, pp. 1–67.

give it such power'.[48] And, later, in more legal positivist terms, from MacIver: '[w]e have now to consider, not the ethical or discretionary limits of an indeterminate power over society, but the positive limits of a particular association, viewed alike in relation to other associations and to the specific means with which it is endowed'.[49]

But if the state was now increasingly regarded as nothing but a particular association or corporation among other associations or corporations of an equal standing, limitations of its power and authority over the social body made it difficult to explain the absence of conflict between those constellations of interest into which the state had now been dissolved. Again, the presence of relative order appeared enigmatic in the absence of the traditional and monist concept of the state.

Finally, a fourth aspect remains to be discussed, namely the idea that the state was a source of moral obligation, and that it could legitimately claim the full moral allegiance of its citizens. What was criticized was not primarily the prevalence of national sentiment, or the fact that citizens sometimes did indeed show allegiance to the state – the wartime context made it hard to doubt this with any sincerity – but rather the notion that citizens owed their existence as moral beings to the state, which was thought to be devoid of moral obligation outside itself, thus being a self-sufficient source of *Sittlichkeit*.

Symptomatically indeed, this argument was frequently directed against what was identified as a distinctively German conception of the state, even if it was sometimes admitted that the moral superiority of the state was an assumption inherent in the traditional concept of the state itself. But before and during the First World War, Anglo-American political science remained blissfully oblivious of its indebtedness to German state theory. Later, however, the war could be interpreted as a clash between different conceptions of the state, each with different political and ideological implications. The 'traditional' state concept was now associated with the Germans, to whom

the State is deemed to be something much more than a mere agent of the people for the protection and promotion of their common or collective interests. It is looked upon as an entity having interests, ambitions, and a will of its own quite distinct from those of its citizens, collectively considered . . . With such a combination of conceptions it was inevitable that the policy of the German State should be one of aggression.[50]

---

[48] A. D. Lindsay, 'The State in Modern Political Theory', *Political Quarterly*, vol. 1, 1914, no. 1, pp. 128–145.

[49] MacIver, *The Modern State*, p. 472.

[50] W. F. Willoughby, *Introduction to the Study of the Government of Modern States* (New York: Century, 1919), pp. 29–31; cf. also Westel W. Willoughby, 'The Prussian Theory of the State', *American Journal of International Law*, vol. 12, 1918, no. 2.

Although the arguments against the assumption of moral superiority were frequently cast in terms of the pernicious impact of monist conceptions on foreign policy, such an argument could just as well be directed inwards, and then against what were perceived as tendencies to irresponsible state intervention into the economy or society at large.[51] As Laski asked rhetorically, 'is there not a tremendous danger in modern times that people will believe the legal sovereignty of a State to be identical with its moral sovereignty?'[52] This fear was even more clearly voiced by Hobhouse, when he characterized the metaphysical concept of the state as

its own end, and the highest duty of the individual is to be a member of the state. Beyond the state there is no higher association and states have no duties to one another or to humanity, but their rise and fall is the process of universal history, which is the ultimate court of judgment before whose bar they come.[53]

The idea that the state was the overarching source of moral obligation could be met on both cosmopolitan and communitarian grounds. But either way, such an ethically inspired critique of the state gave rise to a problem that was but another avatar of the problem of political order. For if the state cannot command the moral allegiance of its citizens on the basis of its inherent moral superiority, from where is this overarching moral authority, so indispensable to social harmony and cohesion, supposed to come? Admittedly, this was '[a] vast and crucial issue, transcending all politics'.[54]

To the early critics of the state, the state concept and the institutional realities of contemporary societies were conceptualized as inseparable, yet their criticism focused on their increasing mismatch. What was criticized was a fusion of ideas and institutions embodied in the state concept, and the political practices rightly or wrongly associated with that concept. The traditional state concept was held to be practically and theoretically redundant because it failed to make sense of perceived changes in modern societies, most importantly the increasing fragmentation of political values and institutions resulting from the celebrated achievements of the day, such as enlarged franchise and the organization of labour.

Yet the pluralist alternative was not easy to articulate, since the problem of political order remained phrased within a vocabulary that privileged monist solutions. Thus political pluralism saw itself as born in practice

---

[51] Laski, *Authority in the Modern State*, pp. 83f., 96f.; see also John Dewey, *Problems of Men* (New York: Philosophical Library, 1946), p. 374; Jacques Maritain, *Man and the State* (Chicago, IL: University of Chicago Press, 1951), ch. 1.

[52] Laski, *Studies in the Problem of Sovereignty*, p. 20.

[53] Hobhouse, *Metaphysical Theory*, p. 33.

[54] Friedrich, 'Deification of the State', p. 30.

well before it could codify itself in any coherent theory that could explain and justify how political order was possible within a society composed of a plurality of semi-autonomous or proto-sovereign institutional spheres. But in an age when political reality had not yet become an inanimate object of scientific curiosity but remained a source of political engagement, the critique of the traditional state concept could be articulated against the backdrop of a presumed convergence between legal and normative ideals on the one hand, and political realities on the other, and this without any profound confusion being felt.

But this was going to change. In what to posterity has been made to look like a successful quest for objectivity and a welcome depoliticization of political science, normative concerns became carefully distinguished from empirical ones. Although criticism of the state proper persisted, it was gradually marked off from the scientific endeavour and became the province of political theory or ideology, as was the problem of political order itself. In this process, state-bashing was retargeted: it became less concerned with the state as an institutionalized idea embodied by a concept, but all the more preoccupied with the concept of the state as an intradisciplinary source of intellectual confusion. Yet this retargeting was possible only after a tacit agreement had been reached that the state, in its traditional guise, had ceased to exist in political reality. The class of phenomena to which the state concept could supposedly refer had successfully been emptied by the early pluralist onslaught.

Again it was Bentley who provided the behaviouralist critique of the state with impetus, long after his *The Process of Government* had been published in 1908 without much impact on the scientific community.[55] In terms that must have been somewhat confusing to many of his contemporaries, Bentley had articulated a new argument against the widespread use of the state concept:

> If an effort were being made here to restate theoretical political science it might be a serious question how far the exclusion of the term 'state' would be justified. Since the object is a very different one – namely, to illustrate the possibilities of the application of a particular manner of statement or scientific method to the material – I am convinced that the gain is vastly more than enough to offset the passing inconvenience to persons accustomed to starting their trains of thought from the word 'state' as they define it. From such persons I ask only the recognition that I am adapting my verbal tools in what I conceive to be the best manner to the task immediately at hand.[56]

---

[55] See John G. Gunnell, 'The Declination of the State and the Origins of American Pluralism', in James Farr, John S. Dryzek and Stephen T. Leonard (eds.), *Political Science in History: Research Programs and Political Traditions* (Cambridge: Cambridge University Press, 1995), pp. 19–40.

[56] Bentley, *The Process of Government*, p. 263n.

What we are told here is not merely that the concept of the state is redundant as an analytical tool, but that the political scientist is logically entitled – not to say obliged – to tailor his or her vocabulary in ways that enhance explanatory power, and this without any considerations apart from those dictated by epistemic or intra-scientific concerns. This statement also presupposes a sharp logical and ontological difference between the theoretical vocabulary of the scientist and the portions of reality to which the terms of this vocabulary are supposed to refer, and that this referential connection can and ought to be rendered unequivocal by stipulative definitions. Today this assumption may not strike us as that bold – but we have to remember that it had not yet been incorporated into the educated folklore of the day, but had barely penetrated philosophical discourse outside Vienna and Cambridge.

But gradually, such a distinction between political concepts and political reality began to permeate the social sciences in the interwar period. As a result, it became possible to assert that truly scientific propositions were verifiable – and later falsifiable – in a way that normative propositions were not, and that the former kinds of proposition ought ideally to be law-like generalizations in order to qualify as candidates for serious scientific discussion. Consequently, the laws of the political world were no longer accorded any causal efficacy of their own, but were reinterpreted as constructs through which the scientist was able to bring order and coherence to an otherwise chaotic mass of observations. The world of Mill and Comte was thus deprived of its naturalistic splendour as its laws were now seen as theoretical propositions circulating in the mind of the scientist rather than inherent in the fabric of political reality. Furthermore, the discovery of such laws was crucial to any explanation of facts, entities which in turn were supposed to be directly accessible to the scientist by means of observation, and existing independently of his or her theoretical vocabulary, thereby constituting the basis for testing generalizations carefully formulated within such a vocabulary.[57]

Largely simultaneously, the impact of legal positivism was increasingly being felt within both jurisprudence and political science, and began to reinforce the same set of distinctions that made the bifurcation into normative and empirical theory possible. The most important of these distinctions was that between a man-made normative order and the

[57] For statements of this position in the social sciences, see for example Stuart A. Rice, *Quantitative Methods in Politics* (New York: Knopf, 1928), especially passages criticizing the concept of the state, pp. 191–4; and later Richard S. Rudner, *Philosophy of the Social Science* (Englewood Cliffs, NJ: Prentice-Hall, 1966); for philosophical defences, see for example Carl G. Hempel, *Aspects of Scientific Explanation and Other Essays in the Philosophy of Science* (New York: The Free Press, 1965); for a summary of its impact in political science cf. also Gunnell, *Between Philosophy and Politics*, p. 23.

observable regularities of the political world; they were no longer seen as two sides of the same coin. In fact, this critical edge of legal positivism was itself directed against what it took to be a confusion of legal, political and sociological notions in the traditional concept of the state. As Kelsen forcefully argued,

[a]ccording to the traditional view, it is not possible to comprehend the essence of the national legal order...unless the state is presupposed as an underlying social reality...[h]owever, if by scientific analysis one is led to the result that there is no sociological concept of the State, the concept of the State is juristic, one by no means denies or ignores those facts which pre-scientific terminology designates by the word 'State.'...[t]hese facts are actions of human beings, and these actions are acts of State only insofar as they are interpreted according to a normative order the validity of which has to be presupposed.[58]

With such restrictions put on scientific discourse, the concept of the state could hardly qualify as a useful part of the analytical toolbox. Its ambiguity and opacity were repulsive to the truly empiricist mind, as was its association with idealist and non-liberal thought in general. Its fusion of legal and political connotations was repulsive to the legal positivist, as was its association with non-democratic legal doctrines. Still, this concept had for a long time been at the centre of attention, first during the formative phase of the discipline, and then later as a focal point of the early pluralist critique. Consequently, the behaviouralist attitude to the concept of the state was marked by an ambivalence right from the start, since it was difficult to dispose of a concept that had been constitutive not only of political discourse in the past, but also of the state tradition targeted by the early pluralists.

But while the first wave of criticism had been successful in so far as few political scientists now believed that the state existed outside the realm of philosophical and legal fiction, the behaviouralist critics nevertheless had to make sense of the fact that this concept had for so long been crucial to disciplinary self-description. For how could one explain that the discipline had been wrestling with a ghost without declaring a fair share of its past null and void, thereby undoing much of the continuity crucial to its present identity? As it turned out, this became a matter of striking a precarious balance between denying the present importance of the state while not forgetting its past. This meant that the new political science had to demarcate itself rigorously from its prescientific past, and posit a sharp discontinuity at the heart of its own identity and within its own history.

[58] Hans Kelsen, *General Theory of Law and State* (Cambridge, MA: Harvard University Press, 1945), pp. 182, 189.

Here the entire range of critical concepts provided by the new philosophies of science and law became instrumental. Apart from making the case for excommunication stronger on the grounds of the inherent ambiguity and opacity of the state concept, the distinction between descriptive and prescriptive propositions – when itself given a prescriptive twist – made it possible to shuffle all talk about the state that did not obey the logical demands of verifiability to the normative and speculative backyards of the discipline.[59] That this entire practice rested upon a paradoxical way of handling the relation between the prescriptive and the descriptive did not occur to the participants in this game, and had it occurred, a swift recourse to the taboos of self-reference would have saved these participants from cognitive embarrassment.

The implications of this can be seen in the various attempts to reduce the concept of the state to observable entities that followed upon the uptake of logical empiricism within political science, however diluted that uptake was. On the one hand, the concept of the state was now declared scientifically illegitimate on the basis of its inherent opacity, its past ambiguity and the indeterminateness of its present reference; on the other, and as seen in the previous section, it was reinscribed as the centrepiece of a tradition itself indeterminate and unverifiable, thought to comprise the prescientific past of the discipline.

Thus, to Catlin, since '[a] behaviourist treatment of Politics, proposing to discover what, if any, are the rules of human social method, will be compelled ... to choose its own crucial researches and to compile its own relevant data',[60] the concept of the state is rather useless to empirical political science, because

[p]olitics is more than the study of the State or of government, since it is impossible to study either, thoroughly and intelligently – viewed from the standpoint of the scientist who inquires into the nature of the structure and of the process of change ... without studying more than either; i.e. without studying the system of human interrelationships called society.[61]

And ultimately, 'belief concerning the nature of the State is a matter of individual taste, and cannot be the basis of a scientific doctrine of Politics'.[62] Thus, since the concept of the state contains both empirical and normative elements, theoretical propositions about the state are not susceptible to testing, and are therefore ultimately meaningless or at

---

[59] See Gunnell, *Descent of Political Theory*, pp. 199ff.
[60] Catlin, *Science and Method*, p. xi.
[61] *Ibid.*, p. 201.
[62] *Ibid.*, p. 329.

least confusing. The concept therefore belongs to the realm of moral and metaphysical speculation.[63]

This desire to excommunicate the concept of the state from the domain of the empirically knowable and reinscribe it into the primitive past of the discipline of politics culminated in Easton's *The Political System* (1953), where he starts by noting the ambiguity of the term 'state':

> The confusion and variety of meanings is so vast that it is almost unbelievable that over the last twenty-five hundred years in which the question has recurringly been discussed in some form or another, some kind of uniformity has not been achieved.[64]

This passage illustrates a fundamental tension within the behaviouralist critique. On the one hand, it was agreed that the basic problem with the state concept was its lack of clear and unambiguous meaning resulting from its lack of unequivocal reference. On the other, it was believed that this concept had nevertheless been at the core of Western political reflection from its start, thereby positing a discontinuity between prescientific and scientific political reflection.

The self-appointed heirs of Carnap and Hempel could not tolerate what to their predecessors had been a fruitful ambiguity reflecting the confusions of political practice. One was now about to attain knowledge about politics, which was something different from knowledge in politics. Yet this critical view of the state concept presupposed not only that the problem of the state had been a continuous source of confusion, but also that this problem could not be solved through a new rigorous definition of the term 'state'. Rather it could be defined away by dismantling the state concept altogether. Thus, Easton goes on to conclude that

> [a]fter the examination of the variety of meanings a critical mind might conclude that the word ought to be abandoned entirely. If the argument is raised that it would be impossible to find a substitute to convey the meaning of this term, intangible and imprecise as it is, the reply can be offered that after this chapter the word will be avoided scrupulously and no severe hardship in expression would result.[65]

Yet there was nothing new about this recommendation, since it had already been incorporated into the official doctrine of the discipline in the 1930s.[66] What was new, however, was the assumption that the connotation of a singular term is ultimately a function of its denotation, so

---

[63] Rice, *Quantitative Methods*, pp. 191–3
[64] Easton, *Political System*, pp. 107–8.
[65] *Ibid.*, p. 108.
[66] Sabine, 'The State'.

that by banishing that singular term from discourse because of its lack of tangible reference, its connotations would simultaneously cease to constitute a problem to scientific analysis.[67] Such an assumption, however, would only make sense against the backdrop of another underlying agreement, namely, that there was no such thing as 'the state' to be found 'out there', that is, in the fresh domain of objectivity constituted by empiricist political science.

In short, state-bashing was now premised on the assumption that one could get rid of the concept of the state – as well as all problems associated with this concept – by getting rid of the term 'state', and that this could be done without any serious implications, either for the way political order was explained and justified, or for the disciplinary identity of political science. Hence, by banishing a contested term from discourse in the name of scientific sobriety and semantic purity, Easton was hoping to '[discover] the connotative meaning, that is, the general properties of any political phenomenon'.[68]

But even if its ambiguity in itself was a sufficient reason to abolish the term 'state' from discourse, this term had other significant shortcomings as well. Thus, even if we could arrive at a precise formal and operational definition of this term – itself highly doubtful – it would nevertheless be a poor analytical guide to political reality, since it would automatically exclude societies devoid of overarching authority from the domain of political inquiry:

[t]hus even if we could reach agreement to adopt as our meaning the most general definition today given to the concept of the state, it must still fall short of providing an adequate description of the limits of political research. By definition it excludes social systems in which there can be no question that political interaction is an essential aspect.[69]

The major drawback of the state concept is thus revealed. It does not serve to identify the properties of a phenomenon that give the latter a political quality. At most, the state concept is usually just an illustration of one kind of political phenomenon, a comprehensive political institution.[70]

Even this critique has a familiar ring, since it singles out the concept of the state as at once vapid and too narrow. The concept of the state does not and cannot exhaust the objective possibilities of the domain of politics, since the concept of politics comprises practices and institutions far beyond the domain of human activity conventionally denoted by the

---

[67] Easton, *Political System*, p. 114.
[68] *Ibid.*, p. 115.
[69] *Ibid.*, p. 111.
[70] *Ibid.*, p. 113.

concept of the state. But whereas earlier versions of this critique had focused on what they took to be an apparent and lamentable mismatch between concept and reality, the behaviouralist version of this argument typically criticizes the concept of the state because of its lack of explanatory power, thus presupposing a divide between theoretical concepts and empirical reality, a divide not as readily accessible to the early pluralists.

On the one hand, this strategy may be interpreted as indicative of a final and happy divorce between a political and a scientific critique of political concepts, paving the way for a detached and objective political science in the service of a mature democracy. On the other hand, it is as much indicative of a politics of depoliticization, and the coming of a new political technology based on the denial of the political contestability of state authority. Hence, by arguing that the concept of the state ought to be banished on grounds that this concept itself is politically contestable, one in fact depoliticizes politics by making the definition of this latter concept a scientific rather than a political question, thus making the entire question of political order a question to be settled by scientific authority rather than through a 'politics' of the political.

Thus, by aspiring to become a science *about* politics rather than a science *in* politics, and by removing a central yet ambiguous concept like that of the state both from the research agenda and from the legitimate domain of conceptual contestation, political science now could lay claims to a political authority of its own. By denying that the state existed, political science was able to produce both the rationale and the detailed empirical knowledge necessary for a political technology whose scope vastly exceeded the methods of governance inspired and legitimized by the early political science. Whereas early political science had built its credentials upon lofty promises of order and progress, postwar political science did so by making itself instrumental to political authority by removing the notion of such authority from contestation through safeguarding its presupposed presence in the conceptual structure of that discipline. Yet this left a lacuna in the understanding of political order to which we now must turn.

The impurity of plurality

Given that the concept of the state was now of limited or no use to political science in its effort to understand and explain political phenomena, this made it difficult to explain and justify the presence of political order, since one of the main functions of the state concept had been to render such an order intelligible in terms of itself. So even if the concept of the state is held to be out of tune with reality or too ambiguous for any serious scientific purposes, its excommunication from discourse opened up a theoretical void that could not easily be filled or explained away.

But the quest for proper conceptual substitutes was constrained by the terms in which criticism of the state concept had been phrased. First, we have seen how the concept of the state was indeed constitutive of early political science, and how this concept later came to constitute the main source of coherence and continuity of a tradition which state-bashers had invented in order to oppose. Thus, a successful strategy of excommunication would risk putting political science out of touch with parts of its own past, thereby risking a net loss of disciplinary identity.

Second, since the concept of the state and the concept of politics had been stuck in definitional symbiosis for quite some time, it was difficult to make sense of the concept of politics without providing an explanation and justification of the presence of political order in other, non-statist terms. Thus, a successful strategy of excommunication had to find a way to make sense of the *sui generis* character of politics without recourse to the concept of the state.

Those who sought to find replacements for the state concept confronted both those problems, but with some differences in emphasis. Whereas those who had argued that what was signified by the traditional state concept had ceased to exist in reality had to furnish some new overarching principle that could explain the relatively harmonious interaction between the components to which the state had been reduced, those who held that the state concept – given its inherent opacity – could not refer to any tangible portion of reality at all, had to do so by reference to some theoretical principle capable of satisfying both the demand for explanatory power and the need for disciplinary identity.

Yet there is a considerable continuity between the different conceptual substitutes suggested by state critics. Here it is evident how much the behaviouralists owed to their early pluralist predecessors, since they both tried to find proper substitutes by reducing the state to what they took to be its basic components, and then sought to account for the relationship and interaction between these components in political terms. Doing this, they found it imperative to dissolve the inherited bond between the concept of the state and the concept of politics, so that the latter could be defined without any reference to the former.

Among the early critics of the state, the way around the state concept went through the theory of the real personality of corporations, and the doctrine of the autonomous legal status of groups in relation to the state. Rather than assuming that corporations and groups owed their existence and legal standing to the legal authority of the state and thus were to an extent fictitious in character, the early pluralist assumed that these entities had existed prior to, or at least could claim rights and liberties independent of, those granted to them by the sovereign state.[71]

As mentioned above, this contention had originally emerged out of a legal and historical doctrine which had assumed the state to be trans-historically present while explaining how it had managed to make other political forms subservient to it during its march forward. From the writings of Gierke and others early pluralists sought to distil a rival pluralist tradition of political thought. But while the ideological implications of this position had never been obvious during the nineteenth century more than as a curiously proto-democratic anomaly, they were capitalized on by state-bashers of the coming generation, however selective their uptake of these writings.[72]

Thus Laski, after some bashing of the 'traditional' concept of the state, goes on to outline his position by describing the pluralist state as a society composed of self-sufficient groups, and in which sovereignty is partitioned on the basis of function. In such a society, '[g]roups ... must be treated as independent units living ... a corporate life that gives birth to special considerations'.[73] The state is but 'one of the associations to which [the individual] happens to belong',[74] and '[i]t is not necessarily any more in harmony with the end of society than a church or a trade-union, or a freemasons' lodge'.[75] Consequently, the pluralistic concept of the state

denies the oneness of society and the state. It insists that nothing is known of the state purpose until it is declared; and it refuses, for obvious reasons, to make a priori observations about its content.[76]

Still, in such a society, the need for reconciliation between competing group interests will inevitably arise. So even if the state is ultimately but one association among others, it must have a will of its own, being at least potentially able to claim superiority over lesser conflicting wills. Consequently, Laski notes that the will of the state

may come into conflict with other wills; and the test of the allegiance it should win is the degree in which it is thought to be more in harmony than its antagonists with the end of social life.[77]

But this certainly does not solve the problem of political order that arises when the state is deprived of its sovereignty, for who is to decide

---

[71] Cf. Vincent, *Theories of the State*, ch. 6.
[72] Coker, 'Technique of the Pluralist State', pp. 186ff.
[73] Laski, *Authority in the Modern State*, p. 77.
[74] Laski, *Studies in the Problem of Sovereignty*, p. 10.
[75] Laski, *Authority in the Modern State*, p. 65.
[76] *Ibid.*, p. 65.
[77] *Ibid.*

upon the proper ends of social life? Laski is characteristically ambivalent about the role of the state, since he wishes to reinterpret this concept along pluralist lines, but he finds it difficult to strip it of all its monist connotations without having to deal with the problem of political order by introducing an equally monist substitute. This problem constantly threatened to make the very concept of a pluralist state an oxymoron. In response to this situation, the concept that at least provisionally came to replace the state was the concept of government, since

the essence of the state turns upon the reciprocal relations of government and citizens. A state, after all, is fundamentally a territorial society divided into government and subjects.[78]

This tendency to reduce the state to its components – whether to groups or individuals – while remaining highly ambivalent about the source and locus of those authoritative decisions necessary to bind that plurality together, the proper scope of those decisions, as well as the ethical standards by which to judge them, was a tendency common to all pluralist writers. To their contemporary critics, this ambivalence left the pluralist theory of the state open to major objections, since it could be interpreted either as inconsistent or anarchic, or at least as suspiciously polyarchic. To the conservative mind of the day, pluralism was but a recipe for social unrest.[79]

Thus, even if pluralist theory was sometimes credited with a more realistic description of the political conditions within modern societies by their critics, it could not furnish any clear-cut theoretical solution to the problem of political order. As one critic put it,

[i]f the state is not all powerful, but the political loyalty only one of many loyalties, more or less equally strong, then obviously something approaching chaos may result, if these coördinate loyalties are numerous and potent and conflicting enough.[80]

Not surprisingly, therefore, that same set of connotations that had carefully been eliminated from the state concept in order to make it chime better with new realities was now frequently but silently reattributed to the concept of government. This, of course, made pluralist doctrine susceptible to another line of criticism, namely, that it was unable to distinguish sharply enough between the concepts state and government, and that it therefore could not deliver what it had promised.

This difficulty in finding a clear-cut solution to the problem of order without reintroducing essential attributes of statehood in forever new

[78] Laski, *Foundations of Sovereignty*, p. 22.
[79] Elliot, 'Sovereign State or Sovereign Group?', pp. 481–90; Follett, *New State*, pp. 258–9.
[80] Ellis, 'The Pluralistic State', p. 404.

semantic guises also led to a criticism that focused on the theoretical futility of pluralism:

> The pluralists, therefore, attempt to abolish sovereignty, but are finally compelled to restore it. And sovereignty ... comes back with a vengeance. The truth is that when pluralism sets out to prove that there is no ultimate authority in society, and that there should not be such authority, it proposes a task which cannot be accomplished ... whatever detailed scheme these pluralists may prefer, and whatever different ethical background they may possess, they all seem to agree that a community is unintelligible unless a community of good is assumed, and, consequently, that while this good demands a definite restriction of governmental action to a specific sphere consistent with the nature of its function, it nevertheless justifies a supreme social power which is substantially all-pervading and unitary in its exercise.[81]

Or, as Coker put it in the *Encyclopedia of the Social Sciences*:

> [i]t appears then that when the pluralists set forth their abstract theory they deny the sovereign power of the state or else characterize the power of something which is properly only ultimate and reserved; but when they devise the specific institutional arrangements to carry out their theory they assign to the state numerous tasks ... [t]hey would retain the state but deprive it of sovereignty. It appears, however, that they accomplish this compromise only in words.[82]

But the main difficulty faced by the pluralist theory of the state resulted from its inability to distinguish logically between descriptive and prescriptive propositions, and this in a period when such a distinction was in the process of becoming the main instrument of self-criticism among political scientists. Whereas few of its critics seriously disputed what pluralists took to be new facts of political life, they frequently enough pointed out that the facts were not necessarily inconsistent with the traditional monist concept of the state, provided that this theory was understood not as a statement of how things really are, but rather as a statement of a legal ideal, firmly separated from political reality. According to their critics, the often radical political recipes of the pluralists did not follow from their accounts of political reality.[83]

The varieties of criticism that started out from this distinction did so in order to expose the pluralist inability to furnish a solution to the problem of political order while replacing the traditional state concept with those of group and government. Thus, and somewhat ironically, by insisting on the prescriptive force of this distinction between the descriptive and

[81] Kung Chuan Hsiao, *Political Pluralism: a Study in Contemporary Political Theory* (New York: Harcourt Brace, 1927), pp. 139–40, 230–1.
[82] Francis W. Coker, 'Pluralism', *Encyclopedia of the Social Sciences* (New York: Macmillan, 1934).
[83] Ellis, 'The Pluralistic State', p. 405; Follett, *New State*, pp. 262, 283; Elliot, 'Pragmatic Politics', pp. 251–75.

prescriptive, those critics did to the pluralist conception of the state what pluralists had done to the traditional state concept – that is, reject it on grounds of its perceived mismatch with 'reality'.

Even if this criticism did very little to save the traditional state concept from intellectual disrepute and excommunication, it did presuppose a statist conception of political order. In those accounts of politics that aspired to be strictly empirical and devoid of normative presuppositions, politics was now defined without reference to higher principles or underlying essences, yet the very possibility of identifying phenomena as political demanded a principle of order that could constitute the basis of descriptive classifications and coherent theorizing. But to the extent that such an order was presupposed in the definition of the political realm, it was also quite unnecessary to justify this conception in the context of empirical theorizing, since it was the presence of such an order that constituted the baseline for further explanation of political phenomena.

Thus, according to Bentley, politics consists entirely 'of the group activities of men; activities that always embody an interest, that never define themselves except in terms of other group activities of the existing society'.[84] But if politics is the sum total of such activities, government is nothing but a 'differentiated, representative group, or set of groups ... performing specified governing functions for the underlying groups of the population ... [g]overnment in this sense is not a certain number of people, but a certain network of activities'.[85]

The facts of government could thus be defined in terms of group activities, and the problem of political order could seemingly be reconceptualized as a purely empirical question. There was simply no need to assume that the principles of theoretical and empirical inquiry had to correspond in any way to the principles of political order itself. Anarchy and chaos were to be conquered by measurement and sober empirical enquiry into the facts of the governmental process in which group interests are articulated and reconciled, not by reference to higher and epistemically unwarranted principles of political order and authority.[86]

Hence, when subjected to the cutting force of the distinction between descriptive and prescriptive theorizing, the problem of political order with which state-bashers had been forced to wrestle could at best be avoided but not solved. The presence of political order came to constitute a largely unreflected premise of descriptive and explanatory accounts of political processes, but the task of justifying this presupposition was relegated to the realm of normative theorizing. As a consequence, within mainstream

---

[84] Bentley, *Process of Government*, p. 258.
[85] *Ibid.*, pp. 260–1.
[86] Catlin, *Science and Method*, pp. 141, 177.

political science the problem of political order was largely rephrased as a problem of theoretical coherence, so that the hallmark of political order was to be accessible to empirical inquiry and explicable in those categories that were used to define the political in the absence of the concept of the state. As we learn from Lasswell and Kaplan,

[p]olitical science, as one of the sciences of interpersonal relations, deals not with 'states' and 'governments' but with concrete acts of human beings... [e]very proposition about the abstraction 'state' can be replaced by a set of propositions referring only to the concrete acts of certain persons and groups. And the same is true of the abstraction 'government'.[87]

But there was still a ghost in the complex machinery of group interests and government, difficult to make sense of without reference to unobservable entities. As the behavioural revolution proceeded, the dream of a consistent group interpretation of the governmental process gradually became difficult to sustain since the problem of political order now cropped up in the guise of unexplained variance. Even if the state had been broken down into its component parts of group interests and government, it was increasingly difficult to explain the relatively harmonious interaction of these groups without reference to some principle of order or source of authority capable of moderating what would otherwise have been irreconcilable differences in the social body.

But if such order does not come from above, it could be conceived of as a spontaneous result of the interaction within a complex system, or as an expression of the fundamental principle of such a system. Truman's *The Governmental Process* (1951) provides a good example of how behaviouralists tried to explain the regularities of political life without reference to the state:

[a] major difficulty allegedly inherent in any attempt at a group interpretation of the political process is that such an explanation inevitably must ignore some greater unity designated as society or the state... [m]any of those who place particular emphasis upon this difficulty assume explicitly or implicitly that there is an interest of the nation as a whole, universally and invariably held and standing apart from and superior to those of the various groups included within it... It is no derogation of democratic preferences to state that such an assertion flies in the face of all that we know of the behavior of men in a complex society.

If these various organized interest groups more or less consistently reconcile their differences, adjust, and accept compromises, we must acknowledge that we are dealing with a system that is not accounted for by the 'sum' of the organized interest groups in the society.[88]

---

[87] Harold D. Lasswell and Abraham Kaplan, *Power and Society: a Framework for Political Inquiry* (New Haven, CT: Yale University Press, 1950), p. 184.

[88] David B. Truman, *The Governmental Process: Political Interests and Public Opinion* (New York: Knopf, 1951), pp. 49–51.

True to the behaviouralist credo, we are entitled to assume the existence of a system behind those observable interactions that together make up the governmental process only to the extent that the former display a sufficient degree of coherence and harmony. Within this view, government itself is not the source of order, but rather the outcome of an anterior and invisible order, provided by 'the unexpressed assumption that the phenomena of politics tend to cohere and to be mutually related'.[89] Consequently, what had previously been explained with reference to an opaque and abstract concept such as the state was now thought to be explainable with reference to the natural coherence of political life, an assumption construed by the political scientist in order to make sense of political practices, but not necessarily foundational in relation to those practices themselves.

But the concept of political system was itself far from unproblematic, since it turned out to be difficult to define its organizing principle without recourse to any of the conventional attributes of the state concept, or to new but semantically equivalent notions. On the one hand, the existence of a system – itself by definition unobservable – could be inferred from the regularities of political practice, themselves and their reproduction seemingly independent of any attribute conventionally associated with the traditional state concept. Thus, when interpreted as an empirical concept with clear and distinct reference, the concept of system refers to the orderly and coherent practices that together constitute the domain of politics, and not to something over and above them. As Easton put it,

[t]he search for recurrent relationships suggests that the elements of political life have some form of determinate relationship . . . [i]n short, political life constitutes a concrete political system which is an aspect of the whole social system.[90]

On the other hand, it is precisely this assumption of a political system that makes it possible to identify the crucial variables and the systematic relationships between these concepts, since 'an initial step in developing systematic theory must be an inquiry into the orienting concepts of the system under investigation', and without some guide 'to indicate when a variable is politically relevant, social life would simply be an incoherent wilderness of activities'.[91] Thus, when interpreted theoretically, the concept of the political system fulfils the same theoretical function as the assumption of *a priori* unity did in the context of traditional state theory.

According to Easton, those 'orienting concepts' necessary to delineating the political from other aspects of social life are furnished by the

[89] Easton, *Political System*, pp. 96–7.
[90] *Ibid.*, p. 97.
[91] *Ibid.*, p. 98.

common sense idea of political life, which equates politics with the making and execution of an authoritative policy for a society. Furthermore, what makes certain social practices distinctively political is the fact that they cohere around or relate to the 'authoritative allocation of values for a society'.[92] Now while the other social sciences also touch upon the allocation of values in society, the subject matter of political science is defined and delimited by the function of the concept of authority in the above definition.

But arguably, such a concept of authority is nothing less than a convenient shorthand used to describe the aspects of political life earlier subsumed under the concept of the state, such as the indivisibility and potential limitlessness of its authority. And by implication, redescribing such an authority in systemic terms amounts to nothing less than making it difficult to question it as authority, let alone explaining or justifying its mysterious presence in the social body. So when stripped of its moral connotations, the concept of authority is simply used to describe the fact that members of a society either obey, or feel that they ought to obey, a certain policy.[93] The presence of such authority, it turns out, 'is a necessary condition for the existence of a viable society', and

[e]very society provides some mechanisms . . . for authoritatively resolving differences about the ends that are to be pursued, that is, for deciding who is to get what there is of desirable things. An authoritative allocation of some values are unavoidable.[94]

Simply put, then, it is the coherence among the observable facts of political life that permits us to speak of a concrete political system, yet it is the assumption of a theoretical political system that permits us to discern this coherence among the facts of political life.[95] Either way, however, the concept of political system is defined by the assumption that it is authority that constitutes such a system as *a* political one – whether empirical or theoretical in nature – by marking it off from other possible social systems, and by making provisional sense of the regularities within it. Hence, the subject matter of politics is ultimately defined and rendered accessible to scientific inquiry by the concept of authority, a concept which is thereby turned into an unquestionable foundation of political science. In the absence of this concept, the subject matter of politics would evaporate into thin air, and become analytically indistinct from other modes of human intercourse.

[92] *Ibid.*, p. 129.
[93] *Ibid.*, p. 133n., Easton here draws heavily on Weber's definition of authority.
[94] *Ibid.*, p. 137.
[95] Cf. Gunnell, *Between Philosophy and Politics*, pp. 78ff.

But in sharp contrast to the early pluralist critique of the state, all questions about the normative justification of such authority are left out of the domain of legitimate scientific inquiry by Easton, while the question of explanation is turned upside down: it is authority that explains, rather than itself standing in need of explanation – the question of the scope and legitimacy of this authority is now the province of normative political theory.[96]

It is no overstatement to say that the view that the state concept is fundamentally redundant to political science remained part of mainstream disciplinary consensus well into the 1980s, when it became increasingly contested.[97] As the *Encyclopedia of the Social Sciences* (1968) had it, 'it is impossible to offer a unified definition of the state that would be satisfactory even to a majority of those seriously concerned with the problem'.[98]

To sum up, during this period, there was a theory of the state that simply stated that the state was not, and implied in this theory was the assumption that the absence of the state ought to be a foundational premise for empirical inquiry into political phenomena, something which was tantamount to presupposing its presence as a condition of the political itself. What was disputed was thus neither the nature and origin of state authority, nor the validity of the philosophical and metatheoretical doctrines that had informed the excommunication of the state from the theoretical and empirical agenda of political science, but rather the exact nature of and relationship between those things that had been introduced as substitutes for the state.

In this chapter we have seen how the state concept, from having been the centrepiece of early political science, soon became singled out as an object of political and philosophical criticism, and was then apparently relegated to the margins of the discipline and its self-understanding. This was done through successive reconstructions of state traditions, and a subsequent effort to liberate the disciplines from the imagined intellectual strictures imposed by such a tradition, however defined. But while wrestling with its own past, political science could not but implicitly reaffirm the centrality of the state concept. During this Promethean quest for scientific rigour and political detachment, the concept of the state was gradually redefined in the hands of its critics. From having signified a fusion of ideas and institutions no longer corresponding to what were perceived as new

---

[96] Gunnell, *Descent of Political Theory*, pp. 199ff.
[97] Cf. Almond, 'The Return to the State'.
[98] Morton H. Fried, 'The State', *Encyclopedia of the Social Sciences* (New York: Macmillan, 1968), p.145.

political realities, the concept was reinterpreted as an intradisciplinary source of confusion and scientific underdevelopment. Within the world of political science, the state ceased to exist because it was defined away as a topic of scientific inquiry.

But as we have seen, the method of denial has largely been futile. Beyond the superficial silence imposed on the state topic within mainstream political science, we find the state concept very much alive underneath existing explanations of the presence of political order. True, the state concept was excommunicated from the theoretical core of political science, and relegated either to the primitive and prescientific past of political reflection, or to the normative and unverifiable margins of political knowledge. But throughout this denial, the presupposed presence of the state continued to condition the possibility of the domain of objectivity and inquiry, partly because the source and locus of political order remained conceived as distinct from the international outside and from the societal inside of modern polities, partly because of the tendency to introduce theoretical and semantical equivalents into political reflection. By taking the presence of such a political order for granted as a baseline fact of political inquiry, the state was ontologized as the secret foundation of any such inquiry and all further theorizing.

4   Recycling the state

According to a widespread view, when the state concept was brought back into focus within political science in the late 1970s, this was a reaction against decades of pluralist neglect. The disappearance of the state from the research agenda was then frequently explained by the impact of empiricism on the study of politics, an epistemology which, at least when dogmatically applied, was believed to rule out any talk of abstract and intangible entities such as the state.[1]

As Skocpol then had it, '[t]here can be no gainsaying that an intellectual sea change is under way, because not long ago the dominant theories and research agendas of the social sciences rarely spoke of state'.[2] We also learn that 'the state is now once again a reality in its own right, endowed with resources, with a material interest and a moral vision which cannot be ascribed to the dominant coalition outside it'.[3]

Naturally this attempt to bring the state back in was met with scepticism by those who had struggled to throw the state out, and was seen as a threat to the scientific achievements of political science.[4] The point of this chapter is not to dwell on this controversy, however, but to describe how it happened that the state was brought back in, and what happened to the state concept in the process. Against the backdrop of the pluralist and behaviouralist onslaught, this is somewhat puzzling. But as I shall argue, the attempt to bring the state back in cannot be understood as a simple reaction against pluralism and behaviouralism, but must be

[1] Cf. R. King, *The State in Modern Society* (Chatham, NJ: Chatham House, 1986), pp. 1–31; J. A. Caporaso, 'The State in a Comparative and International Perspective', in J. A. Caporaso (ed.), *The Elusive State: International and Comparative Perspectives* (Newbury Park, CA: Sage, 1989), pp. 7–16; Terence Ball, *Reappraising Political Theory: Revisionist Studies in the History of Political Thought* (Oxford: Clarendon, 1995), ch. 2.

[2] Theda Skocpol, 'Bringing the State Back In: Strategies of Analysis in Current Research', in Peter B. Evans, Dietrich Rueschemeyer and Theda Skocpol (eds.), *Bringing the State Back In* (Cambridge: Cambridge University Press, 1985), p. 6.

[3] Sergio Fabbrini and Oreste Massari, 'The State: the Western Experience', paper presented at 17th IPSA Congress, Seoul, 1997, p. 20.

[4] See for example Gabriel A. Almond, 'The Return to the State', *American Political Science Review*, vol. 82, 1988, no. 3, pp. 850–74.

seen against the backdrop of previous interpretations of the state concept within Marxist state theory.

Largely contrary to the intentions of those who struggled to bring the state back in, this effort only further contributed to the tendency to turn the state into an unquestioned foundation of political inquiry. As I shall argue, bringing the state back in implied a recycling of a quasi-transcendental state concept. Much like those who had tried to throw the state out, those who brought it back in could not but accept that the state was something categorically distinct from society at large and from the international outside. Thus, and with the benefit of hindsight, it is easy to conclude that if the effort to throw the state out was futile, the effort to bring it back in has largely been perverse in terms of its actual implications for political theory.

But those who wanted to bring the state back in construed the relationship of the state to the societal inside and the international outside differently. If the attempts to throw the state concept out started out from the assumption that the state was by definition autonomous in relation to the societal inside and the international outside, the effort to bring the state back in evolved out of the assumption that the state was dependent upon society. Consequently, those who brought the state back in rarely argued directly against the view that the state was autonomous, but all the more in favour of the assumption that the state ought to be understood as relatively autonomous in relation to a society upon which it was thought to be *a priori* dependent.

While those who wanted to bring the state back in agreed that the problem of the state ought to be taken seriously by political science, they normally began by contending that the state ought to be conceptualized as a dependent variable rather than as an autonomous source of authority in the social body, since the state was regarded as being fundamentally dependent on society rather than conversely. To understand how this logical detour became necessary, however, we must situate the effort to bring the state back in in its proper theoretical context.

As I tried to show in chapter 2, the evolution of the modern state concept took place in close conjunction with that of society. From Montesquieu to Ferguson, the concept of society emerged as distinct from, and as a possible counterpoise to, sovereign authority, a development that culminated in Hegel's subordination of civil society to the state. Largely accepted by later political discourse, this disjunction paved the way for later conceptualizations of the relationship between the state and civil society. What we have been discussing so far is a state concept presupposing state autonomy in relation to the societal inside. Yet a fair share of state theorizing during the twentieth century has evolved out of the reverse assumption: that sovereign authority is profoundly conditioned by the constellations of interest within a society which in turn is supposedly historically or logically prior to the state.

In many textbooks this latter way of relating state and society is depicted as a Marxist or socialist one. This is not necessarily correct, since the notion that the state is dependent upon society has been defended by non-Marxists as well.[5] But this need not bother us much in the present context, since my aim is to make sense of the effort to bring the state back in, not to account either for Marxist state theory in general, or for the general idea of state dependence. Rather, I shall focus on how the effort to bring the state back in emerged out of a distinct way of conceptualizing the state that emphasized its dependence on societal forces. In doing this, I shall proceed in the same way as in the previous chapter. Thus, I shall begin by describing how those who brought the state back in reconstructed the tradition which they opposed, and then continue to analyse their contentions against the kind of state concept embodied by that tradition. Finally I shall have something to say about their ways of reconceptualizing the state, arguing that this merely made it more mysterious.

Reconstructing pluralism

As it is common to view the spirit of modernity as a critical one, it is possible to argue that during the twentieth century the discourse on the state has been critical in so far as it has regarded the state as a reality to be unmasked in the search for a more real reality behind it. But as we have noted, before critical activity can get off the ground, it is necessary to identify a target of criticism – indeed, such an identification is in itself an integral part of the critical strategy.

In this chapter, we shall see this practice at work again. Before the state could be brought back in in its seemingly new guise, the outcome of decades of state-bashing had to be put in critical perspective. Intuitively this might seem a difficult task, since if the upshot of state-bashing had been to banish the state concept from scientific discourse, how could

---

[5] Thus it is fully possible to argue that purported expressions of a general interest – such as the state – are of particularist origin but not necessarily particularist in function, as did Charles A. Beard in *An Economic Interpretation of the Constitution of the United States* [1913] (New York: Macmillan, 1954), p. 13. It is equally possible to regard the state as highly dependent on the structure of society, without committing oneself to any Marxist or socialist notion of class dominance, or the state's dependence on any particular sets of interest. In the previous chapter we were also able to see how those who wanted to throw the state out often pointed to the actual dependence of state institutions upon constellations of interests in society; see, for example, G. D. H. Cole, *Essays in Social Theory* (London: Macmillan, 1950), *passim*.

there then be anything left to oppose? But as we shall see, the target of criticism had less to do with the way state-bashers themselves perceived their enterprise and what they took to be its constructive achievements, but all the more to do with the implications of state-bashing. As a consequence, however, critics were bound to discover that the state concept was very much alive and kicking beneath the celebrations of its demise, if for reasons distinct from ours.

Before we can get into detail about how this tradition of statelessness was constructed by its Marxist critics, a few particularities about Marxist theorizing on the state are worth noting. Within this tradition, there is a need to justify one's theoretical arguments with reference to what the canonical texts of Marx and Engels had to say about the state. Two main positions prevail with respect to those texts. According to the first position, the canonical figures never contributed anything but scattered fragments to a scientific understanding of the state, but a theory of the state can nevertheless be assembled out of these fragments, given the right exegetical effort. According to the second, since there is no coherent theory of the state made explicit in the canonical texts, such a theory has to be inferred on the basis of what the canonical figures had to say about other things.[6]

Both these positions converge on the assumption that the possibility of such a theory of the state hinges on its consistency with what the canonical texts had to say, and such a consistency is in turn perceived to be necessary to justify claims about the continuity of a distinct tradition of Marxist state theorizing. Now this scholastic attitude has provided Marxist state theory with a theoretical context and conceptual resources of its own, but also confined the articulation of such a theory within the boundaries defined by authoritative interpretations of its canonical texts.

Furthermore, and thanks to the ambiguity of these texts and the number of interpretations of them claiming to be authoritative, almost any theory that does not deny that the state is dependent on the basic structure of society, and that does not rule out that this society is in some sense logically or historically prior to the state, can potentially be incorporated into this tradition. As I shall argue in more detail below, many of those

---

[6] For overviews of the state debate within Marxist thought, see Norberto Bobbio, 'Is There a Marxist Theory of the State?', *Telos*, 1978, no. 35, pp. 5–16; Martin Carnoy, *The State and Political Theory* (Princeton, NJ: Princeton University Press, 1984); Boris Frankel, 'On the State of the State: Marxist Theories of the State after Leninism', *Theory and Society*, vol. 7, 1979, nos. 1–2, pp. 199–242; David A. Gold, Clarence Y. H. Lo and Erik Olin Wright, 'Recent Developments in Marxist Theories of the Capitalist State', *Monthly Review*, vol. 27, 1975, no. 5, pp. 29–43, no. 6, pp. 37–51; John Holloway and Sol Picciotto, *State and Capital: a Marxist Debate* (London: Edward Arnold, 1978), pp. 1–31; Bob Jessop, 'Recent Theories of the Capitalist State', *Cambridge Journal of Economics*, vol. 1, 1977, no. 4, pp. 353–73.

who tried to bring the state back in – Marxists or not – assumed things about the state that gave their arguments a Marxist flavour. The first assumption that ties together this discourse on the state is that the state is fundamentally dependent on something external to itself – such as a society or an international system – for its existence. The second assumption is that any denial – explicit or implicit – of such a dependence is sufficient to qualify a theory of the state as an exemplary target of criticism, and that such a denial is constitutive of a tradition construed for critical purposes.[7]

It is to this counter-tradition we now must turn our attention. Since those who brought the state back in frequently looked for textual support in their classics, we might as well start by asking what kind of state concept Marx and Engels themselves could reasonably have opposed, given the historical and philosophical context in which their works were situated, questions which are far easier to answer than the more scholastic questions about what kind of state concept can be distilled from these texts through a decontextualizing reading of them.

Then one thing becomes obvious. What Marx and Engels criticized was not the state in general, but its distinct nineteenth-century appearance, and the then prevailing philosophical justifications of its sovereign authority.[8] For example, one main point of Marx's *Critique of Hegel's Philosophy of Right* (1843) was to demonstrate that the state is not an embodiment of universal interest, but that it is ultimately derivative and expressive of particular interests in society. According to the young Marx, such an inversion of the relationship between state and society was a crucial step in a refutation of Hegel's political philosophy and as he hoped, also conducive to a refutation of Hegel's entire philosophical system.

Within this view, Hegel's main mistake was to have made empirical reality subservient to the concepts of speculative philosophy, so that '[j]ust as the universal as such is rendered independent it is immediately mixed in with what empirically exists, and then this limited existent is immediately and uncritically taken for the expression of the idea'.[9] To Marx, the state is an empirical institution, consisting of a mass of men organized into a political community and subjected to a common political authority, not the realization of an abstract idea hypostasized into an acting subject.[10]

---

[7] Cf. Martin Shaw, 'The Theory of the State and Politics: a Central Paradox of Marxism', *Economy and Society*, vol. 3, 1974, no. 4, pp. 429–50.

[8] See Hal Draper, *Karl Marx's Theory of Revolution*. Vol. I: *State and Bureaucracy* (New York: Monthly Review Press, 1977), pp. 168–93.

[9] Karl Marx, *Critique of Hegel's 'Philosophy of Right'*, trans. A. Jolin and J. O'Malley (Cambridge: Cambridge University Press, 1970), p. 42.

[10] Cf. Shlomo Avineri, *The Social and Political Thought of Karl Marx* (Cambridge: Cambridge University Press, 1968), p. 14.

Conceptualized in this way, the state derives from the structure of society and therefore inevitably reflects the constellation of interests within it. The state cannot lay any legitimate claim to represent or embody any unity over and above these interests and forces.[11] As a consequence, the symbolic expressions of unity and universality associated with the state are in fact arbitrary and contingent, reflecting particular *claims* to universality. To Hegel crown, constitution and bureaucracy symbolized the unity of the state and represented the general will of the people; to Marx they rather testified to a systematic concealment of actual power relations between the classes of civil society, conditioned as those relations were by unequal relations of property. The state is essentially particularity dressed up as universality.[12]

The main upshot of the *Critique* is to show that the state is derivative of something other than itself, upon which it subsequently becomes dependent for its basic identity and claims to authority. The claims to universality advanced by such a state are not to be taken at face value, but should rather be seen as indicative of what is implicitly denied by that concept: that the state is nothing but the expression of an underlying unequal distribution of wealth and power which it simultaneously conceals. This assumption has come to constitute the core of those theories of the state that aspire to be critical.

There is a considerable affinity between the kind of state concept which Marx attacked in his *Critique*, and the kind of state concept which early pluralists sought to dismantle. There is also a striking similarity in the terms of criticism, since both Marx and the pluralists began by problematicizing the relation between the appearance and reality of statehood. But there is an important difference that might help us to account for the differences in outcome. Whereas pluralists sought to get rid of the monist state concept by reducing the state to lesser components, Marx conceptualizes the state as essentially derivative of underlying societal forces. This may sound like splitting hairs, but whereas 'being reducible to' lesser components implies that the state could exist even in the absence of these components, 'being derivative of' implies that the state could hardly exist without these societal forces. As we shall see later in this chapter, this subtle difference has had profound consequences for the fate of the state concept.

When late modern critics tried to identify pluralism as a lasting and coherent tradition of political theory, they felt perfectly free to transpose the critical concerns of Marx on to new theoretical contexts, simply because they did not believe that the context had changed as a result

---

[11] Marx, *Critique*, pp. 8f.; Avineri, *Social and Political Thought*, pp. 17ff.
[12] Marx, *Critique*, pp. 41f., 65f., 79; Avineri, *Social and Political Thought*, p. 13.

of the pluralist onslaught on the monist state concept. It was thus fully possible to argue that as long as the state could be said to exist in political reality, this state was not only necessarily capitalist in nature, but was also justified by a Hegelian conception of it that made it inherently bourgeois. As Mandel confidently expressed it: '[t]he state in late capitalism continues to be what it was in the 19th century – a bourgeois State which can ultimately only represent interests of the bourgeois class'.[13]

Precisely as Marx had interpreted the Hegelian concept of the state in terms of its concealing function, later critics of pluralism have relentlessly done the same to those concepts and theories of the state that could be said to deny that the state is derivative of and therefore dependent on the primordial forces and interests of society. At first glance this strategy looks somewhat misguided, since what such critics opposed was a 'theory of the state' that simply denied that there was such a thing as the state in the first place and that the state concept was therefore wholly redundant to any scientific analysis of political phenomena.

But to deny that the state exists is tantamount to denying that the state could be derivative of and dependent on something outside itself, because something that does not exist can hardly be conceived of as derivative or dependent. From this it is a small, but not entirely permissible, step to conclude that if the state is *a priori* dependent, it must exist. But it was not always necessary to infer that this was the case, since the assumption that the state exists by virtue of its dependence on society was an irrefutable part of its conceptual identity.

Hence those who want to construe a state concept worth opposing on the grounds of its ideological function must either direct their critical claims against the explicit reduction of the state into components such as interest groups or against the implicit but always very vague assumption of the state being present as a principle of political order behind the superficial plurality of interests in society. As it happened, the critique of the pluralist concept of the state was dual track: the reduction of the state to lesser components while retaining assumptions of an equilibrium between them was what made ideological concealment possible. Thus, the fact that the state has been neglected in political analysis, writes Miliband,

does not mean that Western political scientists and political sociologists have not had what used to be called 'a theory of the state'. On the contrary, it is precisely the theory of the state to which they do, for the most part, subscribe which helps to account for their comparative neglect of the state as a focus of

---

[13] Ernst Mandel, *Late Capitalism* (London: New Left Books, 1975), p. 550.

political analysis... [i]ts first result is to exclude, by definition, the notion that the state might be a rather special institution, whose main purpose is to defend the predominance in society of a particular class.[14]

The pluralist theory of the state is thus attacked not because of any failure to explain what it purports to explain, but because it allegedly conceals more than it reveals about the actual distribution of power within society. What is wrong with pluralist theory is not the answers it provides, but the questions it asks; these cannot but yield answers that distort reality. Worse still, if the pluralist reduction of the state to competing interest groups is supplemented by the idea of a government being neutral and impartial in relation to these interests, the neglect of the basic class character of state institutions gives way to active concealment:

[i]n fact, 'elite pluralism', with the competition it entails between different elites, is itself a prime guarantee that power in society *will* be diffused and not concentrated... [o]ne of the main purposes of the present work is in fact to show in detail that the pluralist-democratic view of society, on politics and of the state... is in all essentials wrong – that this view, far from providing a guide to reality, constitutes a profound obfuscation of it.[15]

Whereas pluralists had readily accepted that government is dependent on the articulation of group interests, they had turned this insight into an argument for throwing the state concept out of their theoretical framework. To them, the concept of the state did not explain anything that could not be better explained by reference to the concepts of government and group. But to those for whom the state was *a priori* dependent on something external to itself for its conceptual identity, such denial of the reality of the state was nothing but a gross act of ideological concealment.

According to the critics of pluralism, by reducing the state into its component parts and its external determinants to competing and formally equal interest groups, democratic pluralism had merely served to convey the illusion that modern states were already democratic, and that the fundamental questions of the distribution of power and wealth had already been settled in democratic theory and practice alike. Thus, although Miliband willingly admits that the pluralist theory of the state – that there is such a theory and that this theory is consistent is perfectly evident to him – renders the state 'decisively constrained by forces external to it',[16] the tendency to equate these external constraints with the interplay of

---

[14] Ralph Miliband, *The State in Capitalist Society: the Analysis of the Western System of Power* (London: Quartet Books, 1973), pp. 4–5.

[15] *Ibid.*, p. 6.

[16] Ralph Miliband, 'State Power and Class Interests', *New Left Review*, 1983, no. 138, p. 59.

competing interest groups rather than with competing classes makes it 'a profound obfuscation'.[17]

Gradually the critical claims were further radicalized, and their scope was widened. A fair share of criticism was directed not against any purported failure of pluralism to explain the dynamics of political life in terms of competition between interest groups, but against the implicit attribution of mediating functions to those entities which had been introduced as substitutes for the traditional state concept, such as government or political system. To imply that these entities were neutral in relation to those interests or, worse, to imply that the main function of these was to sustain a harmonious equilibrium between otherwise conflicting interests, was but conservatism dressed up as science. This criticism was not exclusively directed against pluralist substitutes for the state concept, but against system functionalism as a whole, and what was perceived as its inherently conservative presumption of order and stability within society. Thus Poulantzas:

by applying the general functionalist conception of the political system as the central integrating factor of a social system, the political system can be specified as the 'authoritarian distribution of values for the social ensemble' [sic] and the study of the political can be seen as the study of a process of legitimization of the relations of a social system.[18]

From such a point of view, all that mainstream political science had to say about the distribution of power in modern societies was nothing but ideology, designed to mask the actual dominance of a ruling class. According to its critics, the cash value of defining politics as the authoritative allocation of values was to conceal the class basis of all politics. According to the same critics, the empiricist and behaviouralist emphasis on observable units of analysis amounted to an implicit denial of the reality of the capitalist structure of modern society, and was thus nothing but part of a more general strategy of concealment.

By implication, the effort to throw the state concept out was doubly undesirable. Not only did this effort effectively hide the locus and medium of class dominance, but it also deprived its critics of the concept they thought best suited to reveal and criticize this dominance. As such, the mainstream discourse on the state within political science was to be read as symptomatic of the ideology of the bourgeois state and expressive of its ability to conceal its fundamental dependence on the class structure of capitalist society.

---

[17] Miliband, *State in Capitalist Society*, p. 6.
[18] Nicos Poulantzas, *Political Power and Social Classes* (London: New Left Books, 1973), p. 222.

It seems as if every theory of the state which did not *a priori* assume that the state was fundamentally dependent on entities outside itself was false by definition, simply because of the concealing function that could be attributed to it, on the basis of the state autonomy that such a concept could be said to imply by not ruling it out. Apart from the obvious difficulty of attributing truth value to any theory solely on the basis of its function, this conclusion is indeed puzzling and deserves attention.

At this point it might be tempting to note that the efforts to get rid of the state concept had been futile, partly because this concept was pushed down into the muddy foundations of the discipline, and partly because these efforts provoked attempts to restore the centrality of the state. So although there was not very much of a debate between mainstream state-bashers and their new and angry opponents, there was a considerable frustration among the former about what appeared to be the misunderstandings of the latter.[19]

To the mainstream political scientist at this time, the Marxist critique of the pluralist view of the state appears to be misguided, or paranoid, or both. Misguided, because saying that the state is dependent on something other than itself for its existence is not to say what the state *is*, only a way of saying what it is not: a transhistorical entity floating free of time and space – something which nobody at the time was prepared to assert with any sincerity anyway. Paranoid, because this way of conflating validity and function would make it possible to twist every assumption about the state which was incompatible with Marxist dogma into an exemplary pillar of bourgeois ideology, irrespective of its empirical validity.

But there is a real incommensurability buried here, not merely mutual ideological and scientific prejudice. One way to make sense of this incommensurability of state concepts would be to once again recognize the potential affinity between the pluralist and Marxist critiques of the state, and then ask why this did not result in any actual convergence of concerns.

First, if the state really were wholly dependent on something other than itself, then the state concept would seem as redundant to political analysis as those who tried to throw it out had so laboriously argued. If the state really were totally dependent on something other than itself for its existence and function, everything that could be explained with reference to the concept could then, and arguably with greater parsimony, be better explained with reference to those things upon which the state was held to be dependent. If the state could successfully be turned into a dependent variable, the state concept might as well be abandoned completely.

---

[19] Cf. Almond, 'The Return to the State'; David Easton, 'The Political System Besieged by the State', *Political Theory*, vol. 9, 1981, no. 3, pp. 303–25.

Yet this was exactly the kind of conclusion which those who wanted to bring the state back in wished to avoid at all costs, and for obvious reasons. The assumption of the *a priori* dependence of the state upon society at large served critical purposes, but the basic upshot was to assert the theoretical and empirical value of this concept *pace* the pluralists and their effort to throw it out. Those who wanted to bring the state concept back in often phrased their criticism of pluralism in ideological terms, but they nevertheless had a research agenda different from that of the pluralists, one which encouraged inquiry into domains not readily accessible to the latter.

Second, and as I tried to show in the previous chapter, the attempt to throw the state concept out was futile as this concept was invariably replaced with others that were semantically equivalent. However onto-logically innocent these replacements appeared to their proponents, they all catered to the basic need to explain and justify the presence of political order by providing definitions of politics and the political in presumably non-statist terms. It was these conceptual substitutes that now came to be regarded as symbols of authority, themselves expressive of particular interests, which those who struggled to bring the state back in wanted to unpack and unmask in much the same way as the young Marx had un-packed and unmasked the concepts of crown and constitution in Hegel's *Rechtsphilosophie*.

So rather than simply opposing pluralists on ideological grounds, those who tried to bring the state back in were standing on their shoulders, ex-tending the scope of, and thereby also perpetuating, a certain critical discourse that has animated conceptualizations of the state and its au-thority throughout the twentieth century. Thus, as we shall be able to see, the continuity and coherence attributed to the pluralist theory of the state by its critics are but a projection of this critical spirit, and the un-masking tactic it brings to bear on all conceptions of political authority, and all efforts at symbolic substitution.[20]

The first step in this strategy of unmasking was to assert the ontolog-ical reality of the state, since, in order to be susceptible to criticism, the state must be assumed to exist in the first place. The second step was to assert its *a priori* dependence on societal forces, so that the identity of the state could ultimately be seen as derivative of what was allegedly more fundamental. The third step consisted in asserting the relative autonomy of that state in relation to those very same societal forces, a move which looks paradoxical in the face of the first step. Yet as we shall see in the next sections, there is a certain fragile coherence to this strategy.

[20] Cf. Jacques Derrida, *Spectres of Marx: the State of the Debt, the Work of Mourning, and the New International* (London: Routledge, 1994).

Making the case against pluralism

If the state is real but yet ontologically dependent, what does this ontological dependence imply, and what does it rule out? In other canonical texts there is very little to indicate that the state is wholly determined or fully exhausted by its *a priori* dependence on property relations in society. Pushed to extremes, the assertion of total dependence would be the same as equating the state with a passive object devoid of any capacity to act. Such an equation would be at odds not only with much nineteenth-century experience of statehood such as that provided by Bonapartism, but also with any interest in the state as a *sui generis* category of political analysis. From total dependence would ultimately follow total redundance.

But apart from the critical view of the state to be found in the *Critique*, much has been said in favour of those interpretations of the canonical texts that emphasize the active side of the state by turning it into an acting subject. Thus, in the *German Ideology* (1845/1932) we learn that

the State has become a separate entity, beside and outside civil society; but it is nothing more than the form of organization which the bourgeois necessarily adopt both for internal and external purposes, for the mutual guarantee of their property and interests...the State is the form in which individuals of a ruling class assert their common interests.[21]

What is conveyed here is not the idea of a passive object entirely dependent on forces outside itself for its existence, but rather the notion of an entity which has the capacity to act on behalf of these forces. Within this view, the state is not only an inanimate tool in the hands of the ruling class, but has a capacity to act which is derivative of its dependence on that particular class and its interests. Thus, to say that the state is dependent does not necessarily imply that it is totally passive, only that it lacks the capacity to act independently of those interests on which it is dependent for its existence. Accepting this assumption was an important step towards recognizing the analytical value of the state concept, and therefore also crucial to those who wanted to bring the state back in after what they took to be decades of neglect.

Thus, in the rest of this section, we shall see how the attempt to bring the state back in has been conditioned by the view of the state as an agent, however dependent on underlying social forces. As I shall argue, in order to bring the state back in, two potentially conflicting views of the state

---

[21] Karl Marx and Friedrich Engels, *The German Ideology* [1932] (New York: International Publishers, 1947), pp. 59–60.

had to be reconciled within the state concept, ultimately rendering this concept structurally inconsistent: the views of the state as an inanimate object and the state as an acting subject.

Yet this reconciliation had to be effected without implying that the state could be fully autonomous in relation to society. The basic presupposition of dependence ruled out the possibility of the state being a neutral mediator between conflicting interests in society, thus embodying a general interest as opposed to particular ones, since only 'bourgeois ideologies affirm the neutrality of the State, representing the general interest, in relation to the divergent interests of "civil society"'.[22]

This does not mean that the dependency thesis must rule out every possible form of autonomy, however. If the state is not invested with any capacity for action, it becomes close to impossible to make theoretical sense of it at all. It also becomes difficult to explain why political science should bother itself with such a concept, if its capacity to act is purely chimerical. The dilemma which state theory had to confront at this stage was therefore a matter of reconceptualizing the notion of societal dependence so that it became compatible with notions of partial autonomy.

Cast in philosophical terms, the dilemma looked something like this. On the one hand, there was a strong tendency to view the state as an object, its status as an object being defined and justified in terms of its dependence on the basic structure of society, such as the mode of production, and on particular classes within that structure. Making theoretical sense of the state as such an object implied turning it into a dependent variable, and the more successful such an analysis, the less the capacity of the state to act. On the other hand, there was a tendency to view the state as a subject, its status as a subject being defined and justified in terms of its capacity to act upon precisely those forces of society upon which it was assumed to be dependent. Making sense of the state as a subject meant turning it into an independent variable, and the more successful such an analysis was, the less the state's prima facie dependence on the forces of society would seem.

Thus, when cast in these terms, no concept of the state could be articulated without a constant vacillation between an objectivist and a subjectivist interpretation. It would therefore seem that any theory that tried to incorporate both these understandings of the state was likely to give rise to incompatible interpretations of empirical reality, since it is difficult to imagine how such an account could possibly get its causal priorities straight.

---

[22] Nicos Poulantzas, 'The Problems of the Capitalist State', *New Left Review*, 1969, no. 58 p. 72.

At a discursive level, however, this theoretical tension between an objectivist and a subjectivist interpretation looks more like mutual implication, in so far as a subscription to the former notion only seems possible against the backdrop of a tacit acceptance of the latter, and conversely. We have also to bear in mind that both notions could be distilled from the canonical texts of Marxism, texts that provided the effort to bring the state back in with many of its theoretical resources and much of its rhetorical momentum.

If no one could be suspected of believing that the state was an entity autonomous from society, there would be no need to reiterate arguments in favour of its basic dependence, since the main upshot of these arguments was to make claims of state autonomy look like acts of ideological concealment. And conversely, if no one could be suspected of believing that the state was totally dependent on social forces external to itself, then the constant asserting of its capacity for autonomous action in relation to those forces would most probably fail to convince, since that would be to point out the obvious to theorists unconvinced about its *a priori* dependence, namely, that the state – however defined – indeed can and does act, and that this capacity constitutes a minimum requirement for any further definition within this theoretical context. This becomes evident when we encounter political theorists who succeeded in remaining unbothered by efforts to throw the state out and then bring it back in.

But how was the above dilemma handled in theoretical practice? As we shall see, starting out from a crude assumption that the state is an instrument in the hands of the dominant class, the discourse on the state evolves into a plea for the relative autonomy of the state from the dominant class and the structure of society. To my mind, this concept of relative autonomy constituted the crucial element in the effort to bring the state back in, but also, and by virtue of its own incoherence, the main source of its theoretical shortcomings. In the end, relative autonomy gave way to a recycling of a quasi-transcendental concept of the state.

But let us start with the instrumentalist view of the state, and the criticism it provoked. According to a simple instrumentalist theory of the state, the view that the state is a neutral warrant of the general interest is not only an illusion handed out by corrupt political scientists, but part of the politico-philosophical folklore used by the dominant class to legitimize its dominance and to reproduce the mode of production that makes its dominance possible. This concept of the state is thus derivative of a particular kind of empirical state: a bourgeois state sustained by a bourgeois ideology within the same superstructural arrangement.

This argument can be elaborated and substantiated in a variety of ways. As exemplified by Miliband and Domhoff, and contrary to pluralist claims, such a dependence is empirically evident, since the personnel of the state either belong to the same classes that dominate civil society, or have been coopted by these classes. However, Miliband cautiously remarks that

the first step in this analysis is to note the obvious but fundamental fact that this class is involved in a *relationship* with the state, which cannot be *assumed*, in the political conditions which are typical of advanced capitalism, to be that of principal to agent.

But what the evidence of this investigation suggests is that

in terms of social origin, education and class situation, the men who have manned all command positions in the state system have largely, and in many cases overwhelmingly, been drawn from the world of business and property, or from the professional middle class.[23]

Whereas Miliband assumes that these classes are more or less homogeneous in terms of both socioeconomic characteristics and interests, Domhoff breaks them down into a multitude of fractions with rivalling interests. This does not and cannot weaken his general case, however, since he defines a 'governing class' as

a social upper class which own a disproportionate amount of the country's wealth, receives a disproportionate amount of a country's income, and contributes a *disproportionate number of its members to the controlling institutions and key decision-making groups of the country.*[24]

This version of instrumentalism presupposes two things. First, it presupposes that the members of the dominant class are not only represented within the state and its institutions, but that they also have a common interest and that they can use the state in order to forward that interest. Second, it presupposes that this interest is known to the members of the dominant class rather than merely ascribed to them by the observer, and that they do intentionally forward these interests by means of their privileged position within the state. Thus, for the state to be an object in the hands of the dominant class would necessitate this class, and each of its members, being agents in their own right; that is, that they possessed not only knowledge of their interests but also the intentions and capacity to act quite rationally upon these. That this is indeed the case has been

---

[23] Miliband, *The State in Capitalist Society*, pp. 51, 61.
[24] G. William Domhoff, *Who Rules America?* (Englewood Cliffs, NJ: Prentice-Hall, 1967), p. 5. My italics.

obvious to many proponents of this thesis:

[i]n modern society, which is based on the antagonism between capitalist bourgeoisie and proletariat, state power is held in an absolute way by the bourgeoisie, which does not share it with any other class.[25]

Apart from this direct dependence of the state upon members of the dominant class, another version of this argument takes the state to be dependent on the economic resources of that class rather than upon the actual will of its members. Within this view, the power of the dominant class over the state resides in the dependence of the latter upon tax revenues, and the ability of the former to withhold investment should the state act contrary to their interests.[26] Accordingly, the dominant class does not have to control the state directly, nor does it have to exercise its clout intentionally upon the state, since the uneven distribution of wealth makes the state likely to comply intentionally with what it perceives to be the wishes of the dominant class.

Phrased in this way, the instrumentalist thesis admits to the empirical possibility that the state could be appropriated by classes or interests other than those dominant in society as a whole. Hence, turning the state into an object dependent on particular classes and their interests naturally begs the question of whether this relationship is necessary, or if the state is neutral in so far as it could also be used by other social classes in order to further their interests, provided that they could gain access to the state and its institutions.[27]

It was this kind of conclusion that provoked criticism both from systems theorists and from structuralists. According to critics such as Offe and Poulantzas it is precisely the possibility that other social classes could appropriate the state for their purposes that makes the instrumentalist view of the state insufficient. Even if it is granted that there is an 'empirical preponderance of those which represent and implement interests oriented toward the process of accumulation' within the state, instrumentalism is quite unable to 'demonstrate the structural necessity of this state of affairs'.[28] Viewing the state merely as an object means yielding too much to the bourgeois and pluralist conception of state power, since 'concepts and notions are never innocent, and by employing the notions

[25] Etienne Balibar, 'The Dictatorship of the Proletariat', *Marxism Today*, vol. 21, 1977, no. 5, p. 151.
[26] Carnoy, *State and Political Theory*, p. 52.
[27] Jessop, 'Recent Theories of the Capitalist State', p. 356.
[28] Claus Offe, 'Structural Problems of the Capitalist State, Class Rule and the Political System', in Klaus von Beyme, *German Political Studies*, vol. I (London: Sage, 1974), p. 33.

of the adversary to reply to him, one legitimizes them and permits their persistence'.[29]

Thus, to the critics of instrumentalism, conceiving the state merely as an object is not sufficient if we want to understand its entire range of functions in capitalist societies. The instrumental relation between the state and the dominant class is conceptualized in subjective terms, that is, as fundamentally dependent on the subjective interests and actual intentions of that class. In that case, the capacity of the state to act would depend solely 'on the extent to which class struggle and pressure from below challenge the hegemony of the class which is dominant in such a society'.[30] Hence, there is a 'flagrant theoretical inconsistency [in] the simplistic and vulgarized conception which sees in the state the tool or instrument of the dominant class'.[31]

To sum up the structuralist objection: turning the state into an object makes it difficult to account for what the state does, so its capacity to act must be regarded as dependent on the dominant classes in society which infuse the state with the capacity to act on their behalf or behest. Doing this necessitates the dominant classes having been conceptualized as acting subjects in their own right, fully equipped with interests, intentions and a capacity to act rationally. The net effect of such a theoretical move is to make the state dependent upon the existence of classes conceived of as subjects, while simultaneously conceptualizing this dependence in terms of their capacity to dominate the state and influence its policies more or less intentionally. Thus, the relationship between the state and the social classes dominating it must itself be defined in terms of the defining attributes of these classes, that is, in terms of their interests and intentions.

And conversely: as soon as we start to define this dependence with reference to structural features of the society in which the state is situated rather than with reference to the intentions and interests of the dominant classes, the state is turned into an acting subject, capable of responding intentionally and perhaps even rationally to the demands of these structures. Hence, making the state dependent on subjects such as classes turns it into an object, and this objectification in its turn makes its relation to these classes reducible to their subjective attributes. Contrary to this, the structuralist proposal to view the state as dependent on objective structures holds out the promise of turning the state into a subject while making its relation to these structures wholly objective by rendering it independent of the intentions and interests of a particular class or group.

---

[29] Poulantzas, 'Problems of the Capitalist State', p. 70.
[30] Ralph Miliband, 'State Power and Class Interests', p. 60.
[31] Poulantzas, *Political Power and Social Classes*, pp. 256, 257, 284–5.

Halfway to its solution, the basic dilemma posed by objectivist and subjectivist interpretations can now be restated like this. If the instrumentalist theory of the state turns the state into an object by focusing on specific agents such as classes as the main source of its dependence, the structuralist or systems theory of the state turns it into an acting subject by focusing on its dependence on those objective structures that also give rise to social classes. Consequently, solving the dilemma now becomes a matter of showing how structural dependence conditions state autonomy, rather than cancelling it out. Since this may sound enigmatic to those of us who are trained to view agency and structure in terms of tension rather than direct implication, the underpinnings of the structuralist turn deserve some elaboration.

It took two ontological moves to bring the structuralist turn to bear on the state problem. First, since it is difficult to go structuralist while remaining faithful to the basics of empiricist epistemology, the latter had to be disposed of in order to assert the reality of structure. Objective structures are not accessible to experience in the same way as subjective interests and the declared intentions of concrete agents, so making the case for structural dependence necessitates a shift away from the immediately given to the underlying and unobservable mechanisms of society. This begs the further question of how it is possible to infer the existence of such structures from their effects or surface manifestations. In order to permit any such inference, this shift in turn requires yet another reversal of the relationship between concepts and the portions of reality to which they are supposed to refer, given an empiricist framework of inquiry. As a result, the concept of the state takes on a certain priority in relation to its institutional manifestations within the structuralist scheme, so that the former can now be said to embody rather than represent the latter.

Before we go into detail, it is important to note that this episode coincided neatly with the critique of empiricism within Marxist theory in general. Empiricism could now confidently be theorized as a part of bourgeois ideology, since by insisting that the basic units of analysis should be observable, it cut off epistemic access to the unobservable structural essence of capitalist society. Cutting off such access to the hidden but nevertheless very real structures of capitalist society was tantamount to denying their existence, and this denial was but another act of ideological obfuscation and concealment.[32]

Against this backdrop it was easy to conclude that unobservables ought to do the job of explanation all by themselves. The concept of structure

---

[32] For a critique along those lines, see Louis Althusser and Etienne Balibar, *Reading Capital* (London: New Left Books, 1970), pp. 37–41.

was now identified less with the order of signs where it first had emerged, and gradually more with the order of invisible causal forces. Simultaneously, structures were no longer interpreted in purely descriptive terms, but more in generative terms. Structures, says Godelier,

> should not be confused with visible 'social relations' but constitute a *level of reality* invisible but present behind the visible social relations. The logic of the latter, and the laws of social practice more generally, depend on the functioning of these hidden structures and the discovery of these last should allow us to 'account for the facts observed'.[33]

It is tempting to see this as a retreat back into the long lost living museum, but that would be undue simplification. But if structures are not immediately given to experience, how do we know that they exist and perform the kind of generative function they are assumed to perform in relation to the more tangible and observable facts of the sociopolitical world? The standard solution was provided by Althusser, according to whom '*the whole existence of the structure consists of its effects*, in short that the structure, which is merely a specific combination of its peculiar elements, is nothing outside its effects'.[34]

This brings us to the question of concepts. Even if we were to attain knowledge of these structural effects, that would not permit us to conclude that the structure that produced them existed independently of these effects, let alone to understand the precise causal relationship between that structure and its observable effects. To do these things necessitates the prior possession of the concept of that structure, since within this framework all knowledge depends on the prior construction of the concept of its object. That is, and contrary to the empiricist understanding of the relationship between concepts and reality, concepts do not primarily refer to preconstituted classes of objects, but are conditions of knowledge by constituting such classes and domains as objects of knowledge.[35]

When transposed to political science, such an ontology made it possible to reconceptualize the state as essentially dependent on the economic structures of society, while rendering it wholly independent of the direct influence of particular classes. Armed with a concept of the state signifying a relation in the overall structure of capitalist society, the state could now be understood as capitalist by definition, since it was situated in a capitalist society whose essential structures it helped to

---

[33] Maurice Godelier, 'System, Structure, and Contradiction in *Capital*', *Socialist Register*, 1967, p. 92.
[34] Althusser and Balibar, *Reading Capital*, p. 189.
[35] *Ibid.*, pp. 183–5.

sustain and reproduce by virtue of its structural position alone. Hence, within a structuralist view of the state, the state is still essentially a class state, but has to be conceived of as relatively autonomous in relation to the dominant class in order to be able to serve the interests of that class by contributing to the reproduction of a capitalist mode of production.

According to Poulantzas, the source of this relative autonomy is exactly the objective dependence of the state and the political upon the social and economic structures of society, rather than its subjective dependence on particular class interests.[36] Thus, the relation between the dominant class and the state can be conceptualized as

an *objective relation*. This means that if the *function* of the State in a determinate social formation and the *interests* of the dominant class in this formation coincide, it is by reason of the system itself: the direct participation of the members of the ruling class in the State apparatus is not the *cause* but the *effect*, and moreover a chance and contingent one.[37]

Consequently, such a state 'can only truly serve the ruling class in so far as it is relatively autonomous from the diverse fractions of this class, precisely in order to be able to organize the hegemony of the whole of this class'.[38] Here the state is conceptualized as dependent on forces outside itself, since the existence of such dependence hinges on an inferential relation between the concept of structure and the concept of the state rather than on what specific states or dominant classes do in any empirical reality; that there exists such a thing outside and independently of concepts is not evident as long as we remain within the structuralist framework. Rather the converse – what states and classes *can* possibly do is circumscribed by the totality of concepts which define the structures in which they are situated, since states and classes are but relations that obtain within these structures, and thus wholly relative in relation to them and, ultimately, to the concepts defining them. And fully consistent with the dream of a structure devoid of subjects, all agency is defined in relational terms and thus conceptualized as derivative of the structure itself. It should now be plain how and why it was possible and necessary to assert state autonomy by insisting on its fundamental dependence on the structures of capitalist society.

Simply put, the concept of the state and the concepts which together define the social structure of society are in turn defined in terms of each

---

[36] This is not to imply that Poulantzas is to be interpreted as a die-hard structuralist. For a discussion, see Bob Jessop, 'On the Originality, Legacy, and Actuality of Nicos Poulantzas', *Studies in Political Economy*, vol. 34, 1991, no. 1, pp. 75–107.

[37] Poulantzas, 'Problems of the Capitalist State', p. 73.

[38] *Ibid.*

other. The same goes for the possibility of attaining knowledge of such a state: since structural dependence is integral to the conceptual identity of the state, and since such a state concept is a necessary condition for the attainment of knowledge of the state, the resulting knowledge cannot be expected to yield anything but a confirmation of the state's structural dependence.

Since one crucial function attributed to the state is to legitimize the mode of production and the class structure, this implies that those theories of the state that deny this structural dependence cannot but contribute to this legitimizing and reproductive function, be it in the shape of a bourgeois political science or – hardly discernible from it – in the guise of liberal democratic folklore.[39] Wholly consistent with this need for legitimacy, the state presents itself

as a popular-class-state. Its institutions are organized around the principles of the liberty and equality of 'individuals' or 'political persons'. Its legitimacy is no longer founded on the divine will implied by the monarchical principle, but on the ensemble of formally free and equal individuals–citizens and on the popular sovereignty and secular responsibility of the state towards the people.[40]

The story the state has to tell about itself is nothing but ideology, and the myth of the state as a neutral embodiment of a general interest is functionally necessary to conceal its profound class character while throwing the dominated classes a bone in order to secure continued dominance:

[t]he notion of the general interest of the 'people', an ideological notion covering an institutional operation of the capitalist state, expresses a real fact: namely that this state, by its very structure, gives to the economic interests of certain dominated classes guarantees which may even be contrary to the short-term economic interests of the dominant classes, but which are compatible with their political interests and their hegemonic domination.[41]

But the structuralist state also has to face the need to sustain the accumulation processes in society, since without the necessary economic resources, it would be difficult to buy consent and support the quest for ideological legitimacy. Thus, as Offe has reminded his fellow theorists, there is a trade off between the goals of accumulation and the quest for legitimacy necessary to maintain cohesion in society.[42] The 'capitalist state has the responsibility of compensating the process of socialization

---

[39] See Amy Beth Bridges, 'Nicos Poulantzas and the Marxist Theory of the State', *Politics and Society*, vol. 4, 1974, no. 2, pp. 161–90.

[40] Poulantzas, *Political Power and Social Classes*, p. 123.

[41] *Ibid.*, p. 190–1.

[42] Claus Offe, 'Advanced Capitalism and the Welfare State', *Politics and Society*, vol. 2, 1976, no. 4, pp. 479–88.

triggered by capital, which constitutes a threat to the capital relation'.[43] Hence, the need for mass loyalty and legitimacy

obliges the State apparatus to execute its class-bound functions under the pretext of class neutrality and to provide its particular exercise of power with the alibi of general interests [since] an openly practiced class character of political governance which is apparent as such involves the risk of class-polarization and a politicization of the class struggle.[44]

Again we are able to notice how the critique of the state concept is a critique of its ideological function rather than its explanatory power, and how this critique spills over into a theory of the state that focuses upon its need for legitimacy and its function as a source of cohesion:

the State can only *function* as a capitalist state by appealing to symbols and sources of support that *conceal* its nature as a capitalist state; the existence of a capitalist state presupposes the systematic *denial* of its nature as a *capitalist* state.[45]

As we noted in the previous section, every theory of the state that would deny its structural dependence is ideological in nature and thus false by definition. And conversely, every theory that would assert the fundamental dependence of the state on society is valid to the extent that it can show that theories that deny this fundamental dependence are in fact themselves dependent upon that state, since within this view, the state as well as state theories are inseparable within the superstructure. By the same token, all concepts of the state which are not determined by an *a priori* dependence by being derived from the logic of capital or the class structure are part of the giant cover up operation of capitalism. This goes not only for those pluralist conceptions of the state which are premised on the idea that the state is independent of society, but also for those concepts which contain a denial of their own fundamental dependence upon the capitalist state.

In those theories in which the state is rendered dependent upon the objective structures of society rather than upon the subjective interest of particular classes, the scope for state autonomy in relation to these forces seemingly looms larger than in the former kind of theory, since its structural dependence inevitably raises questions of how and why these structures are reproduced, questions invariably answered by defining the state as an agent whose identity and agency are both enabled and constrained by those structures.

[43] Claus Offe, 'The Crisis of Crisis Management: Elements of a Political Crisis Theory', *International Journal of Politics*, vol. 6, 1976, no. 3, p. 49.

[44] Offe, 'Structural Problems', p. 47.

[45] Claus Offe, 'The Capitalist State and the Problem of Policy Formation', in Leon N. Lindberg, Robert Alford, Colin Crouch and Claus Offe (eds.), *Stress and Contradiction in Modern Capitalism* (Lexington, MA: D. C. Heath, 1973), p. 127.

Since the state faces the enormous task of maintaining both the capitalist mode of production and the class structure that sustains it, its existence as an independent agent indeed looks vital for the survival of the entire social system, in so far as it is able to counter the self-destructive tendencies inherent in capitalism. But does it really matter what actual states – presumably specific instantiations of the state concept – do for the way that the concept of the state has been defined within the context of Marxist political discourse?

Not really. Quite irrespective of whether we take the state to be dependent on the will of the dominant class or on the objective structures of capitalist society, it does not really matter what the state does, or what this in turn does to society in terms of unintended consequences, since its dependence upon things other than itself is an analytical assumption about the basic conceptual identity of the state rather than an empirical hypothesis about the 'specific referents' of its concept. Likewise, the ideological function of other state concepts and their apparent 'falsehood' is inferred from this analytical assumption, since their function and their validity are but the other side of the *a priori* assumption of dependence.

In its instrumentalist version, this assumption is rendered immune to empirical counter-instances either by defining the dominant class in terms of its position within the state or by making the instrumental dependence a matter of definition by assuming that the interests of the state and those of the dominant class naturally and inevitably coincide. Hence, only if the members of a given state did dispossess themselves and the dominant class would we be entitled to question the empirical validity of this version of state dependence. In the structuralist version, the only possible empirical disproof of dependence and the only evidence of any real autonomy from the structures of society would be if a given state did abolish capitalism overnight or deliberately tried to create massive social disorder.[46]

Thus, the state seems able only to reproduce capitalist social relations, never to transform them in any substantial way without simultaneously ceasing to be a state, since the state concept is defined in terms of its relation to the total structure of capitalist society. Defined in this way, the state cannot remain identical with itself while ceasing to be dependent on something other than itself, since such a dependence is a condition of its possibility and a condition of the validity of those theories analysing this dependence. Yet already at this point it seems as if the state concept is

[46] A. Van den Berg, *The Immanent Utopia: From Marxism on the State to the State of Marxism* (Princeton, NJ: Princeton University Press, 1988), pp. 301ff.; Frankel, 'On the State of the State', p. 206.

necessary in order to explain the presence of relative political order within capitalist societies, however dependent the state is made to look, and however ideologically undesirable any notion of state autonomy would be.

As we saw above, the main contention of the structuralist critique of the instrumentalist view of the state was that instrumentalists had failed to demonstrate that the subservience of the state to the interests of the dominant class was necessary. According to their critics, this failure was tantamount to denying the *a priori* dependence of the state on either the dominant class or the structure of capitalist society, and this would in turn be to admit the possibility of its autonomy in relation to both.

To concede that there is indeed nothing necessary about state dependence would have forced the adherents of this thesis to accept the validity of pluralist findings, since for explanatory and ideological purposes it would have been quite sufficient to postulate a tendency towards a conflict of interests within the political system, behind which any semantic equivalent to the state concept could have been introduced in order to explain away what would then have looked like anomalous cases of reconciliation between different class interests. Had explanatory power alone been the issue, it would have been quite sufficient to turn Easton and Parsons on their heads by substituting an assumption of conflict for an assumption of harmony as the ordering principle in the political system. But this, of course, would have made it difficult to bring the state back in, since it would then have looked redundant.

Much in the same way that pluralists once criticized the view that the state was *sui generis* and wholly autonomous in relation to society, and ended up arguing that the concept of the state was redundant, those who started to bring the state back in criticized this former view by implying that the state was dependent while arguing that the state concept was therefore indispensable as a category of political analysis. But there is a clear tension between these two convictions. On the one hand, there is the basic view that the state exists, and is identical with itself as an object of inquiry only by virtue of being dependent on something other than itself. On the other hand, there is the insight that if the state is conceptualized as wholly dependent on something other than itself, this threatens its analytical value as an independent theoretical and empirical concept. Thus, as we shall see in the next section, the effort to bring the state back in while insisting on its necessary dependence results either in a dissolution of the state into society or, if some coherent notion of autonomy is retained in order to avoid this outcome, in a set of rather conventional and statist assumptions about the state as a source and locus of sociopolitical order.

The relativity of autonomy

Hitherto I have argued that the effort to bring the state back in was conditioned by an *aporia* between two conflicting views of the state within the same theoretical discourse. This renewed interest in the state took place against the backdrop of tensions already present in the canonical texts of Marxism, which could lend support both to the view that the state was ontologically dependent upon society and to the view that the state had the capacity to act within that very same society. I have also tried to show that attempts to reconcile these views have implied that the state, however ontologically conditioned by its fundamental dependence, was nevertheless necessary in order to explain and justify the presence of political order, in this particular case the class structure of late modern capitalism.

Yet there is more to it than that, something which becomes plain if we venture beyond criticism of existing conceptions of the state and instead analyse the ways in which the state has been reconceptualized by those struggling to bring it back in, and how those reconceptualizations in turn changed its place and function within the larger theoretical context. As I shall argue in this section, these reconceptualizations have not only had the intended consequence of bringing the state back into focus, but have also and unwittingly brought with them strong statist commitments while removing the state from the scope of rigorous theoretical analysis.

Returning once more to the canonical texts, it is possible to find support for a third view of the state, namely, that the state is the ultimate source of order in society. Within this view, the function of the state is not reducible to its repression of the dominated classes and its ability to conceal that domination, but implies a maintenance of political order necessary to maintain both a capitalist mode of production and the class structure that goes with it. The most famous expression of this notion is to be found in *The Origin of the Family, Private Property, and the State*. According to Engels, in order that

classes with conflicting economic interests, shall not consume themselves and society in fruitless struggle, a power, apparently standing above society, has become necessary to moderate the conflict and keep it within the bounds of 'order'; and this power arisen out of society, but placing itself above it and increasingly alienating itself from it, is the state.[47]

It has been possible to read into this passage a vague promise of a final reconciliation between the state as object and the state as subject, between the state as wholly dependent and the state as fully autonomous. From this point of view it becomes hard to argue that the state is capable

---

[47] Friedrich Engels, *The Origin of the Family, Private Property, and the State* (London: Lawrence and Wishart, 1972) p. 229.

of autonomous action only by virtue of its dependence upon the class structure or the mode of production, since a fair degree of autonomy from these seems necessary in order to explain the existence of order within society, which would otherwise be consumed by class struggle. Rather than being an instrument or a functional requisite, the state now appears as a biased moderator.

The state, as it were, is an essential source of cohesion in the social body, capable of resolving class antagonism by means of repression and concession.[48] But to say that the state must have a certain degree of autonomy from class interests does not mean that it is fully independent from them, only that a degree of independence is necessary for serving some interests by reconciling them with others, thereby maintaining the cohesion of society as a whole.

While this assumption is rarely expounded in texts where the main task is to criticize the institutions of capitalist statehood, it constitutes the backbone of most explanations of why capitalist societies tend to hold together and why revolutions so rarely occur in them despite social antagonism. But if the state is defined by its dependence on something other than itself and is simultaneously thought to be responsible for the continued existence of that other – capitalist society – we must now ask what this responsibility does to the identity of the state concept.

It is clearly insufficient to define the state as a mere object. Whenever it is interpreted as an object, the state seems to dissolve at closer inspection, much in the same way as it did in the pluralist analysis of the state, but with the significant difference that it now dissolves into a society constituted by class relations rather than by competing interest groups. It then becomes difficult to make sense of the state as a unity. But making sense of its unity, however, is absolutely necessary if we want to attribute agency to the state, and such attribution of agency in turn is indispensable if we want to conceptualize the state as a source and locus of political order.

Thus, in order for the state to be intelligible as an agent in its own right, a firm line of demarcation must be drawn between the state proper and the society upon which it is in some sense dependent; yet every such line of demarcation must be conceived of as sufficiently flexible to accommodate the transitions between different modes of production that occur in history according to a materialist interpretation. In the rest of this section, I shall analyse different solutions to the dilemma created by defining the state as being both autonomous and dependent, while making sense of its unitary character.

Let us start with the tendency for the state to become absorbed by society. To instrumentalists like Miliband, what can possibly be appropriated

---

[48] Jessop, 'Recent Theories of the Capitalist State', pp. 355ff.

by the dominant class thus appears to be not one instrument, but many. Thus, according to him, the state 'is not a thing . . . it does not as such exist. What "the state" stands for is a number of particular institutions which, together, constitute its reality, and which interact as parts of what may be called the state system.'[49] In Miliband's analysis, the government, the administrative apparatus, the judiciary and parliamentary assemblies together constitute the state. It is these 'institutions in which "state power" lies, and it is through them that this power is wielded in its different manifestations by the people who occupy the leading positions in each of these institutions'.[50]

If the state concept is ultimately but a shorthand for a plurality of institutions and the people supposedly controlling them, it seems as if this concept could be disposed of, precisely as pluralists earlier had concluded. This conclusion was also accepted implicitly by most critics of pluralism before the effort to bring the state back in had gained momentum within political science. For example, neither Mills nor Domhoff bothered to articulate any distinct concept of the state, but remained content to argue that local as well as federal political institutions were indeed dominated by members of the business elite, or unconsciously adapted themselves to its interests.[51] This apparent neglect of the state could perhaps partly be explained by the relative 'statelessness' of American political experience, and partly by the epistemic standards of the day. If not wholly redundant, the concept of the state was at least dispensable when actual decision-making and policy formation were analysed at the level of specific institutions. Consequently, the debate with pluralists such as Dahl came to concern which elite wielded most clout in what issue area, rather than whether 'the elite' dominated 'the state' or not.

But what makes it possible to speak of this set of institutions as a system? Again the concept of system is introduced as an antidote to the theoretical incoherence that the absence of the state concept gives rise to. The very term 'system' seems to imply that some minimum coherence can be attributed to the plurality of institutions conveniently subsumed under the state concept. Thus, in order to retain some basic meaning of this concept, some principle of unity must be found which makes it possible to speak of the component institutions of the state in terms of a system as opposed to an incoherent multitude. Furthermore, such a principle must be defined in terms other than those used to define the social class upon which the state is held to be dependent, since to make the coherence of

---

[49] Miliband, *The State in Capitalist Society*, p. 46.
[50] *Ibid.*, p. 50.
[51] Domhoff, *Who Rules America?*, *passim*; C. Wright Mills, *The Power Elite* (New York: Oxford University Press, 1956), *passim*.

the state dependent upon the homogeneity and cohesion of that social class would result either in the crudest of tautologies, or undercut all reasons for retaining the state concept as an analytical category, since it would then be impossible to distinguish between the state and those parts of society upon which it was dependent.

Having dissolved this distinction, the notion of class power could now easily be substituted for that of state authority without any loss of explanatory power. Indeed, there are strong Occamite reasons in favour of such a substitution, since if the distinction between state and society becomes too blurred while the state is believed to be dependent on social forces, the state may as well go to the dogs. Doing this, however, would entail those who wanted to bring the state back losing one important reason for doing so. At this point, those who wanted to retain the state concept while treating it as a dependent variable had little choice but to become closet Weberians or half-hearted decisionists. Thus, to Miliband, behind the plurality of institutions of the state lurks a very real locus of authoritative decision-making, since it is 'ultimately a very small group of people in the state – often a single person – who decide what is to be done or not done'.[52]

We might therefore tentatively reiterate the conclusion that it is theoretically difficult to make sense of the state concept as a dependent variable while arguing that the same concept refers to a unitary institution or any coherent set of institutions which must therefore enjoy a certain autonomy from particular classes as well as from the total ensemble of social relations. Thus, on the one hand, if the state is thought to be wholly dependent on the mode of production or the dominant class, one is left with the problem of explaining what makes the state a state rather than an incoherent bundle of separate institutions, either to be analysed as superstructural epiphenomena of an underlying structure, or as mere tools in the hands of the dominant class. On the other hand, if coherence is attributed to these institutions on the basis of some organizing principle that draws them together independently of external forces in society at large, then a first and irreversible step is taken towards treating the state as a subject, capable of acting either in its own interest, and then also possibly in opposition to all other constellations of interests in society, or in the interest of society as a whole, and then in possible opposition to at least some other constellations of interests, including those of the dominant class – which is precisely what was assumed by the pluralists.

Again structuralism provided a way of handling this dilemma by stripping the state concept of empirical content and turning it into a condition

---

[52] Miliband, 'State Power and Class Interests', p. 61.

of knowledge of itself understood in relational terms. According to the basic structuralist thesis, the state stands in an objective relation to the dominant class, and has as its primary function to maintain the cohesion of the entire social structure by reproducing the mode of production together with the class division which makes the state necessary if then also necessarily dependent. As Poulantzas argues, the main function of the capitalist state is to be a

factor of cohesion between the levels of a social formation. This is precisely the meaning of the Marxist conception of the state as a factor of 'order' or 'organizational principle' of a formation: not in the current sense of political order, but in their sense of the cohesion of the ensemble of the levels of a complex unity, *and as the regulating factor of its global equilibrium as a system* ... [t]he state prevents political class conflict from breaking out [and] prevents classes and 'society' from consuming themselves ...[53]

As a minimum requisite, the state must be able to act independently of the dominant class in order to serve that class by organizing its political hegemony.[54] But in order to do this, the state must be understood as a unity in its own right, a unity which it is difficult to conceptualize while remaining consistent with the *a priori* assumption of the state's dependence. If the state displays internal unity and coherence, this is not a result of its subservience to the interests of a particular class, but because such a unity derives from its relationally defined and objective position in capitalist society as a whole.

The state, writes Poulantzas, 'forms an *objective system* of special "branches" whose relation presents a *specific internal unity* and obeys, to a large extent, *its own logic*'.[55] In order to maintain this role while obeying its own logic, the state has to be relatively autonomous in relation to the dominant class and its competing fractions, much in the same way as the political has to be relatively autonomous in relation to the economic base. To Poulantzas, the capitalist state has 'relative autonomy as a constitutive feature of its concept'.[56]

But it is still difficult to conceptualize the state as a unity in its own right, since having been defined as a relation in a larger structure of objective relations, it must also ultimately be derived from that structure and, having been derived from it, it is difficult to conceive of its unity in terms other than those of structural conditions necessary for its existence. On the one hand, if the unity of the state is seen as derivative of the capitalist mode of production, it becomes difficult to conceptualize the

[53] Poulantzas, *Political Power and Social Classes*, pp. 44–5, 50.
[54] Poullantzas, 'Problems of the Capitalist State', pp. 73–4.
[55] *Ibid.*, p. 75.
[56] Poulantzas, *Political Power and Social Classes*, p. 261.

nature of this autonomy other than in terms of its ability to reproduce the conditions of that mode of production. Taken seriously, this kind of autonomy resembles that of a bee in a beehive, which is free to fly about according to its own whims, but which nevertheless unwittingly yet inevitably ends up reproducing the larger organism of which it forms an indistinguishable part. Acting otherwise, the bee would undermine the conditions of its own existence by undermining those of the beehive. The relatively autonomous state, consisting of little else but a set of structural relations, turns out to be relatively autonomous as a result of its absolute dependence on those relations which together constitute its conceptual identity. Thus, the state

protects and sanctions a set of *rules* and *social relationships* which are presupposed by the class rule of the capitalist class. The state does not defend the interests of one class, but the *common* interest of all members of *capitalist class society*.[57]

Within this view, the fact that the state is derivative of the same structure – the mode of production – which it simultaneously reproduces does not necessarily imply that the state lacks the capacity to act according to its own interest, only that the institutional self-interest that makes it tick is in turn 'conditioned by the fact that the state is *denied* the power to control the resources which are indispensable for the *use* of state power'.[58] In order to perform this essential reproductive function, the state must have some degree of autonomy from the social structure from which it necessarily derives. And conversely: the only reason why the state needs this autonomy is in order to be able to fulfil its reproductive functions. But again we have to face the prima facie insoluble dilemma between the attempt to make sense of the state as a unity in its own right, vested with the capacity to act autonomously, and the imperative to regard its existence as derivative of and dependent on something other than itself.

On the other hand, if the state is taken to be derivative of the class structure of society, its relative autonomy is 'inherent in its very structure ... in so far as it is the resultant of contradictions and of the class struggle ... within the State itself – this State which is both shot through and constituted with and by these class contradictions'.[59] In this case, the agency of the state is essentially dependent on the logic of class relations, to the extent that it becomes close to impossible to account for its unity,

[57] C. Offe and W. Ronge, 'Theses on the Theory of the State', *New German Critique*, 1975, no. 6, p. 139.

[58] *Ibid.*, p. 140.

[59] Nicos Poulantzas, 'The Capitalist State: a Reply to Miliband and Laclau', *New Left Review*, 1976, no. 95, p. 74.

since the question of what brings these contradictions together into a co-herent structure must either be left unresolved – so that the state concept dissolves into the sum total of class contradictions – or solved with ref-erence to a second-order source and locus of unity situated somewhere within the structurally fragmented state. Given these options, what can the concept of relative autonomy reasonably mean?

The exact meaning of this notion has been contested, a fact which has not prevented it from becoming a catchword for all those disputing the not-so-widespread idea that the state is a mere object in the hands of the dominant class. As Jessop has remarked, the concept of relative autonomy

seems to operate just as an abstract, formal concept serving nothing but a di-acritical function in demarcating the approach preferred by its advocates from the crude reductionism and from an absolute autonomization of different insti-tutional orders...In this sense, it does...embody a *contradictio in adjecto*: either a system or political agent is autonomous or it is not.[60]

But even if we generously interpret autonomy as an attribute that can vary along a continuum, it is indeed doubtful whether those using this concept within the present theoretical context have done so in a consistent way. As we have noted, in its structuralist or systems theory versions, the relatively autonomous state is no longer object or subject, but is turned into a relation, either between the mode of production and the rest of society, or between social classes, themselves defined in relational terms. As we have also noted, the structuralist state has no essence apart from those relations together composing it, nor does it constitute a unitary actor in itself, since it is derived either from the mode of production and the logic of the capital relation or from the class structure of society and the class struggle.

As such, it becomes nothing but a 'condensation of a balance of forces', with no capacity to act independently of the mode of production that conditions the class struggle that permeates it. When the state happens to act, this is either the result of the reproductive logic of the former or a momentary outcome of the latter as it manifests itself between different class factions within the state.[61]

But if the state is nothing but a relation between things themselves defined in relational terms, the relative autonomy of the state must consist in the relative autonomy of a relation in relation to other relations, an idea which it is difficult to make sense of other than in rather esoteric terms. Yet Poulantzas maintains that state policy is nevertheless likely

[60] Bob Jessop, *State Theory: Putting the Capitalist State in its Place* (Cambridge: Polity Press, 1990), pp. 101–2.

[61] Nicos Poulantzas, *Classes in Contemporary Socialism* (London: New Left Books, 1975), p. 98; Nicos Poulantzas, *State, Power, and Socialism* (London: New Left Books, 1978), pp. 135–6.

to be coherent as a result of the hegemony of particular factions of the dominant class within the state. This takes us back to square one, since if the coherence of the state and its policy are nevertheless guaranteed by the presence of a hegemonic fraction within it, this is only to again assert what was initially denied by the same theory, namely, that the state contains a single source and locus of power capable of overriding other rivalling loci of power within as well as without it. This amounts to nothing less than the introduction of yet another state inside the state in order to explain the unitary character of the latter and the relative coherence of its output. Without such an assumption, the state concept is bound to face dissolution into a bundle of institutional components, and will therefore ultimately be superfluous as an analytical concept. With such an assumption a first step towards infinite regress is taken.

Thus, the ultimate source of state unity in modern societies is neither the capitalist mode of production nor the class structure it brings into play, but is to be sought within the state itself. It is the presence of such a state within the state that draws the mode of production and the class structure together into a coherent system of social relations, thus making these relations derivative of the state rather than conversely, since the

> state is related to a 'society divided into classes' and to political domination, precisely in so far as it maintains, in the ensemble of structures, that place and role which have the *effect* of dividing a formation into classes and producing class domination.[62]

So behind the state permeated by class struggle there seems to be a hard core of the state left which produces this struggle at least to the same extent as it is produced by it. Thus, reconceptualizing the state in terms of class contradictions seems rather futile, since it either does violence to the assumption of state unity, or necessitates the assumption of a state within the state, the former being both the source of the class struggle within the latter as well as its ultimate arbiter. Hence, by stripping the state of its accidental attributes, the structuralist or systems theorist interprets the concept of the state as if it had an essence behind the contingencies resulting from its place in capitalist society only to discover either that this essence itself evaporates into class contradiction or factionalism or, even more reluctantly, that this essence is essential to the existence of the social relations from which the state concept was derived in the first place. Thus, the structuralist unwittingly but easily ends up as a die hard *étatiste*.[63]

---

[62] Poulantzas, *Political Power and Social Classes*, p. 51.
[63] Van den Berg, *Immanent Utopia*, pp. 339, 351; cf. Bob Jessop, *Nicos Poulantzas: Marxist Theory and Political Strategy* (New York: St Martin's, 1985), pp. 72–4, 333–4; cf. Carnoy, *State and Political Theory*, pp. 121–2.

Simply put, behind the accidents of statehood ensuing from the state's structurally determined place in modern capitalist societies, it is possible to discover either unity or diversity but certainly not both at the same time. Either we are bound to discover multiple competing forces inside the state – but this leaves us without any way of making clear theoretical sense of the seeming coherence of its output – or we are forced to assume, consciously or not, a principle of order and coherence that serves to explain this unity and the prima facie coherence of its policy output: this is the indivisible remainder that Marxist theories of the state leave us with.

Hence, in the final analysis, structuralists and systems theorists are compelled to reintroduce very familiar assumptions about the state in order to make sense of its unity and its capacity to act, assumptions which are clearly at odds with their initial declarations of intent and theoretical stipulations – and the discursive cash value of doing this is perverse indeed, since it amounts to reinstating good old indivisible sovereignty in the heart of a theoretical tradition which founders on the assumption of its utmost dispensability.[64]

But what if we simply give up the assumption that the conceptual identity of the state is constituted by its *a priori* dependence of forces external to itself? The price paid for such a move is a certain loss of critical edge, since it was this assumption that made it possible to interpret the traditional concept of the sovereign state as well as its pluralist replacements as nothing but veils concealing the true nature of the capitalist state. In short, giving up this assumption would be to cut off the connection to the critical spirit of Marxism, and to capitulate to the intellectual demands of bourgeois ideology.

To my mind, this is exactly what happened when the state was finally brought back into theoretical focus, and gradually received renewed attention within mainstream political science. Yet the state concept that was brought back in had very few similarities with that earlier propounded by instrumentalists and structuralists. The state was now an 'autonomous structure – a structure with a logic and interests of its own not necessarily equivalent to, or fused with, the interests of the dominant class in society or the full set of member groups in the polity'.[65]

For a moment, the discovery that the state could be conceptualized as autonomous looked brand new. To Nordlinger, giving up the notions of societal dependence and the invariable functions of the state was necessary in order to reconceptualize it along more traditional Weberian lines while preserving the analytical distinction between state and society: 'the

---

[64] Cf. Poulantzas, *State, Power, and Socialism*, p. 13.
[65] Theda Skocpol, *States and Social Revolutions* (Cambridge: Cambridge University Press, 1979), p. 27.

democratic state is not only frequently autonomous insofar as it regularly acts upon its preferences, but also markedly autonomous in doing so even when its preferences diverge from the demands of the most powerful groups in civil society'.[66]

It was precisely such divergence that had been ruled out by definitional fiat by those who had paved the way for the resurrection of the state concept within mainstream political science. But what was thus brought back in was not in itself very new: its perceived newness is best explained as an unintended consequence of previous neglect. The state was never brought back in in some new guise. Rather it was all a matter of recycling. What was recycled had in fact been present all the time, and had conditioned the possibility of modern political science since its birth; the state concept had now regained most of its original nineteenth-century connotations after laborious yet ultimately counterproductive efforts to get rid of these once and for all.

In their own terms, therefore, the efforts to unveil and reconceptualize the inherited and supposedly bourgeois state concept were not very successful, since the original problem of political order which the concept of the state was once introduced to solve cropped up again and inevitably inside the theoretical context of critical state theory, and was then subjected to closet Weberian solutions not unlike those resorted to by those who had earlier tried to throw the state concept out.

Views about the analytical primacy of the state and its autonomy had been present among those historically oriented macrosociologists who had remained relatively unbothered by either the pluralist or the Marxist debates about the state concept. To Hintze, for example, it had long been obvious that '[society] is the natural foundation of the state', but has not been 'generated by the state, nor is the state merely a natural outcome of the developing social system'.[67] Similarly, to Tilly, the success of the state as a form of political organization depended precisely on a gradual concentration of power in the hands of institutions which became increasingly autonomous in relation to society as a consequence.[68]

If these authors had analysed the formation of modern states in their societal contexts, thus implying the existence of a divide between state

---

[66] Eric A. Nordlinger, *On the Autonomy of the Democratic State* (Cambridge, MA: Harvard University Press, 1981), p. 1.

[67] Otto Hintze, 'The State in Historical Perspective', in Richard Bendix (ed.), *State and Society: a Reader in Comparative Political Sociology* (Berkeley, CA: University of California Press, 1973), p. 155.

[68] Charles Tilly, 'Reflections on the History of European State-Making', in Charles Tilly (ed.), *The Formation of National States in Western Europe* (Princeton, NJ: Princeton University Press, 1975), pp. 27–32; cf. also Joseph R. Strayer, *On the Medieval Origins of the Modern State* (Princeton, NJ: Princeton University Press, 1970).

and society, it was equally obvious to them that the state was analytically distinct from, yet conditioned by, an international context composed of a plurality of such relatively autonomous entities. The major sources of disagreement then came to concern explanatory priorities and the temporal sequence between the state and the societal contexts in which it was embedded. Did the prima facie internally autonomous state shape societal development more than it was shaped by it, and did the prima facie externally autonomous state shape its international environment more than it was shaped by it?

When the state concept was once again a legitimate object of theoretical reflection, posing and answering such questions came to be regarded as paramount to our understanding of the modern state and its future fate. To Giddens, for example, the rise and consolidation of state power over society is inseparable from and simultaneous with the constitution of a reflexively monitored state system.[69] What was new with this view was that the state and the international system were seen as mutually constitutive rather than as opposed in terms of principle and content.[70]

But as I have argued elsewhere, the way these questions were commonly phrased precluded any questioning of the state concept itself, since the twin divides between the state and the international and the state and society were tacitly presupposed by the practice of questioning.[71] In the next chapter, I shall analyse another strategy in dealing with the state: dissolving it by dissolving the divides which constitute it as an object of knowledge.

[69] Anthony Giddens, *A Contemporary Critique of Historical Materialism*, vol. II: *The Nation-State and Violence* (Cambridge: Polity Press, 1985), pp. 255–93.

[70] Cf. David Held, *Political Theory and the Modern State: Essays on State, Power, and Democracy* (Cambridge: Polity Press, 1989), ch. 8; Dieter Grimm, 'The Modern State: Continental Traditions', in F.-X. Kaufmann, Giandomenico Majone and Vincent Ostrom (eds.), *Guidance, Control, and Evaluation in the Public Sector*, (Berlin: De Gruyter, 1986), pp. 89–109.

[71] Jens Bartelson, *A Genealogy of Sovereignty* (Cambridge: Cambridge University Press, 1995), ch. 2.

5 Dissolving the state

In previous chapters we have seen how those who fought hard to throw the state concept out from scientific discourse did so by arguing that since there is more than one locus of authority within a given polity, the state concept can and should be replaced by other concepts taking this multiplicity into account. Within this view, the state concept can ultimately be reduced to those of government, group or system without any attendant loss of theoretical meaning or explanatory power. We have also seen how those who tried to bring the state back in did so by arguing that even if the state was ultimately derivative of a society composed of multiple economic and social forces, the state concept was nevertheless necessary when explaining the constitution and reproduction of that society as a whole.

Yet beyond this disagreement, both these views are in profound agreement that the state – however defined – must be understood as distinct from the international system of states and from domestic society. And as a consequence of this agreement, they also share the conviction that the state is, or at least once was, *the* ultimate source of authority within that society and, by implication, that there is no authority over and above the international plurality of such sovereign units. Sovereign statehood and international anarchy are widely believed to be two sides of the same coin.

To most modern political scientists the analytic divide separating the domestic from the international seems to be an indispensable categorization of political life. Without such a distinction being made between inside and outside it would be impossible to distinguish between what are arguably different forms of political life. Without this possibility, the entire topic of political science would threaten to lose much of its coherence. And without such coherence, political science would find it increasingly difficult to make sense of modern political experience. With such a loss of meaning, many modern political practices would lose their rationale and legitimacy, since they presuppose that the state is intelligible in terms of its difference from the state of nature prevailing on the outside. But subscribing to such a neat categorization means that a world without states becomes as hard to envisage in the presence of such a distinction as a world of states would be in its absence.

Yet what we are facing today is nothing less than a broad intellectual movement in favour of a dissolution of these analytic boundaries. In this chapter I shall analyse the efforts to bring about such a dissolution, and its implications for our way of understanding the state and the problem of political authority. As I have argued earlier, the modern discourse on the state is a critical discourse in so far as it has been held together by a strong urge to doubt the reality of the state and find an underlying, more real reality under the veil of appearance. I also take this critical spirit to be a defining property of modern political thought. As I subsequently argued, whereas its modern critics have questioned the theoretical meaning and empirical reference of the state concept, they have invariably failed to question the state all the way down. Whereas those who tried to throw the state out ended up reinserting semantic equivalents of this concept into the core of their theories, the effort to recycle the state ended up with an indivisible remainder. Thus, and contrary to their stated intentions, critical gestures have merely reaffirmed the importance of the state as the foundation of modern political discourse, since late modern political rationality seems to presuppose such a silencing of the question of the foundations of authority in order to remain operative.

Now those who have struggled to dissolve the distinctions that condition the possibility of statehood have frequently done so in the hope of finding a way beyond the state. Undertaken in the hope of releasing political imagination from the strictures imposed by state experience, the effort to dissolve the state typically begins by arguing that the state is wholly contingent upon the distinctions that define its possibility, and that these distinctions are in turn contingent upon political discourse, rather than on any non-discursive reality.

In this chapter I shall focus on those theories that assume the state to be contingent upon discourse. Such theories are invariably critical of earlier usages of the state concept on the grounds that these presuppose that the state is already given to political knowledge, and that this kind of presupposition has to be undone by deconstructing those distinctions between the state, domestic society and the international realm which have conventionally been accepted as a baseline for further theorizing.

After briefly describing the contours of the contingency argument, I shall proceed by analysing two different ways of rendering the state contingent. Whereas the first version takes the external aspects of the state as its main target, the second directs its critical energies against the internal aspects of the state; whereas the former problematicizes the state as an agent in an international context, the latter problematicizes the state as an agent in a domestic context. I shall end this chapter by arguing that each of the above ways of criticizing the state takes for granted what the other struggles to problematicize, and that this in the end jeopardizes their common ambition to reconceptualize the problem of political order without the concept of the state.

Reconstructing modernity

As we have seen in previous chapters, most critical accounts of the state presuppose an account of its history. The meaning of the state concept seems inseparable from its historicity within discourse: either the state concept is taken to be present as an organizing concept throughout a given discourse across time or it is regarded as a manifestation of the unique characteristics of that discourse.

When the state concept was made foundational and constitutive of early political science, the history of political theory and practice was reconstructed in quite narrowly statist terms, as if the state had always been around. Consequently, the study of politics and political thought could be defined in terms of the state and its transhistorical presence. When the state was thrown out, these accounts were replaced by narratives debunking the state-centric view of politics and political science, while being supportive of a disciplinary identity centred on notions of government or political system. Apparently, even Aristotle had something to say about 'the political system'. When the state was later brought back in, these latter accounts of the state were reconstructed as strategies of concealment, and replaced with new stories of the state that emphasized its fundamental dependence on capitalist society.

But however supportive or debunking, the above accounts simply take for granted that the state could exist in an objective and robust way; what is sometimes disputed is the ontological status of the state, not the possibility of its existence, since these accounts invariably presuppose that the state is identical with itself as an object of knowledge, thereby implying that the state concept is also a consistent concept. Now this is exactly what makes these accounts profoundly problematic in the eyes of those who want to deconstruct the ontological conditions of possible statehood, thus subjecting the possibility of statehood to the kind of doubt from which it had arguably been immunized by earlier forms of criticism. In this latter respect, modern political science seems far removed from the conceptual contestability advocated by the bright side of the Enlightenment, and much closer to the forbidden impossibility of questioning authority during its aftermath.

Arguably, the quest for scientific rigour has removed the problems of authority and identity from the domain of legitimate contestation, and instead introduced solutions to these problems among the premises of rational inquiry and intelligibility. Not only are political problems phrased as if the state were necessary to their solution, but the resulting solutions also reproduce those master distinctions that mark the state off from domestic society and the international system. And whenever accepted at face value, these solutions will circumscribe political imagination and render it statist; they will engender problems and strategies of government that build protective shields around what is but a virtual centre in that imagination; they will necessarily make the state look both totally ambiguous yet absolutely indispensable to modern political discourse.

Any attempt to dissolve the state would therefore necessitate a release of political imagination from this concept, and this would be tantamount to saying that the state is wholly contingent and therefore ultimately dispensable. But what would such contingency of the state entail?

Let us start with the concept of contingency, which circulates in this theoretical context in at least two senses. First, to say that something is contingent is to say that it lacks essence.[1] To say that something lacks essence is to imply that it has resulted from the reification of something which is ultimately nothing but an interpretation of other interpretations. Second, to say that something is contingent is to say that it lacks necessity, and saying that is to imply that things could have been otherwise had history taken another course at some critical juncture; for a being to be contingent is to have the potential not to be, as Agamben would put it.[2] Thus, to say that the state lacks necessity is to say that the state has been forced upon us by historical accident. And finally, to say this is to imply that the problem of political order is open to brand new solutions in a brand new future.

But to say that something is contingent in either or both of these senses of course begs the question of what it is contingent upon. Here the standard answer is provided by the concept of discourse. To say that the distinctions that condition the possibility of the state are contingent upon political discourse implies that the state has been construed out of conceptual resources handed down to us by that discourse, and that the state, together with all concepts that help define it as an object of knowledge

---

[1] For an influential statement, see Richard Rorty, *Contingency, Irony, and Solidarity* (Cambridge: Cambridge University Press, 1989), chs. 1–2.

[2] Giorgio Agamben, 'Bartleby, or On Contingency', in *Potentialities: Collected Essays in Philosophy* (Stanford, CA: Stanford University Press, 1999), pp. 243–72.

and action, is ultimately a function of a series of speech acts or a system of statements.[3]

This awareness that communities may lack necessity and essence is not peculiar to late modern political thought, and it is sometimes even held to be constitutive of the modern way of conceptualizing the possibility of community. By the same token, and as we have seen in chapter 2, the idea that communities are born in time, that they are exposed to the corrosive effects of time and finally will also wither in due time are salient themes in both ancient and early modern historiography.[4]

If previous chapters lent some credibility to the idea that the spectres of both Hegel and Marx have continued to haunt political discourse during the twentieth century, this chapter will show us how much political modernity and its critics owe to Nietzsche; the modern way of saying that things widely perceived to be necessary, essential, universal and timeless are in fact contingent is a way of criticizing those political promises which are based on necessity, universality or timelessness for being incapable of realization. This further entails that arguments from contingency themselves derive much of their rhetorical force from those very promises or expectations they set out to criticize: any act of criticism that struggles to expose the contingency of things has the identity of those things as its own foundation. As Zizek has argued, questioning necessity and essence

---

[3] It is important to distinguish between these two meanings of the term discourse, since they have very different implications for the study of political thought. In the present context, however, these differences need not bother us too much, since I shall focus more on the general implications of discourse analysis for the state concept than on the methodological requirements of such an analysis. For statements of the above positions, see, among others, J. G. A. Pocock, 'The Concept of Language and the *Métier d'Historien*: some Considerations on Practice', in A. Pagden (ed.), *The Languages of Political Theory in Early Modern Europe* (Cambridge: Cambridge University Press, 1987), pp. 19–38; Michel Foucault, 'The Discourse on Language', in *The Archaeology of Knowledge* (New York: Pantheon Books, 1972), pp. 215–37; Michel Foucault, 'Politics and the Study of Discourse', in Graham Burchell, Colin Gordon and Peter Miller (eds.), *The Foucault Effect: Studies in Governmentality* (London: Harvester, 1991), pp. 53–72. For commentaries on the difference between a hermeneutics of speech acts and orthodox discourse analysis; see Hubert L. Dreyfus and Paul Rabinow, *Michel Foucault: beyond Structuralism and Hermeneutics* (Chicago, IL: University of Chicago Press, 1982); Gilles Deleuze, *Foucault*, trans. S. Hand (Minneapolis, MN: University of Minnesota Press, 1988).

[4] Cf. Louis Dupré, *Passage to Modernity: an Essay in the Hermeneutics of Nature* (New Haven, CT: Yale University Press, 1993); John G. Gunnell, *Political Philosophy and Time: Plato and the Origins of Political Vision* (Chicago, IL: University of Chicago Press, 1987); David Gross, 'The Temporality of the Modern State', *Theory and Society*, vol. 14, 1985, no. 2, pp. 53–82; Ernst Kantorowicz, *The King's Two Bodies: a Study in Medieval Political Theology* (Princeton, NJ: Princeton University Press, 1957); J. G. A. Pocock, *The Machiavellian Moment: Florentine Political Thought and the Atlantic Republican Tradition* (Princeton, NJ: Princeton University Press, 1975).

is only possible within a framework of self-identity, so even if we succeed in demonstrating the impossibility of any particular identity, that demonstration nevertheless presupposes that self-identity is a distinct possibility, as opposed to a mere name for its own impossibility.[5]

This becomes plain if we take a look at the two rhetorical strategies used in order to bring about the desired dismantling of the state concept. Although they are frequently made to look new by their proponents, both are in fact intertwined with that which they criticize: political modernity. The first is that of denaturalization. When applied to a given thing, the denaturalizing gesture turns it from a natural kind into an artifice of culture. Denaturalization rids beings of their givenness; everything previously thought to be primordial or authentic is deprived of its foundational simplicity and rendered the outcome of human practice. The second is that of temporalization. When applied to a given thing, this releases it from the necessities of recurrence or progress. Temporalization deprives beings of their sameness and their apparent immutability; everything previously thought to be constant and unchanging is deprived of its self-sameness and turned into the sum total of its historical manifestations.[6]

Denaturalization typically begins by an abstract analysis – aided by a whiff of intuition – that permits the political philosopher to distinguish the essence of political order from what is merely accidental to it, and also to realize that his predecessors were all wrong in their attribution of essence to that order. Hence, one starts with present identities and present modes of authority, and tries to show that most of their apparent sameness and givenness are the results of discursive habits, and goes on to argue that their purported essence is nothing but accident mistaken for essence. For example, almost everything that Hobbes regarded as essential to man in a state of nature devoid of social bonds was turned into a matter of social accident by Rousseau; yet both remained convinced that their respective interpretations of the state of nature provided *the* pure beginning from which the emergence of authority could be explained and justified by recourse to precontractual identities.[7]

---

[5] Slavoj Zizek, *For They Do Not Know What They Do: Enjoyment as a Political Factor* (London: Verso, 1991), p. 37.

[6] This way of phrasing denaturalization and temporalization of course owes much to Friedrich Nietzsche, ' "Guilt", "Bad Conscience" and the Like', in *On the Genealogy of Morals* (New York: Vintage, 1969), pp. 57–96 and *The Will to Power*, ed. Walter Kaufmann (New York: Vintage, 1968).

[7] Cf. Jean-Jacques Rousseau, 'L'État de Guerre', in C. E. Vaughn (ed.), *The Political Writings of Jean-Jacques Rousseau*, vol. 1 (Cambridge: Cambridge University Press, 1915). For comments, see William E. Connolly, *Political Theory and Modernity* (Oxford: Basil Blackwell, 1988), ch. 3; Maurizio Viroli, 'The Concept of *Ordre* and the Language of Classical Republicanism in Jean-Jacques Rousseau', in Pagden, *The Languages of Political Theory in Early Modern Europe*, pp. 159–78.

Since then, this gesture has been repeated tirelessly since everything apparently natural and given can be denaturalized and turned into a result of prior accidents.

Temporalization conventionally proceeds by arguing that a given identity not only has a history of its own, but in fact is nothing but the outcome of its history when viewed from the present. It is thus historicization played backwards, since it seeks to undo all myths of pure origins and ultimate foundations. Therefore, temporalization starts by pointing to the essential impurity of the identity to be temporalized, and then goes on to explain its present impurity as a result of historical forces beyond the control of the identity thus constituted, and concludes by affirming the possibility of reclaiming its lost purity in time. As we might recall, what Marx and Hegel did to their predecessors was to historicize *their* visions of political community into conditions of the present, thereby opening that present up to future perfection. While their interpretation of this end state certainly differed, neither Hegel nor Marx questioned the possibility of its attainment, since both narrated the past in terms of its inherent ability to transcend itself.[8] Perhaps the main expression of temporalization in modern political philosophy has been the perpetual postponement of this transcendence; as Nietzsche teaches us, 'the cause of the origin of a thing and its eventual employment and place in a system of purposes, lie worlds apart'.[9]

When brought to bear on the state concept, denaturalization and temporalization make it possible to reconstruct the history of the modern state concept as being defining of political modernity, since political modernity itself could be seen as simultaneous with the emergence of the master distinction between the domestic and the international which keeps the state in place.[10]

Yet arguably, denaturalization and temporalization both bring problems that eventually frustrate the attempt to dissolve the state and rethink the general conditions of authority. If we argue that the state concept is contingent upon the distinctions that together help define it and render it meaningful in diverse contexts, and that these distinctions are in turn contingent upon discourse and its classifying powers, this of course begs the question of the contingency of that discourse. If taken to be fully contingent only upon itself, this leaves us with few conceptual resources to explain what might possibly lurk beyond the modern state,

---

[8] See for example John F. Rundell, *Origins of Modernity: the Origins of Modern Social Theory from Kant to Hegel to Marx* (Cambridge: Polity Press, 1987).

[9] Friedrich Nietzsche, ' "Guilt", "Bad Conscience", and the Like', p. 77; see also Mark Warren, *Nietzsche and Political Thought* (Boston, MA: MIT Press, 1988), ch. 3.

[10] See for example Peter Wagner, *A Sociology of Modernity: Liberty and Discipline* (London, Routledge, 1994), pp. 37–59.

let alone justify those hopes of transcendence that are nourished by the denaturalizing and temporalizing gestures. Rather, and as we shall see below, when pushed to extremes, the contingency argument jeopardizes our ability to envisage new constellations of authority beyond the modern state.

In the following sections, I shall describe what has happened to the state concept when exposed to the twin forces of denaturalization and temporalization, and what this implies for our understanding of the problem of political order. I shall start by analysing some attempts to denaturalize the state in its external aspect, that is, as a sovereign entity situated in an international context composed of a plurality of such sovereign entities. I shall then continue by describing some attempts to temporalize the internal aspect of the state, that is, as a sovereign locus of authority situated in a domestic context composed of a plurality of societal forces.

Denaturalizing the state

Surprisingly, one of the first efforts to denaturalize the state concept came from within a field whose intellectual identity had been strongly conditioned by the state concept from its start and throughout its subsequent evolution.[11] Even during the heyday of pluralist state-bashing, international relations theory seemed immune to efforts to dispose of the state concept, and very few seriously disputed that the proper subject matter of academic international relations was the intercourse of states within a larger system or society of states.

In its mainstream versions, international relations theory had defined the international system and its structure in terms of the component states and their sovereignty, and the former was sometimes regarded as immutable thanks to the purported transhistorical character of the latter.[12]

---

[11] Jens Bartelson, *A Genealogy of Sovereignty* (Cambridge: Cambridge University Press, 1995), ch. 6; Brian C. Schmidt, *The Political Discourse of Anarchy: a Disciplinary History of International Relations* (Albany, NY: SUNY, 1998), chs. 2–3; Brian C. Schmidt, 'Lessons from the Past: Reassessing the Interwar Disciplinary History of International Relations', *International Studies Quarterly*, vol. 42, 1998, no. 3, pp. 433–59. See also Torbjørn L. Knutsen, *A History of International Relations Theory* (Manchester: Manchester University Press, 1997), pp. 2, 33 and *passim*.

[12] For an analysis, see Jens Bartelson, 'Second Natures: Is the State Identical With Itself?', *European Journal of International Relations*, vol. 4, 1998, no. 3, pp. 295–326; Jack Donnelly, 'Realism and the Academic Study of International Relations', in James Farr, John S. Dryzek and Stephen T. Leonard (eds.), *Political Science in History: Research Programs and Political Traditions* (Cambridge: Cambridge University Press, 1995), pp. 175–97. For classical examples, see Raymond Aron, *Peace and War: a Theory of International Relations* (London: Weidenfeld and Nicolson, 1962); Hedley Bull, *The Anarchical*

Although the power, interests and intentions of individual states were supposed to vary across time and space, the token state was a universal and perennial category capable of subsuming the most diverse of political forms, from Sparta via quattrocento Milan to the Soviet Union. In other words, within international relations theory the state concept had retained much of the organizing power it had once enjoyed within early political science, and this precisely because it had never been opened up to empirical investigation. Rather, it was truly primitive in the sense that it had long helped to define both disciplinary self-understanding as well as its subject matter, without ever itself constituting an object of inquiry. Academic international relations has rarely felt any need to analyse the state, simply because its presence has been its unquestioned point of departure.[13]

If the ontological status of the state concept was ever disputed within academic international relations, this was most frequently on the grounds that the assumption of unitary agency associated with this concept was empirically unwarranted, and that it constituted an obstacle to a detailed understanding of the dynamics of foreign policy formation, or that the facts of interdependence had made such monist assumptions increasingly obsolete.[14] As Ringmar describes this situation, the state either vanished into thin metaphysical air or was dissolved into an incoherent bundle of components.[15] In other words, criticism of the state concept was conducted along lines similar to those of the early pluralists wrestling with the spectres of Hegel: the monist state concept was criticized from within a monist framework, and replaced by a plurality of components themselves defined in monist terms.

In its search for intellectual redemption at the end of the Cold War, international relations encountered historical sociology. As we might recall from chapter 4, the effort to bring the state back in had furnished that field with a state concept defined in terms of relative autonomy. It

Society: a Study of Order in World Politics (London: Macmillan, 1977); Hans Morgenthau, Politics Among Nations: the Struggle for Power and Peace (New York: Knopf, 1985); Kenneth N. Waltz, Theory of International Politics (Reading, MA: Addison-Wesley, 1979).

[13] A few notable exceptions ought to be mentioned: Bonce Andrews, 'Social Rules and the State as a Social Actor', World Politics, vol. 27, 1975, no. 4, pp. 521–40; Fred Halliday, 'State and Society in International Relations: a Second Agenda', in H. C. Dyer and L. Mangasarian (eds.), The Study of International Relations (London: Macmillan, 1989), pp. 40–59.

[14] Classics in this respect include Graham T. Allison, Essence of Decision: Explaining the Cuban Missile Crisis (Boston, MA: Little, Brown, 1971); Peter Gourevitch, 'The Second Image Reversed: the International Sources of Domestic Politics', International Organization, vol. 32, 1978, no. 4, pp. 881–911; Robert O. Keohane and Joseph Nye, Power and Interdependence: World Politics in Transition (Boston, MA: Little, Brown, 1977).

[15] Erik Ringmar, 'On the Ontological Status of the State', European Journal of International Relations, vol. 2, 1996, no. 4, pp. 439–66.

was this 'relative autonomy' which had made the state concept look so new and promising to a generation of historical materialists who had been accustomed to view the state in terms of its *a priori* dependence on society.

By the same token, mainstream international theory, it seemed to its opponents, had construed the international sphere as *a priori* timeless and immutable, and had tailored history to fit by means of a presentist interpretation of a largely alien – that is stateless – past. According to those critics, a misguided quest for scientific rigour had not only put an end to historical sensitivity, but impoverished our understanding of the state by simply taking it for granted.[16] The result was an effort to marry off international relations theory and historical sociology that never really got off the metatheoretical ground; yet it was plain that the state could no longer be treated simply as a synchronic invariant, but had to be opened up to diachronic analysis.[17]

Another, and in our present context more important, source of denaturalization came from the gradual spread of epistemic doubt within the discipline itself. Coinciding with the end of the Cold War, epistemic scepticism was not primarily targeted at the state concept, but rather against the political rationality of international relations as a whole. To its critics, international relations theory had not only failed to make sense of a major transformation of world politics, but had also been legitimizing the cynical practices of power politics, and had uncritically contributed to their dissemination. Furthermore, it was guilty of having imposed Western values disguised as universal ones upon a pluralist and multicultural world.[18]

---

[16] For early arguments to this effect, see among others Richard K. Ashley, 'The Poverty of Neorealism', in Robert O. Keohane (ed.), *Neorealism and its Critics* (New York: Columbia University Press, 1986), pp. 255–300; Robert W. Cox, 'Social Forces, States, and World Orders: beyond International Relations Theory', in Keohane (ed.), *Neorealism and its Critics*, pp. 204–54; Robert G. Gilpin, 'The Richness of the Tradition of Neorealism', in Keohane, *Neorealism and its Critics*, pp. 301–21; John Gerard Ruggie, 'Continuity and Transformation in the World Polity: towards a Neorealist Synthesis', in Keohane, *Neorealism and its Critics*, pp. 131–57.

[17] See for example David Dessler, 'What's at Stake in the Agent–Structure Debate?', *International Organization*, vol. 43, 1989, no. 3, pp. 441–73; Alexander Wendt, 'The Agent–Structure Problem in International Relations Theory', *International Organization*, vol. 41, 1987, no. 3, pp. 335–70; Alexander Wendt and Raymond Duvall, 'Institutions and International Order', in E.-O. Czempiel and James N. Rosenau (eds.), *Global Changes and Theoretical Challenges: Approaches to World Politics for the 1990s* (Lexington, MA: Lexington Books, 1989), pp. 51–73.

[18] Early examples in this genre include R. B. J. Walker, 'East Wind, West Wind: Civilizations, Hegemonies, and World Order', in R. B. J. Walker (ed.), *Culture, Ideology and World Order* (Boulder, CO: Westview, 1984), pp. 2–22; R. B. J. Walker, 'World Politics and Western Reason: Universalism, Pluralism, and Hegemony', in Walker, *Culture, Ideology and World Order*, pp. 182–216.

At this point, we must step back for a moment and ask what conditions the possibility of this kind of criticism, and why it came to converge on the state concept. Two peculiarities of international relations theory are then important.

First, and as we have noticed throughout this book, all criticism has to be undertaken in the name of some political subjectivity, or from a perspective congenial to the eventual formation of such a subjectivity in time. In the context of international relations, this necessary backdrop was seemingly lacking, since the international sphere had conventionally been characterized in terms of a plurality of such communities but not as a community in itself. Indeed, such a lack of common ethical subjectivity had to an extent been constitutive of the very meaning of the international domain. The ethical possibility of criticism was thus circumscribed by the fact of fragmentation right from the start.[19]

Second, and as we have seen throughout this book, rewriting existing histories of the state concept is a powerful means of reconceptualizing the state. Within international relations, historiography had long been both implicit and statist. On the one hand, it was widely felt that international theory, due to the peculiar nature of the international realm, lacked much of the wealth and coherence of domestic political thought, and that it was therefore difficult to subsume under a series of perennial problems, or under the metanarratives of evolution or progress. On the other hand, those political philosophers who had been incorporated into the canon of domestic political thought had unfortunately remained remarkably silent on the topic of international relations, so its history had to be construed on the basis of scattered remarks, diplomatic correspondence and legal documents.[20]

So in order for such a rewriting to be possible, there had to be such a thing as a distinct tradition of international theorizing that could be subjected to historical criticism. What was evident, however, was that the possibility of reconstructing such a tradition hinged on the presence of the state, and that histories of international theory were as dependent on that presence as the identity of academic international relations itself.[21]

---

[19] For this way of characterizing the background understanding of international relations theory see Chris Brown, *International Relations Theory: New Normative Approaches* (London: Harvester, 1992), pp. 52–82. See also Thomas W. Pogge, 'Cosmopolitanism and Sovereignty', *Ethics*, vol. 103, 1992, pp. 48–75; Yael Tamir, 'Who's Afraid of a Global State?', in Kjell Goldmann, Ulf Hannerz and Charles Westin (eds.), *Nationalism and Internationalism in the Post-Cold War Era* (London: Routledge, 2000), pp. 244–67.

[20] J. L. Holzgrefe, 'The Origins of International Relations Theory', *Review of International Studies*, vol. 15, 1989, no. 1, pp. 11–26; Martin Wight, 'Why is there No International Theory?', in Martin Wight and Herbert Butterfield (eds.), *Diplomatic Investigations* (London: Allen & Unwin, 1966), pp. 17–34.

[21] Jens Bartelson, 'Short Circuits: Society and Tradition in International Relations Theory', *Review of International Studies*, vol. 22, 1996, no. 4, pp. 339–60; Brian C. Schmidt, 'The

So when the state concept became exposed to denaturalization, this must be seen as the result of a double discursive intervention, targeted at the nexus that tied an inherited disciplinary identity together with a kind of historiography that was used to legitimize that identity, and used that identity to justify politically incorrect practices. That nexus was the concept of the sovereign state. Since both the concept of the international sphere as well as existing narratives of the origin of international theory presupposed the presence of the state, denaturalizing the state became integral to a critique of the political rationality of international relations. And that critique had to contend

with a widely shared readiness to interpret community ahistorically and monistically as a fixed thematic unity, a kind of essence, an identity transcending and uniting manifest differences in the world of human practice. Such interpretive dispositions, we shall note, put community in opposition to pluralism, each negating the other.[22]

While being immanent, this kind of critique is based on the possibility that the international domain could be different from the way it is, lest the critical gesture should lose its bite. Yet its very immanence entails a tacit denial of transcendence. Thus, in order to remain critical without ceding its international perspective, critics had to imagine a community in the midst of a radical plurality and reconcile this image with the possibility of transcending it, something that gave way to self-entrapment: the more statist international theory was made to look, the more difficult it became to make sense of an international political order beyond the state. Hence, if the very ontology of the international sphere seemed to rule out the possibility of transcendence, and if the existence of the state was taken to be integral to the possibility of the international domain, the sovereign state had to be untied from both the international and domestic contexts:

[t]he sphere of *domestic* politics ... is the sphere in which community is most fully realized. It is the domain wherein the intersubjective foundations of action lend authority to the state as the monopolist of coercive means, the primary arbiter of social conflict, and the ultimate agent of social action on behalf of society as a whole.[23]

Within this view, there is nothing necessary or timeless about the state. Nor does it exist in any robust sense outside political discourse. The state concept does not refer to any transhistorical substrate or constellation of

Historiography of Academic International Relations', *Review of International Studies*, vol. 20, 1994, no. 4, pp. 349–67.

[22] Richard K. Ashley, 'The Geopolitics of Geopolitical Space: toward a Critical Social Theory of International Politics', *Alternatives*, vol. 12, 1987, no. 4, p. 406.

[23] *Ibid.*, p. 412.

forces, but is nothing but the outcome of a series of discursive accidents peculiar to the modern age. It is merely an interpretation of earlier interpretations of authority and identity, resulting from successive clashes over the proper definition of political community. The state itself is nothing but

a product of history, tied up with a specific social formation, and cannot be regarded as a permanent feature of the human condition. Even as it came into being at a particular point in time, it will and must disappear when it has exhausted its institutional potentialities or proved inadequate to new challenges.[24]

From this perspective, criticism of international relations becomes urgent, since 'the discursive structure of the modern theory of international relations can be understood as an expression of the claim to state sovereignty rather than as an attempt to explain the consequences of state sovereignty'.[25] But to say that there is nothing necessary, essential, universal or timeless about the state of course begs the question of how it has been constituted as distinct from something other than itself. Clearly, there is a difference between saying that the state is contingent, and demonstrating that this is the case by showing that it is contingent upon something which itself is contingent, or can be rendered as such. To pose this question is to ask what the state is contingent upon, and how the distinctions between domestic society, the state and the international system have been drawn in and through political discourse. And when answering these questions, it is necessary to account for how this construct – the sovereign state – has been rendered a natural kind, taken for granted and removed from the scope of conventional theoretical criticism. It is thus not sufficient to show that the state is the outcome of undue reification; one must also provide an account of how such an interpretation has become constitutive of political reality.

According to critical international theory, it is the categorical distinction between the domestic and the international that conditions the possibility of statehood. This divide has made the international and domestic spheres appear to be in timeless disjunction, marked by a profound ethical difference yet stuck in ontological interdependence – the political map of the world may change, but there remains an essential difference between what goes on inside states and what goes on between them, and this difference is what makes modern politics modern.[26]

[24] Bhikhu Parekh, 'When Will the State Wither Away?', *Alternatives*, vol. 15, 1990, no. 3, p. 259.
[25] R. B. J. Walker, 'From International Relations to World Politics', in J. Camilleri, A. P. Jarvis and A. J. Paolini (eds.), *The State in Transition: Reimagining Political Space* (Boulder, CO, Lynne Rienner, 1995), p. 33.
[26] See among others William E. Connolly, 'Identity and Difference in Global Politics', in James Der Derian and Michael J. Shapiro (eds.), *International / Intertextual Relations:*

This argument has been developed in two different yet largely complementary versions. In the first version, the constitution and reproduction of sovereign statehood takes place right in our present, right in the contemporary discourse of international relations, and by means of the total structure of the conceptual oppositions it brings into play. In the second version, the constitution of the state takes place through the sequential unfolding of the same conceptual oppositions throughout the gradual emergence of international relations discourse. I shall briefly describe both of these versions below, as exemplified by the works of Ashley and Walker respectively.

To Ashley, the constitutive divide between the domestic and the international is drawn and sustained by the discursive practices of realist power politics, and the sovereign state is situated in the narrow discursive space between these spheres. The condition of possibility of these domains and their separation is sovereign man – man interpreted as a transcendental subject and a condition of knowledge.[27] Thus, domestic society is demarcated from the international realm, and the sovereign state is demarcated from both by being inserted in between them by virtue of its embodiment of the sovereignty of man. Thus, the state is man writ large as much as man is the microcosm of the state, since both instantiate the rationality and autonomy intrinsic to all modern subjectivity. And all modern discourses, writes Ashley,

presuppose the necessity of a state as an agency of rational law and violence whose legitimacy obtains in its deployment of violent means to bring an external 'anarchy' under control and secure the conditions of sovereign man's autonomous being within domestic bounds. All variants thus take a paradigm of sovereign man to provide a principle of differentiation, a specific Cartesian principle by which it becomes possible to distinguish between an inside and an outside: a domestic field of rational being, where man freely submits to the state, and a dangerous external domain of anarchic forces that the state must tame in defense of sovereign man.[28]

Thus, sovereign man and sovereign state go hand in hand:

In modernist discourse, the sovereignty of the state, including the duty to obey the law it speaks, does not derive from any source external to man. Rather, the state's sovereignty obtains in its establishing as the principle of its law those historical

Postmodern Readings of World Politics (Lexington, MA: Lexington Books, 1989), pp. 323–42; R. B. J. Walker, 'The Prince and "The Pauper": Tradition, Modernity, and Practice in the Theory of International Relations', in Der Derian and Shapiro, *International/Intertextual Relations: Postmodern Readings of World Politics*, pp. 25–48.

[27] This view is derived from Michel Foucault, *The Order of Things: an Archaeology of the Human Sciences* (London: Routledge, 1991), pp. 318–43.

[28] Richard K. Ashley, 'Living On Border Lines: Man, Poststructuralism, and War', in Der Derian and Shapiro (eds.), *International/Intertextual Relations: Postmodern Readings of World Politics*, pp. 259–321.

limitations that modern reasoning man knows to be the necessary conditions of his free use of reason. It consists, more succinctly, in subordinating *raison d'état* to the reason of man, making the former the guarantee of the possibility conditions of the latter.[29]

By denying the contingency of the boundaries that constitute the state as identical with itself, the discourse of power politics effectively reproduces them. The reification of the sovereign state is ultimately based on a concealment of its constructed and contingent character, and this construction takes place in and through the community constituted by realist power politics. Hence, the community of realist power politics is a community ultimately held together through a collective denial that implicitly affirms what is explicitly denied: the possibility of community outside the domestic context, since, according to Ashley, 'domestic society signifies the limits in space and time in which modern reasoning man can secure the absolute foundations that his will to total knowledge requires'.[30] Hence, the distinctions between the domestic, the state and the international are expressions of this community, which is rendered functional and cohesive by projecting these distinctions on to the world and forcing its inhabitants to accept them as part of unthought folklore. This is done through a double rhetorical move:

The first move invokes an unsurpassed commitment to a Western order of discourse, which is disposed to regard all limits only as its own essential project for a universal rational mastery. The second move defers the universal fulfilment of this commitment by invoking history. It invokes a commitment to the historical and particularistic view . . . that the margins of community are real, always present, and always of profound political significance.[31]

The result of this double move is in turn double. First, it differentiates the international field of practice from the domestic one and places them in ethical opposition to each other. Second, it represents the outcome of its activity as existing independently of human knowledge and practice. Doing this, the double move constitutes a domain of objects – states – and renders them accessible to theoretical and empirical investigation.[32] Ultimately, therefore, the modern state appears as the outcome of the discursive differentiation of political space into two distinct spheres, the domestic and the international. Through this differentiation, the state is given, both as an acting subject and as an object of investigation.

[29] Richard K. Ashley, 'The Powers of Anarchy: Theory, Sovereignty, and the Domestication of Global Life', in James Der Derian (ed.), *International Theory: Critical Investigations* (London: Macmillan, 1995) p. 110.
[30] *Ibid.*, p. 100.
[31] Ashley, 'Geopolitics of Geopolitical Space', pp. 415–16.
[32] *Ibid.*, pp. 418–19.

In Ashley's reading, modern man and the modern state are not only analogous by virtue of being modelled on each other, but they also implicate each other discursively and are constructed out of the same conceptual resources by means of the same logocentric practices. These practices are embodied in a discourse of power politics that singularly subordinates modern political life to the narrative of domestication, and imposes the sovereign state as the privileged source of identity and authority by carefully distinguishing it from the forces of anarchy that hold sway on its outside.

To Walker, theories of international relations 'are interesting less for the substantive explanations they offer about political conditions in the modern world than as expressions of the limits of contemporary political imagination'.[33] Again, the explanatory claims of mainstream international relations are downplayed in favour of an emphasis on their constitutive function. Rather than explaining what they take to be their *explanandum*, these theories are actually constitutive of what they purport to explain. In this context, their constitutive function also means that these theories impose limits on our ability to envisage a political reality different from that they portray simply because this possibility of representation is wholly internal in relation to the world thus constituted.

According to Walker, the most important expression of the limit of political imagination is the principle of state sovereignty. Its importance derives from the fact that state sovereignty is thoroughly constitutive of the modern political order and yet is itself constituted in and through political discourse.[34] Thus, in order to understand the modern state, we must situate it in a broader problematic and ask what problem the state once evolved as a response to. But

in order to advance claims about universality in human affairs, it is not obviously helpful to do so without coming to terms with the conditions under which prevailing claims about universality have emerged in the context of a historically specific particularity that has in turn affirmed its own capacity to resolve all relations of universality and particularity.[35]

Within this view, the sovereign state enjoys no existence outside the discursive practices of international relations. Yet if both the modern state and the international system are profoundly contingent upon those

---

[33] R. B. J. Walker, *Inside/Outside. International Relations as Political Theory* (Cambridge: Cambridge University Press, 1993), p. 5.

[34] Cf. Lene Hansen, 'R. B. J. Walker and International Relations: Deconstructing a Discipline', in Iver B. Neumann and Ole Wæver (eds.), *The Future of International Relations: Masters in the Making* (London: Routledge, 1997), pp. 316–36.

[35] Walker, 'From International Relations to World Politics', p. 29.

discursive practices, they nevertheless represent a historically specific solution to a more perennial problem, that of human community:

> state sovereignty is in effect an exceptionally elegant resolution of the appar-
> ent contradiction between centralization and fragmentation, or, phrased in more
> philosophical language, between universality and particularity.[36]

This resolution is carried out spatially as well as temporally. Spatially,
sovereignty suggests a firm demarcation between inside and outside, between the domestic and the international as distinct spaces. In the latter
sphere, political community is a manifest possibility. As such, 'it embodies
an historically specific account of ethical possibility in the form of an answer to questions about the nature and location of political community'.[37]
Hence, within states, we are able to observe how universal values such
as justice, freedom and democracy are articulated and translated into
institutional reality.

Outside states, there is no such community. The international domain
is devoid not only of central authority, but also of shared values and universally accepted institutions. In the international realm, there is anarchy
and plurality, and thus also discord and a constant risk of war. Thus,
the universalist concepts articulated in the domestic sphere are hardly
meaningful beyond the borders of the sovereign state since their ultimate
point of reference is the domestic community, which also constitutes their
limit.

Efforts to extend their application beyond their original context are
therefore futile. Thus, whereas politics is possible within domestic communities, relations between states are devoid of such an inherent ethical possibility.[38] Thus, through the spatial demarcation presupposed by
modern political theory and international relations discourse, universalist concepts are particularized since their meanings are circumscribed by
the context of their emergence and application. This implies that pluralism itself is universalized in the structure of international life, and that
the spatial limitation of community is itself twisted into a universal value
within an order of sovereign states.[39] Interpreted in this way, the principle
of state sovereignty implies a denial of 'the possibility of any other resolution of the relationship between universality and particularity because

---

[36] R. B. J. Walker, 'Security, Sovereignty, and the Challenge of World Politics', *Alternatives*, vol. 15, 1990, no. 1, p. 10.
[37] Walker, *Inside/Outside*, p. 62.
[38] *Ibid.*, ch. 3.
[39] Walker, 'Security, Sovereignty', p. 13; Walker, *Inside/Outside*, p. 63. For a discussion of
the ethical implications of this view, see Jens Bartelson, 'The Trial of Judgment: a Note
on Kant and the Paradoxes of Internationalism', *International Studies Quarterly*, vol. 39,
1995, no. 3, pp. 255–79.

of the way it affirms the presence of political community in territorial space'.[40]

In temporal terms, the resolution effected by sovereignty suggests a demarcation between a domain of progress and a domain of recurrence and repetition. Within the domestic community, the realization of universal values is thought to be possible over time. In such a context, the dominant historical narrative will be one of progress or evolution. Outside states, no such possibility exists, and neither progress nor evolution are open options. Rather, the history of interstate relations is one of recurrence, moral stagnation and profound immutability; individual states may come and go in history, and their power and interests may change, but the basic structure of the international realm will remain the same. Even so, this resolution denies and excludes alternative possibilities 'because it fixes our understanding of future opportunities in relation to a distinction between history and progress within statist political communities and mere contingency outside them'.[41] Ultimately, the resolution carried out by the principle of state sovereignty

affirms a specific account of who we are – citizens of particular states who have the potential to work toward universal standards of conduct by participating in statist political communities – and denies the possibility of any other alternative.[42]

The spatial and temporal demarcation created by the principle of sovereign statehood itself reflects and is contingent upon a more general subordination of the temporal dimension of politics to the spatial one, carried out within modern political discourse. To Walker, this indicates a more profound mutation in the structure of sociopolitical concepts:

[n]ot only does the principle of state sovereignty reflect a historically specific resolution of questions about the universality and particularity of political community, but it also fixes that resolution within categories that have absorbed a metaphysical claim to timelessness.[43]

To Walker, the limits of the sovereign state are also the limits of political imagination, since 'in speaking about challenges to our understanding of political community, we run into the limits of our own ability to speak of

---

[40] Walker, 'Security, Sovereignty', p. 13.
[41] Ibid., p. 14.
[42] Ibid., p. 12.
[43] R. B. J. Walker, 'Sovereignty, Identity, Community: Reflections on the Horizons of Contemporary Political Practice', in R. B. J. Walker and S. H. Mendlovitz (eds.), Contending Sovereignties: Redefining Political Community (Boulder, CO: Lynne Rienner, 1990), p. 172.

politics at all'.[44] Yet simultaneously, transcending the limits posed by the sovereign state is urgent if we want to understand the present, since

> questions about political identity, and thus about the legitimation of various forms of inclusion and exclusion, are no longer adequately answered in the territorial terms we have inherited from early-modern Europe and reproduced so readily in the name of state and nation.[45]

But however urgent its transgression may seem, there is no easy way beyond this limit, since 'ways of speaking about state sovereignty reproduce certain assumptions and resolutions of philosophical and political questions that are constitutive of state sovereignty itself',[46] and 'the categories through which we might attempt to pose questions about the political are precisely those that have been constructed in relation to the state'.[47] So even if the state concept seems outdated, it reflects more profound metaphysical commitments within Western political discourse, which 'rest on a claim to be able to fix a point of identity – a universality in time and space – against which all differences in space and time can be measured, judged, and put in their place'.[48]

But as a result of this laborious deconstruction, we find ourselves imprisoned within the same state which deconstruction promised to dissolve. Both Ashley and Walker denaturalize the state by rendering it an artifice of discourse, yet their accounts of how the distinctions that condition its possibility have emerged invite a certain circularity, and that circularity spills over into a fundamental closure. To Ashley, the discursive practices that condition the possibility of the sovereign state also founder in the presupposed presence of state authority and identity, since the communitarian bond formed by power politics presupposes the state as its prime medium of articulation and dissemination. To Walker, the sovereign state is rendered a historically specific solution to the more perennial problem of political community, yet what makes that problem look perennial is the fact that it is abstracted from the modern solution to it: the state.

In the final analysis, by rendering the state contingent upon contemporary discursive practices or upon a specific resolution of the relation between the universal and the particular, both Ashley and Walker become predisposed to discern the ghosts of statism in every concept upon which the state is held to be contingent. Yet arguing that the state is contingent

---

[44] Walker, 'Sovereignty, Identity, Community', p. 168.
[45] Walker, *Inside/Outside*, p. 22.
[46] Walker, 'Sovereignty, Identity, Community', p. 169.
[47] Walker, 'From International Relations to World Politics', p. 25.
[48] Walker, 'Sovereignty, Identity, Community', p. 175.

upon things themselves contingent upon the presupposed presence of the state is equivalent to saying that the state is an inescapable limit of the political imagination, and therefore tantamount to demonstrating its necessity.

To my mind, this tells us less about the limits of political imagination but all the more about the limits of deconstruction. The strategy of denaturalization presupposes that we can fix a divide between what is really real and what has been rendered as real through a reification of appearances. Deconstruction presupposes that we can undo the oppositions responsible for previous and arbitrary rearrangements of those divides that condition the possibility of the state and constitute it as real. When pushed to its logical limits, deconstruction cannot but affirm the binary oppositions and constitutive divides it sets out to denaturalize, and will therefore inevitably bring us back to the original foundations of authority, since it is based on the possibility of justifying authority by exposing *its* critical limit.[49]

In order to gain momentum, denaturalization must cultivate the possibility of something unconstructed against which it can measure and justify its critical claims. By virtue of their international perspective, Ashley and Walker succeed in dissolving the state as conventionally conceptualized within international relations theory. What their perspective seems to preclude, however, is a dissolution of the state as conventionally conceptualized within domestic political theory. Indeed, and as noted above, their very ability to problematicize the state hinges on the possibility of subverting this difference from without, that is, from a viewpoint external to the state.

The state is thus dissolved from the outside in rather than from the inside out. This is not to say that Ashley and Walker take internal sovereignty for granted, but rather to say that by interpreting the state as an abstract space situated in between the domestic and the international, they nevertheless construe this space as itself distinct from domestic society, and leave this divide and the conditions of its possibility unexplained. The state thus exists in timeless disjunction with society, and the authority to demarcate and define the proper boundaries of political life within the state is held in abeyance. Hence, even if the state is made to look contingent from without, some of its original mystery is retained within the core of the concept.

By implication, the denaturalizing critique takes place in a temporality opened up between the two deaths of the state. The state has already

---

[49] Cf. Jacques Derrida, 'Force of Law: the "Mystical Foundation of Authority"', in D. Cornell, M. Rosenfeld and D. G. Carlson (eds.), *Deconstruction and the Possibility of Justice* (New York and London: Routledge, 1992), pp. 3–67.

gone through its first death in so far as it has lost its aura of permanence within theoretical discourse. Yet supposedly, most of us are still blissfully unaware of this fact, thinking and acting as if the state were still here to stay. The task of those trying to dissolve the state is to make us aware of this first death, thereby bringing about its second and more conclusive death – the state is dead but nobody knows that it is dead.[50] Phrased differently, the institutional realities of the state may already have withered away, but its spectres continue to haunt us and pose an obstacle to our understanding of the brave new world beyond it. Hence, to critical international theory, the state concept is to us what ideas of empire were to the Renaissance: a fiction which has not yet entirely lost its power to generate reality, or a reality not yet fully turned into fiction; a truth which remains seen as a lie.[51]

But if political practices have already transgressed the limits defined by the state, critical international political theory leaves us with very few intellectual resources with which to understand that new world whose possibility it assumes. So once again, this act of criticism accomplishes a kind of closure similar to that of which it accuses uncritical international theory. Whereas the latter made the state look inescapable by virtue of its necessary, universal and timeless nature, the former makes the state look inescapable by insisting on its foundational presence in the political imagination, however lamentable that presence in turn is made to look.

Temporalizing the state

If the upshot of critical international theory was to show that there is nothing natural about the compartmentalization of modern political space into the two distinct spheres of domestic and international politics, the upshot of the efforts of those who struggle to temporalize the state is to show that it is but one possible constellation of authority in the historical evolution of technologies of power.

The temporalizing gesture is primarily directed against the internal aspects of sovereign statehood and their seemingly timeless or transhistorical character. Where critical international theory denaturalized the external aspects of statehood by making them contingent upon the categorical and spatial distinction between the domestic and the international, temporalization suggests a historical relativization of political authority across time.

---

[50] Cf. Zizek, *For They Do Not Know What They Do*, pp. 63–5.
[51] Cf. Frances A. Yates, *Astraea: the Imperial Theme in the Sixteenth Century* (London: Routledge and Kegan Paul, 1975).

If critical international theory wrestled with the distinction between the domestic and international contexts of politics, those who have struggled to temporalize the state have directed their critical attention to the distinction between the state and civil society. Intuitively, therefore, it would seem that the denaturalization and temporalization are likely to yield complementary conclusions about the nature of the state and its future fate, since the one problematicizes what the other omits from its critical perspective, and vice versa.

Perhaps the best way to make sense of temporalization is to start with what it opposes. As we may recall from previous chapters, the distinction between the state and civil society has been intensely contested in successive rhetorical battles over the relationship between the state and civil society.[52] Yet these battles seem to demand that interlocutors are in agreement that there are natural kinds called 'the state' and 'civil society', and that the line of demarcation separating them, albeit historically flexible, is nevertheless indispensable to our understanding of modern politics. What is left to debate is the position of this line, as well as what kind of transactions can possibly take place across it, and what they imply in terms of political order.

The main points of disagreement are well known. On the one hand, whereas pluralist political science struggled to replace the state with the concepts of government or political system, it was nevertheless forced to discriminate between the political and the non-political; doing this meant reintroducing distinctions that those latter concepts were thought to have made redundant. On the other hand, those who struggled to bring the state back in frequently did so by rendering the state *a priori* dependent on civil society just in order to be able to assert its relative empirical autonomy from it.

Now both these strategies converge on three assumptions. First, that both the state and civil society exist in some objective and robust way. Second, that state and society are ontologically different if not opposed entities. Third, that the analytical divide separating them is necessary to our understanding of both, and that our understanding of both in turn is necessary for our understanding of what politics is ultimately all about: the proper relationship between the state and civil society, or between the political and the prima facie non-political.

To those who want to temporalize the state, all this looks naive, and testifies to an ideological deadlock within the discourse on the state. First, by uncritically assuming that state and society exist by virtue of being distinct – whether society is seen as prior to or derivative from the state,

---

[52] For a full account of this debate, see Jean L. Cohen and Andrew Arato, *Civil Society and Political Theory* (Cambridge, MA: MIT Press, 1992).

or conversely – participants in the state debate take for granted what is but a point of convergence between liberal and socialist ideology – an agreement whose existence should be explained rather than taken for granted. Second, by assuming that the divide separating the state from the society is analytically necessary, they tend to overestimate the importance of the state concept by presupposing that central authority is a necessary condition for the existence of political order. Third, by investing the state with a certain necessity, they end up with historical accounts of the state which portray it as either inherently expansive, or as wholly subordinated to the forces of civil society. But what happens if we move beyond those agreements?

Doing this is the point of Foucault's famous remark that the King's head must be cut off.[53] According to Foucault, we must get rid of the paralysing fiction of sovereignty if we are to understand the exercise of power in modern societies, which is otherwise likely to remain veiled behind the barren formalisms of legal and political theory.[54]

As I shall argue, however, the ensuing effort to temporalize the state by rendering the distinction between state and civil society contingent upon the changing discursive practices of governmentality merely restores at a new level those concepts and problems that this strategy promises to dispose of once and for all. As we shall be able to note, such a beheading of political theory does not preclude the possibility that the body can remain alive and well after the decapitation; or even if we successfully rid political discourse of the concept of sovereignty, there is a distinct possibility that its ugly head will reappear where we least suspect to find it.

Yet if we follow this recommendation and put the state concept within brackets, several intellectual benefits ensue immediately. Rather than starting from the classical questions of sovereignty – that is, from questions of the proper exercise of power – we might instead ask questions about how sovereignty has in fact been exercised, and how questions about its exercise have been phrased and rephrased from early modernity onwards. Doing this would be tantamount to asking how concrete political practices shape and are shaped by answers to the more basic question of how to govern, and how to govern effectively. Within such a perspective, the state is nothing more than

a specific way in which the problem of government is discursively codified, a way of dividing a 'political sphere', with its particular characteristics of rule, from

---

[53] Michel Foucault, 'Truth and Power', in Colin Gordon (ed.), *Power/Knowledge: Selected Interviews and Writings 1972–1977* (New York: Pantheon, 1980), p. 121.

[54] Michel Foucault, 'Governmentality', in Burchell *et al.*, *The Foucault Effect: Studies in Governmentality*, pp. 87–104.

other 'non-political spheres' to which it must be related, and a way in which certain technologies of government are given a temporal institutional durability and brought into particular kinds of relations with one another.[55]

From this point of view, the state has none of the inherent capacities conventionally ascribed to it, and it lacks both the essence and necessity tacitly attributed to it by modern state theory. Consequently, the entire discourse on the state is something that stands in need of explanation, rather than a discourse that is able to explain the phenomenal reality of the state, since it

presents the state as a small, all-powerful apparatus which obstructs the freedom of individuals and threatens the development of social forces. The state, in this context, is an instance separate from, and exercising a repressive, negative power over, the social body, which, for its part, is endowed with an originally virtuous essence.[56]

By the same token, uncritical subscription to the distinction between state and society is bound to lead to a thoroughly ideologized understanding of political discourse.[57] This distinction explains nothing, but has itself to be explained. Furthermore, the state concept distorts our analysis of actual power relationships by subsuming them under a singular and transhistorical mode of authority, since

[t]he forms of power that subject us, the systems of rule that administer us, the types of authority that master us, do not find their principle of coherence in a State, nor do they answer to a logic of oppression or domination or the other constitutive oppositions of liberal political philosophy – least of all, its ways of dividing the political from the non-political.[58]

Consequently, if an exclusive focus on the state is permitted to distort our historical vision, we could not hope to make sense of present political realities either:

the political vocabulary structured by oppositions between state and civil society, public and private, government and market, coercion and consent, sovereignty and autonomy and the like, does not adequately characterize the diverse ways in which rule is exercised in advanced liberal democracies.[59]

---

[55] Nikolas Rose and Peter Miller, 'Political Power Beyond the State: Problematics of Government', *British Journal of Sociology*, vol. 43, 1992, no. 2, pp. 176–7.

[56] Pasquale Pasquino, 'Theatrum Politicum: the Genealogy of Capital-Police and the State of Prosperity', in Burchell *et al.*, *The Foucault Effect: Studies in Governmentality*, p. 108.

[57] Pasquino, 'Theatrum Politicum', p. 116.

[58] Nikolas Rose, 'Government, Authority and Expertise in Advanced Liberalism', *Economy and Society*, vol. 22, 1993, no. 3, p. 286.

[59] Rose and Miller, 'Political Power Beyond the State', p. 174.

Now a full temporalization of the state does not just necessitate a substitution of questions of government for questions of state: this kind of substitution is familiar from earlier pluralist and anthropological analyses of the state concept.[60] It would also necessitate a wholesale relativization of the state concept, so that the state can be rendered a historically contingent mode of government, rather than a general prerequisite of the possibility of governance; consequently, the concept of sovereignty must be treated as a juridico-political fiction, and then carefully contextualized in all its historical variety. We are then bound to discover that behind the transhistorical appearance of the concept of sovereignty lies a profound circularity:

[i]n every case, what characterizes the end of sovereignty, this common and general good, is in sum nothing other than submission to sovereignty. This means that the end of sovereignty is circular: the end of sovereignty is the exercise of sovereignty. The good is obedience to the law, the good for sovereignty is that people should obey it. This is an essential circularity which whatever its theoretical structure... we always come back to this self-referring circularity of sovereignty or principality.[61]

There is no obvious escape out of this circularity as long as we remain within the confines of the concept of sovereignty. But as soon as we step outside it, the problem of government can be phrased more coherently and substituted for those of state and sovereignty. Where theories of sovereignty try to draw a firm distinction between the power of the state and other forms of power, because their task is to explain and justify a disjunction between them, the study of governmentality seeks to understand continuity between them. When this disjunction between the state and society is understood as historically flexible rather than as given, the institutions of the state can be bracketed off, and treated as wholly simultaneous with and expressive of varying techniques of government, rather than as their implicit justification or theoretical explanation.[62] The state must be taken for what it is: 'an historically variable device for conceptualizing and articulating rule... or... as a means of contesting the nature and limit of political power'.[63]

If sovereignty is no longer *the* question of political theory, the problem of power can no longer be phrased in terms of command and obedience

---

[60] Cf. John Hoffman, *Beyond the State: an Introductory Critique* (Cambridge: Polity Press, 1995), ch. 3.

[61] Foucault, 'Governmentality', p. 95.

[62] Colin Gordon, 'Governmental Rationality: an Introduction', in Burchell *et al.*, *The Foucault Effect: Studies in Governmentality* pp. 1–51.

[63] Rose, 'Government, Authority, and Expertise', pp. 288–9.

to sovereign authority. Rather, within this view, power becomes a question of the multiple practices that coexist within each specific art of governing, and their correlation within a larger matrix of knowledges and technologies.[64] Instead of focusing upon the institutions of the modern state, and explaining their transformation in terms of underlying causes, the study of government attends to the ways authorities have posed and still pose questions about the exercise of power.[65] Hence, the question of government is primarily a question about how to govern and by what means:

> Government is defined as a right manner of disposing things so as to lead not to the form of the common good... but to an end which is convenient for each of the things that are to be governed. This implies a plurality of specific aims... I believe we are at an important turning point here: whereas the end of sovereignty is internal to itself and possesses its own intrinsic instruments in the shape of its laws, the finality of government resides in the things it manages and in the pursuit of the perfection and intensification of the processes which it directs; and the instruments of government, instead of being laws, now come to be a range of multiform tactics.[66]

According to Foucault, the art of government is concerned with the conduct of conduct. It is an activity 'aiming to shape, guide, or affect the conduct of some person or persons'.[67] Governmental power is concerned with the relation between actions rather than with the intentional or causal relations between agents. Integral to this conception is the idea that power conditions the possibility of political subjectivity, so that each particular technique of government has its correlate in a peculiar form of individual and collective identity. Each particular way of ruling both necessitates and sustains different techniques of the self, and each such technique of the self in turn enables and constrains the possibilities of ruling.[68] As Foucault puts it, 'if one wants to analyse the genealogy of the subject in Western societies, one has to take into account not only techniques of domination, but also techniques of the self. Let's say that one has to take into account the interaction of these two types of techniques.'[69]

---

[64] Cf. Michel Foucault, 'The Subject and Power', afterword to Hubert L. Dreyfus and Paul Rabinow, *Michel Foucault: Beyond Structuralism and Hermeneutics* (Berkeley, CA: University of California Press, 1982), pp. 208–26; Foucault, 'Truth and Power', pp. 122ff.

[65] Rose and Miller, 'Political Power Beyond the State', p. 177.

[66] Foucault, 'Governmentality', p. 95.

[67] Gordon, 'Governmental Rationality', p. 2.

[68] Michel Foucault, 'The Political Technology of Individuals', in Luther H. Martin, Huck Gutman and Patrick H. Hutton (eds.), *Technologies of the Self: a Seminar with Michel Foucault* (London: Tavistock, 1988), pp. 145–62.

[69] Michel Foucault, 'Truth and Subjectivity', The Howison Lectures, quoted in Graham Burchell, 'Liberal Government and Techniques of the Self', *Economy and Society*, vol. 22, 1993, no. 3, p. 268.

Politics beyond the state

The temporalization of the state gives rise to problems of its own. If the state – along with the divide that separates it from civil society – is contingent upon political discourse, this of course begs the question of how it emerged and by what rhetorical means it was constituted. Second, and more problematically, it begs the question of how this concept came to be taken for granted within political discourse, and why it has continued to cast its spell over the political imagination even after it supposedly lost its power to organize extra-discursive reality. It is to these questions we now must turn.

Since a large part of the effort to temporalize the state consists in rewriting the history of the state concept, we must now take a closer look at that rewriting and its outcome. If the state concept itself explains nothing, it must be explained; in order to be persuasive and coherent, such historical accounts have to explain how this concept has emerged and why it has lingered on within discourse.

The authors discussed above are disposed to regard the state concept as wholly derivative of underlying variations in the art of government. According to Foucault, the art of government first emerged towards the end of the sixteenth century, and then in response to the twin forces of political centralization and religious dissidence brought about by the Reformation. Before that moment, neither the state nor any recognizable art of government was present within political discourse. In his reading of Machiavelli's *Il Principe*, Foucault points to the fact that the prince stood in a relation of singularity and externality to his possession, the state. But since he does not form part of it, the theme of government does not present itself from within this perspective, which is that of the ruler identifying with his possession, the state. Yet gradually, the state takes on a life of its own, separate from that of rulers as well as ruled. This moment is decisive for the emergence of a new political rationality centred not on the person of the prince, but rather on the state or polity as a whole. The concept of reason of state was used to convey the idea that the state is or should be governed according to principles intrinsic to it and which cannot be derived from any other source, human or divine. The state has its own immanent rationality, and the art of government must discover and systematically employ its principles in order to be successful in creating and upholding order as well as security against the threats posed by external enemies.[70]

---

[70] Michel Foucault, 'Omnes et Singulatim: towards a Criticism of "Political Reason"', *The Tanner Lectures on Human Values 1981* (Salt Lake City, UT: University of Utah Press, 1981), pp. 221–54.

According to Foucault, the invention of reason of state not only enabled but also constrained the full development of the art of government. The problem of sovereignty and its exercise, whether phrased in theoretical terms or in terms of principles of political organization, blocked off the articulation and refinement of this art, which remained subservient to the legalistic themes cultivated in the discourse on sovereignty. During this period the art of government remained modelled upon the family or household as the unit in which management of things and people was possible. The challenge faced by the art of government was how to extend the scope of these governmental techniques from the family to society as a whole.[71]

These efforts to extend the scope of possible government found various expressions within the absolutist and mercantilist state. Both the rise of statistics and the articulation of a distinct science of police were conducive in this respect. Both, however, were premised on the identity between the state – as defined by legal doctrines of sovereignty – and the rest of the community. The intractable problem of reason of state and its various offspring was how to obtain sufficiently detailed knowledge of the reality to be governed in order to render it governable. Since everything potentially fell within the purview of the governable in absolutist doctrine, the exhaustive quest for knowledge and control extended to every part of society, covering a heterogeneous class of practices and objects.[72]

Later, as mercantilism waned, the introduction of the concept of population as an object of both knowledge and power made such an extension of household government possible, and at the same time this took place outside the juridical framework defined by the problem of sovereignty. The new category of population implied that the domain where known techniques of household management could be employed was vastly extended:

[P]rior to the emergence of population, it was impossible to conceive the art of government except on the model of the family, in terms of economy conceived as the management of family; from the moment when, on the contrary, population appears absolutely irreducible to the family, the latter becomes of secondary importance to population, as an element internal to population.[73]

This unblocking of the art of government also coincides with the birth of political economy, since this for the first time constitutes the economic sphere as a domain of reality, and marks it off from that of politics. From the eighteenth century onwards, political economy becomes the preferred

---

[71] Foucault, 'Governmentality', pp. 98–9.
[72] Foucault, 'Omnes et Singulatim', pp. 246–51.
[73] Foucault, 'Governmentality', p. 99.

science and dominant technique of intervention in order to cope with problems pertaining to its corollary datum, population. This is also the formative moment of civil society as a sphere of activity, wholly distinct from, albeit stuck in complex interdependence with, the state. Whereas the rise of statistics and of the science of police had been premised on the virtual identity between the state and the body politic as a whole, political economy effected a disjunction between state and society, and hence made it possible to define the latter as a target of governmental tactics. In the words of Meuret, political economy

> succeeded in imposing itself because it offered, through a redefinition of the economy and the state, new rules of the game to its players – the state, capitalism, and the public . . . [w]e should think of it as a diplomatic treaty, a compromise each player agrees to because its nature appears such as to protect each of them from the other two. [74]

Thus, civil society, far from being a domain either preceding the emergence of the state or being fabricated by it, is to be interpreted as the correlate of the practices of government made possible by political economy, the category of society itself being conducive to the exercise of power rather than being its 'natural' counterpoise. The concept of society is thus closely correlated with these practices of government, as is the corollary state concept. The rest is a matter of ideology, in which the state is portrayed as something constantly threatening to colonize civil society or at least being stuck in perennial opposition to it.[75]

Thus, according to Foucault and his followers, the construction of civil society as a presumably autonomous sphere was one of the major inventions of the liberal art of government. Rather than being a natural domain for spontaneous interaction and exchange between free agents – as classical liberal rhetoric would have it – civil society is an offspring of a peculiar technique of government that proceeds by autonomization of individual subjects as well as of society as a whole. The idea of civil society hence presupposes 'a specification of the objects of government in such a way that the regulations they need are, in a sense, self-indicated and limited to the end of securing the conditions for an optimal, but natural and self-regulating functioning'.[76]

---

[74] Denis Meuret, 'A Political Genealogy of Political Economy', *Economy and Society*, vol. 17, 1988, no. 2, p. 228.

[75] Graham Burchell, 'Peculiar Interests: Civil Society and Governing "The System of Natural Liberty"', in Burchell *et al.*, *The Foucault Effect: Studies in Governmentality*, p. 141.

[76] Burchell, 'Peculiar Interests', p. 127; cf. also Colin Gordon, Afterword to *Power/ Knowledge*, in Gordon, *Power/Knowledge*, pp. 229–59.

Thus, the distinction between state and civil society emerged within a distinct problematic, and in response to historically specific problems of governance. With the coming of classical liberalism and *laissez-faire*, the identity of individual subjects and their relation to the political order became defined by the concepts of interests and rights. Whereas the category of interest had been construed in response to the perceived threat that unruly passions posed to the sociopolitical order and its stability, the concept of right had been derived from the legalist discourse on sovereignty. The problem posed was how political power was to be exercised within a polity inhabited by such bifurcated subjects, and civil society provided the solution. By means of it

an art of government can be defined which does not have to sacrifice its globality or specificity. It makes possible an art of government which has neither to withdraw from a sector of the unified domain of political sovereignty nor to submit passively to the dictates of economic science.[77]

The reification of civil society into a natural kind seems to be a necessary condition for its smooth functioning. If not perceived as bedrock reality by its inhabitants, civil society would not be susceptible to governmental tactics. Simply put, effective government presupposes a domain of objects and subjects to be governed, and the concept of civil society delineates such a domain and thereby makes it accessible to strategic intervention; civil society is the end of governmental activity, yet its being perceived as a natural kind constitutes an important means of achieving this end.[78]

But during the twentieth century, the schematic distinction between state and civil society gradually loses its power to organize the art of government. After a brief but intense battle over the state and its powers, the topic seems to dissolve, as does the state itself. Nor is it any longer possible to conceptualize civil society as distinct from the political sphere and as a natural counterpoise to an inherently interventionist and expansionist state. As Donzelot and Ewald have argued, during the twentieth century the activities of government themselves begin to acquire a complexity and extension similar to that formerly attributed to the activities of civil society, thus rendering these spheres functionally indistinct yet still ideologically opposed.[79]

---

[77] Burchell, 'Peculiar Interests', p. 138.

[78] Burchell, 'Liberal Government', p. 272.

[79] Jacques Donzelot, 'The Mobilization of Society', in Burchell *et al.*, *The Foucault Effect: Studies in Governmentality*, pp. 169–79; Jacques Donzelot, *L'Invention du Social* (Paris, 1984); François Ewald, 'Insurance and Risk,' in Burchell, *et al.*, *The Foucault Effect: Studies in Governmentality*, pp. 197–210.

The late modern relationship between state and society is best under-stood in terms of supplementarity, in which the problems perceived by each automatically become the problems of the other. So if the distinc-tion between the state and civil society has been both relativized and ideologized in modern political practice, modern polities have become inherently pluralist in the sense that state and society permeate each other to the extent that they have become virtually impossible to dis-tinguish. What we have is a will to govern which lacks definite locus but permeates the entire social body. The state has, as it were, been governmentalized.[80]

End of story. The upshot of this account should now be clear. The state and civil society are nothing but contingent manifestations of underlying techniques of power that condition and instrumentalize them in the art of government. Within this view, the state as we have come to know it – as the source of identity and locus of authority within the social body – is a juridico-political fiction that long ago ceased to correspond to the realities of power in modern societies, and whose only function since has been to conceal and legitimize those realities. The state concept is thus but a temporary expression of a ubiquitous will to govern.

But from where does that will come, and where does it reside? The answers to these questions tend to be ambiguous and contradictory. Fol-lowing the logic of temporalization, the state has gradually been replaced by a multitude of different loci of power. There is no overarching source of authority in the sense of a singular centre from which governmental practices radiate, only a will to govern that runs through the polity at large, and which produces multiple loci of power. Yet a centre can only become a centre

through its position within the complex set of technologies, agents and agencies that make government possible. But, once established as a centre, a particular locale can ensure that certain resources only flow through and around these tech-nologies and networks, reaching particular agents rather than others, by means of passage through 'the centre'.[81]

This way of accounting for political order gives rise to a dilemma sim-ilar to that of pluralism, since with a plurality of governmental centres, the question remains of what keeps them in check and bestows their acts with the minimum of coherence necessary for the maintenance of polit-ical order. The beheading of political theory thus leaves us either with a multitude of petty heads, or with the old Eastonian trouble of explaining

---

[80] Foucault, 'Governmentality', p. 103; cf. Rose and Miller, 'Political Power Beyond the State', pp. 191ff.
[81] Rose and Miller, 'Political Power Beyond the State', p. 189.

the relative coherence of political practices without recourse to any over-arching and state-like source of that coherence.

Furthermore, while temporalizing the state helps us make sense of the meaning and experience of statehood as seen from within, it does not and cannot question its own perspective, any more than denaturalization could come to terms with its external viewpoint. The remains of the royal body therefore seem fully capable of a life of their own: even when we rid ourselves of the concept of sovereign authority as the defining charac-teristic of political community, the identity of particular communities as distinct from each other, and as distinct from other possible forms of po-litical life, is assumed as a necessary backdrop to the ensuing explanations of how the political practices of governmentality change over time. Simply put, the temporalization of the distinction between state and society pre-supposes that the distinction between the domestic and the international is preserved, since the entire drama of changing governmentalities is staged within a bounded space which has always already been carved out, and then invariably in response to changing conditions within that very space or in the relationship between such spaces. Thus the initial prob-lematic is restored, since external sovereignty is treated as a transhistorical constant which delineates the space of possible temporalization.

To sum up then: to say that the state is contingent is to say that the state either lacks essence or necessity or both, and that it therefore also consti-tutes but one particular and historically specific constellation of authority and community, constituted in and through political discourse. For the state to be contingent means the state having the potential not to exist. To say this is to imply that history could have taken an entirely differ-ent course, with no experience of statehood conditioning the subsequent meaning of political discourse, and imprisoning us within the confines of statism.

And this in turn is to presuppose that we have reached or are about to reach the end of the state, since the possible absence of the state con-ditions the possibility of its contingency. The state is just an accidental compartmentalization of political space about to be undone by the com-plex forces of globalization, or was nothing but a momentary blip on the screen of history, to be replaced by forever fresh political technologies.

But as we have seen, both denaturalization and temporalization here reach their limit. They are unable to tell us what might possibly lurk beyond the modern state, since by subsuming the totality of political concepts under the meaningful experience of statehood, they leave us with few conceptual resources with which to create or justify new and presumably non-statist constellations of authority and identity. So what were allegedly the limits of the state turn out to be the limits of criticism.

Whereas the above strategies help us realize that the state is but a contingent solution to a more general problem of political order and that most modern formulations of that problem in turn have been conditioned by the state concept, they are themselves quite unable to provide an escape route out of this conceptual structure, since being strategies of immanent criticism, they invariably assume what they set out to criticize: the necessity of the state being identical with itself. This possibility is the starting point as well as the prime target of criticism, and manifests itself in two assumptions: the self-identity of authority and the authority of self-identity.

Whereas denaturalization made the distinction between the domestic and the international appear contingent upon discourse, and the identity of the state in turn contingent upon that distinction, it could not but preserve its authority to demarcate itself from the domestic. By the same token, whereas temporalization made the distinction between the state and society appear contingent upon discourse, and the authority of the state in turn contingent upon that distinction, it could not but preserve its identity in relation to the international. The state is thus dissolved either from the outside in or from the inside out, but never in both directions simultaneously, and since the dissolving gesture itself seems to be based on the poetics of inside and outside, the state remains very much in place, albeit in a very ghostly shape.

This leaves those who want to find ways beyond the state with the theoretical challenge of effecting a double dissolution; a dissolution that would disentangle our notions of authority and identity from the state concept once and for all. Doing this would be tantamount to rephrasing the entire problem of political order, thus disposing of statist interpretations of authority. But this is hardly possible within the present theoretical context, since it would violate the initial conditions of the self-identity to be subjected to criticism: its target would vanish in front of the eyes of the critic, as would its very politicity. So perhaps criticism itself, rather than the state, is the problem.

6   Conclusion

According to the main argument of this book, the state concept has been both constitutive of and foundational to large parts of modern political science, making statism – understood as the presupposed presence of the state – a salient feature of modern political discourse, whether we like it or not. This argument was formulated against the backdrop of a more philosophical claim about the role of criticism in sustaining the constituting authority of the state by transgressing the discursive prohibition against questioning the ultimate foundations of authority. In order to substantiate this claim with textual evidence, the rest of the book focused partly on the formation of scientific political discourse, and partly on those parts of political discourse that have since then been critical of the state.

So what can we conclude from this analysis of the discourse on the state during the past century? First, we have seen how the state concept emerged within modern political discourse as a point of condensation by virtue of its ability to contain a series of profound dualities within that discourse. From having been abstracted from rulers as well as ruled, this concept acquired a certain historicity that made possible a symbolic identity between rulers and ruled within the state, expressed through the self-enoblement of the Third Estate into Nation, and Hegel's later conceptualization of this fusion as a condition of modern political subjectivity at large. This concept, passing through the hands of the German historicists, was both empirical and transcendental: empirical in so far as it denoted a uniform object of inquiry, transcendental in so far as it conditioned the possibility of a domain of knowledge that was to become the fertile ground out of which an autonomous science of politics later could emerge, firmly focused on the state as an object of inquiry.

The concept of the state came to constitute a strategic resource and the very foundation of a modern science of politics by furnishing the quest for disciplinarity with identity, autonomy and authority. As I have argued, modern political science became logically interconnected with that concept through a transference of symbolic attributes between the emergent field of knowledge and its object of inquiry. The concept of the state not only provided the focal object of that science, but was also a condition of its being distinctively 'political' and 'scientific'. Hence, the state has not been constituted in and through political discourse, but rather the other way around: the presupposed presence of the state has constituted this discourse as at once scientific and political. And through this development, or so I argued, the concept of the state was removed from the domain of the politically contestable, as was the question of authority in general. Already at this rather early stage, scientification represents a reversal of *Sattelzeit* hopes of contestability and democratic transparency in political discourse, and brings a superficial substitution of scientific authority for political authority to bear on that discourse.

After the turn of the last century, or so it appears, the state concept becomes a theoretical battleground, and is intensely contested as to its meaning, reference and analytical value. Starting with the pluralist onslaught, a conviction gradually emerges that the fictitious character of the state conceals the true pluralistic nature of modern political life, and that this concept is therefore redundant to any scientific understanding of politics as well as to democratic political practice. Provided with an impetus from logical empiricism and legal positivism, this critique gradually shifts from a mere denial of the reality of the state to a relentless questioning of the analytical value of the concept on the grounds of its inherent opacity and ambiguity. Finally we find the state concept being replaced by a succession of semantic equivalents, themselves implying statist solutions to the problem of political order within what supposedly was purified and stateless discourse. At this stage, the quest for a scientific understanding of politics removed itself from concerns that were themselves 'political'; but however redundant the state concept was made to look, the more unquestionable the presence of the state within the problematics of that science became.

Partly as a response to what looked like an ideological concealment of actual power relations within the capitalist societies, the state was brought back into analytical focus. Being defined by its *a priori* dependence on the socioeconomic forces of civil society, and partly by its ability to conceal these realities, the state concept was gradually redefined to encompass a degree of autonomy necessary to explain the reproductive requirements of the capitalist political order sustaining it. However, the effort to bring the state back in succeeded in one way because it failed in another: only when the ambition to conceptualize the state in critical terms had been abandoned could the concept be brought back in; and yet there was an indivisible remainder of unexplained political authority left at the core of critical state theory. The net effect of this unmasking gesture was thus perverse in its own terms, in so far as it contributed to a reaffirmation of the same concept whose presence had initially constituted the main target of critical state theory.

The above kinds of critical discourse accepted the same constitutive distinctions – between the state and the international, and the state and society – that had once emerged simultaneously with the modern state concept. What the latest generation of state critics has attempted is nothing less than a wholesale undoing of this entire conceptual edifice, commonly identified with political modernity. Arguing that the above distinctions and the categories thus distinguished are wholly contingent upon a political discourse, which in turn is contingent upon nothing but itself, these critics sought either to denaturalize the state from without or to temporalize the state from within. Either way, however, the same master distinctions that conditioned the possibility of the state reemerged, either in terms of a disjunction between state and society, or in terms of the self-identity of the polity, thus jeopardizing the intended outcome of the critical project.

Yet beneath this entire polemic we find a series of tacit agreements about what to disagree about. First, during the twentieth century, theorists dealing with the state concept have gone about their critical project as if the state were 'out there', yet representing something opaque to be unmasked in order to find its underlying 'truth'. This might seem trivial, but reveals what in fact is a contradictory attitude to the object of criticism. The state is invariably interpreted as both identical with itself and real enough to merit critical attention, yet this criticism has as its ultimate task to demonstrate the fictitious character of the state by reducing its conceptual identity to something allegedly more basic and real, be it group interests, governmental processes, political systems, social classes or discursive practices. The objective reality and self-identity of the state is thus as much a condition of criticism as it is its ultimate target: if no one could be suspected of believing the state to be self-identical and somehow real, the criticism would not only lose its bite but also its rationale. A critical theory of the state would then look as relevant and useful to us as a critical theory of unicorns. That is, the political subject in whose name criticism is undertaken is itself based on the authority to demarcate that subject from its other, posited as a presence on either the inside or the outside of the state, so that ultimately, criticism shares the conditions of possibility of its object.

Second, we have been able to see that by accepting the conceptual self-identity of the state as a starting point of that criticism, the critical strategies devoted to its reconceptualization themselves amount to a reaffirmation of the importance of the state concept within political discourse. Put differently, we have seen how the critical efforts have turned the concept singled out for criticism into a foundational and inescapable presence within political discourse. So, far from having escaped the mythical foundations of state authority as constituting authority by subjecting it to the secular rituals of scientific criticism, the mystery of the state has been preserved largely thanks to this critical spirit, and its capacity to hold the discourse on the state together throughout the theoretical discontinuities that it has gone through.

Third, the fact that the state concept has constituted a theoretical battleground in its own right has not implied that the state concept itself has been an apple of discord in any substantial sense. Rather, it seems as though the presence of the state concept has conditioned the theoretical discord without itself being subjected to it. The state concept has been able to function as a battleground by itself being removed from contestation by the way the battle has been fought. Thus, and contrary to the belief that a scientification of political discourse would bring the blessings of transparency to the system of political concepts and the conditions of their usage, both the scientification and the critique of this ambition seem to have produced similar results in terms of a net decrease in contestability. It is fully possible to disagree over the proper meaning and reference of the state concept and thus also about the ontological status of the state; but it is virtually impossible to envisage constellations of authority and community beyond the state without ceasing to be either political or scientific, at least in any recognizably modern sense of those latter terms.

Yet it would be grossly unfair to turn the above observations against the critics of the state, since they have merely sought to do what Kant wanted to forbid and make impossible all at once. They wanted to bring the critical project of modernity closer to completion by emancipating us from any remnants of constituting authority, and stripping political science from predemocratic political metaphysics. In fact, they have all been right in doing what they have done, but they have been humanly unaware of what their doings in turn have done. We have to judge them by Christian standards, not Freudian or Lacanian ones. But we are now in a better position to understand the politics of the Kantian prohibition: to forbid what anyway is held to be impossible is a matter of making that something impossible by tempting the transgression of that which is forbidden, and which only can exist by virtue of being produced through transgression. To my mind, this is exactly what has happened within the critical discourse of the state, and this also constitutes its political rationality; being nothing but a succession of transgressive speech-acts provoked by the prohibition to criticize authority, and being aimed at exposing the unsacred origins of authority by reducing it to the undoubtedly mundane and tangible, the discourse on the state has unwittingly but inevitably created the impossibility it set out to undo. Simply put, systematic disbelief in the material reality of the state is the main condition of its symbolic reality, and its symbolic presence within discourse is the main condition of its functioning as real: the authority of the state resides precisely in the ritual unmasking of it that is authorized by the critical spirit of modernity itself, an authorization that has turned it into a perceived necessity.

Therefore, to criticize the state for not corresponding to or representing something really real 'out there' is to miss the point entirely, simply because the reality of the state consists precisely in being already symbolically present before the conceptualization of the 'out there' of the political scientist. Thus our late modern monarchomac is able to know with perfect certainty that the state does not represent an independent reality, that it does not exist apart from the plurality of components that compose it, the multitude of classes whose antagonism sustains it, or the discursive practices that constitute it. In short, the state critic is fully entitled to feel confident that the state is opaque, ambiguous, fictitious and constructed all the way down. But precisely by virtue of this very certitude, the state critic is as free to think and act as if the state existed as the ordinary citizen subjects in whose name the critic speaks and whom he or she promises to emancipate from their subjection to the ponderous reality of the state, and this always in the name of some imagined political community lurking beyond the state. For how can a mere fiction ever be a threat to one's freedom?

This brings us over to the question of the proper identity of the state. The eigenvalue of the state concept is nothing but a certain relationship that authority entertains with itself: that of presupposing itself as a condition of itself; of constituting itself as a constituted by positing a difference between appearance and reality within itself as a condition of itself, thereby successfully appearing as one in the world. Therefore, ultimately, the state must remain a fiction in order to operate as real, and can only remain a fiction as long as it is taken as real, and it is only taken as real as long as its reality is open to some doubt. And corollary: the truth of the state is a truth whose validity resides in being taken as a lie; it is only as long as the state is seen as a 'deception' that it can continue to exercise any authority. So contrary to what the company of state critics tend to believe, authority is always virtual and symbolic, and the way to sustain this virtual and symbolic authority is not through reification of something that is really not that real, but rather through critically and systematically doubting its reality as measured against something really more real. This, I contend, is very much what late modern political science has been doing when criticizing the state.

So at the end of the day the question of the reality of the state turns out to be irrelevant to questions of its obsolescence or permanence. Returning to Weber, we are now in a position to see how the famous claim to a legitimate monopoly of force already presupposes primordial and symbolic authority as the condition of its success, and how the authority necessary for that success resides in the claim itself, and not in the legitimacy it creates as a consequence of its success. The Weberian state does not and cannot exist in the substantial and robust sense of later state theory, but exists only as a claim whose ultimate fulfilment is and must be held in suspense as the condition of its success. The state is thus not 'out there' but rather 'in here', in the constitutive self-referentiality of its concept. From a Weberian viewpoint, the state is thus ultimately nothing but a claim to authority that authorizes itself by containing its negation in the form of hypothetical rival claims to the same authority: otherwise the state would not need to be a claim but could as well be defined as a fact capable of realization. As we have seen, the critique of the state is nothing but the symbolic embodiment of that rival claim within discourse.

Therefore, we would only have arrived at the end of the state at the very moment it lost its symbolic authority. This would be the moment when its contestation had become utterly pointless because it had become too real to be rendered apparent, and yet totally transparent to the critical spirit then ruling it. This will be the point when the founding of the critique of the state is repeated in a brief moment of terror, holding all of us at gunpoint: 'the state is dead, long live the state!'

But where does this analysis of the proper identity of the state leave us with respect to the problem of political order, and the possibilities of conceptualizing political order beyond or without the state? We have seen how statism constitutes the phantasmic support of the authority of the modern state, and how our statist intellectual predispositions are reinforced rather than undermined by the critique of the state. This implies that the possible outcomes of the ongoing transformation of world politics will remain effectively hidden to us only as long as we remain critical of the state. Being critical of the state not only affirms its symbolic authority, but also implies that new forms of political order can only be conceptualized after, and then perhaps as a consequence of, the total demise of the old state-centric one. But things never die simply as a consequence of their obituary having been written in advance, nor are new things born out of the prophesied demise of old ones.

Political discourse and political order rarely evolve in tandem, and their respective evolutionary paths are never unilinear or uniform. If we are today living through what many commentators believe is a profound transformation of the modern political order – the possible demise of the modern state as the privileged source and locus of political authority and community – we could hardly expect this to be indicated by a discursive silence or an intensified criticism of the state within political discourse. Rather, the most likely discursive correlate of such an institutional crisis would be exactly what we are experiencing today within globalization theory: a resurgence of interest in the state, sustained by reification and nostalgia, and coupled with a feeling of discursive entrapment. Only when the fear of statism finally subsides will the state as the *foci imaginarii* of political theory.

Bibliography

Adams, Henry B., 'Is History Past Politics?', *Johns Hopkins University Studies in Historical and Political Science*, series 7, vols. III–IV (Baltimore, MD: Johns Hopkins University Press, 1895).

Agamben, Giorgio, 'Bartleby, or On Contingency', in *Potentialities: Collected Essays in Philosophy* (Stanford, CA: Stanford University Press, 1999).

Homo Sacer: Sovereign Power and Bare Life (Stanford, CA: Stanford University Press, 1998).

Potentialities: Collected Essays in Philosophy (Stanford, CA: Stanford University Press, 1999).

Allison, Graham T., *Essence of Decision: Explaining the Cuban Missile Crisis* (Boston, MA: Little, Brown, 1971).

Almond, Gabriel A., 'The Return to the State', *American Political Science Review*, vol. 82, 1988, no. 3, pp. 850–74.

'The Return to the State', in Gabriel A. Almond, *A Discipline Divided: Schools and Sects in Political Science* (Newbury Park, CA: Sage, 1990), pp. 189–218.

Althusser, Louis and Balibar, Etienne, *Reading Capital* (London: New Left Books, 1970).

Andrews, Bruce, 'Social Rules and the State as a Social Actor', *World Politics*, vol. 27, 1975, no. 4, pp. 521–40.

Antoni, C., *From History to Sociology: the Transition in German Historical Thinking* (Detroit, MI: Wayne State University Press, 1959).

Aristotle, *Physics* (Bloomington, IN: Indiana University Press, 1969).

Aron, Raymond, *Peace and War: a Theory of International Relations* (London: Weidenfeld and Nicolson, 1962).

Ashcraft, Richard, 'German Historicism and the History of Political Theory', *History of Political Thought*, vol. 8, 1987, no. 2, pp. 289–324.

Ashley, Richard K., 'The Geopolitics of Geopolitical Space: toward a Critical Social Theory of International Politics', *Alternatives*, vol. 12, 1987, no. 4, pp. 403–34.

'Living on Border Lines: Man, Poststructuralism, and War', in James Der Derian and Michael J. Shapiro (eds.), *International/Intertextual Relations: Postmodern Readings of World Politics* (Lexington, MA: Lexington Books, 1989), pp. 259–321.

'The Poverty of Neorealism', in Robert O. Keohane (ed.), *Neorealism and its Critics* (New York: Columbia University Press, 1986), pp. 255–300.

'The Powers of Anarchy: Theory, Sovereignty, and the Domestication of Global Life', in James Der Derian (ed.), *International Theory: Critical Investigations* (London: Macmillan, 1995), pp. 94–128.

Austin, John, *The Province of Jurisprudence Determined* [1832] (Cambridge: Cambridge University Press, 1995).

Avineri, Shlomo, *Hegel's Theory of the Modern State* (Cambridge: Cambridge University Press, 1979).

The Social and Political Thought of Karl Marx (Cambridge: Cambridge University Press, 1968).

Bachelard, Gaston, *The Poetics of Space* (Boston, MA: Beacon Press, 1994).

Badie, Bertrand, *La Fin des Territoires* (Paris: Fayard, 1995).

Bagehot, Walter, *Physics and Politics: Or Thoughts on the Application of the Principles of 'Natural Selection' and 'Inheritance' to Political Society*, 3d edn (London: Henry S. King, 1875).

Balibar, Etienne, 'The Dictatorship of the Proletariat', *Marxism Today*, vol. 21, 1977, no. 5.

Ball, Terence, *Reappraising Political Theory: Revisionist Studies in the History of Political Thought* (Oxford: Clarendon, 1995).

Ball, Terence, Hanson, Russell L. and Farr, James (eds.), *Political Innovation and Conceptual Change* (Cambridge: Cambridge University Press, 1989).

Barker, Ernest, 'The Discredited State: Thoughts on Politics Before the War', *The Political Quarterly*, vol. 7, 1915, no. 5, pp. 101–26.

'The Superstition of the State', *Times Literary Supplement*, July 1918.

Barnard, F. M., 'National Culture and Political Legitimacy: Herder and Rousseau', *Journal of the History of Ideas*, vol. 44, 1983, no. 2, pp. 231–53.

Barrow, Clyde W., *Critical Theories of the State: Marxist, Neo-Marxist, Post-Marxist* (Madison, WI: University of Wisconsin Press, 1993).

Bartelson, Jens, *A Genealogy of Sovereignty* (Cambridge: Cambridge University Press, 1995).

'Making Exceptions: some Remarks on the Concept of *Coup d'État* and its History', *Political Theory*, vol. 25, 1997, no. 3, pp. 323–46.

'Second Natures: Is the State Identical With Itself?', *European Journal of International Relations*, vol. 4, 1998, no. 3, pp. 295–326.

'Short Circuits: Society and Tradition in International Relations Theory', *Review of International Studies*, vol. 22, 1996, no. 4, pp. 339–60.

'The Trial of Judgment: a Note on Kant and the Paradoxes of Internationalism', *International Studies Quarterly*, vol. 39, 1995, no. 3, pp. 255–79.

Baudrillard, Jean, *The Illusion of the End* (Cambridge: Polity Press, 1992).

Bauman, Zygmunt, *Globalization: the Human Consequences* (Cambridge: Polity Press, 1998).

Legislators and Interpreters (Oxford: Polity Press, 1987).

Modernity and Ambivalence (Cambridge: Polity Press, 1991).

Beard, Charles A., *An Economic Interpretation of the Constitution of the United States* [1913] (New York: Macmillan, 1954).

Bender, J. and Wellbery, D. (eds.), *Chronotypes: the Construction of Time* (Stanford, CA: Stanford University Press, 1991).

Bendix, R., (ed.), *State and Society: a Reader in Comparative Political Sociology* (Berkeley, CA: University of California Press, 1973).

Bentley, Arthur F., *The Process of Government: a Study of Social Pressures* [1908] (Bloomington, IN: Principia Press, 1935).

Berlin, Isaiah, *Vico and Herder: Two Studies in the History of Ideas* (London: Hogarth Press, 1976).

Bevir, Mark, *The Logic of the History of Ideas* (Cambridge: Cambridge University Press, 1999).

Blondel, Jean, *The Discipline of Politics* (London: Butterworths, 1981).

Bobbio, Norberto, 'Is There a Marxist Theory of the State?', *Telos*, 1978, no. 35, pp. 5–16.

Bosanquet, Bernard, *The Philosophical Theory of the State* [1899] (London: Macmillan, 1951).

Bouchard, Donald F. (ed.), *Language, Counter-memory, Practice: Selected Essays and Interviews by Michel Foucault* (Ithaca, NY: Cornell University Press, 1977).

Bowen, R. H., *German Theories of the Corporate State* (New York: McGraw-Hill, 1947).

Bridges, Amy Beth, 'Nicos Poulantzas and the Marxist Theory of the State', *Politics and Society*, vol. 4, 1974, no. 2, pp. 161–90.

Brown, Chris, *International Relations Theory: New Normative Approaches* (London: Harvester, 1992).

Brunner, O., Conze, W. and Koselleck, Reinhart (eds.), *Geschichtliche Grundbegriffe: Historisches Lexicon zur Politisch-Sozialen Sprache in Deutschland*, vols. I and VI (Stuttgart: Klett-Cotta, 1972–1997).

Bull, Hedley, *The Anarchical Society: a Study of Order in World Politics* (London: Macmillan, 1977).

Burchell, Graham, 'Liberal Government and Techniques of the Self', *Economy and Society*, vol. 22, 1993, no. 3, pp. 267–82.

'Peculiar Interests: Civil Society and Governing "The System of Natural Liberty",' in Graham Burchell, Colin Gordon and Peter Miller (eds.), *The Foucault Effect: Studies in Governmentality* (London: Harvester, 1991), pp. 119–50.

Burchell, Graham, Gordon, Colin and Miller, Peter (eds.), *The Foucault Effect: Studies in Governmentality* (London: Harvester, 1991).

Burgess, John W., *The Foundations of Political Science* [1892] (New York: Columbia University Press, 1933).

Political Science and Comparative Constitutional Law (Boston, MA: Ginn & Co., 1890–1).

'Political Science and History', *American Historical Review*, vol. 2, 1897.

'The Study of the Political Sciences in Columbia College', *International Review*, vol. 1, 1882.

Bury, J. B., *The Idea of Progress: an Inquiry into its Origin and Growth* (New York: Dover Publications, 1955).

Campbell, D. and Dillon, M. (eds.), *The Political Subject of Violence* (Manchester: Manchester University Press, 1993).

Caporaso, J. A., 'The State in a Comparative and International Perspective', in J. A. Caporaso (ed.), *The Elusive State: International and Comparative Perspectives* (Newbury Park, CA: Sage, 1989), pp. 7–16.

Caporaso, J. A. (ed.), *The Elusive State: International and Comparative Perspectives* (Newbury Park, CA: Sage, 1989).

Carnoy, Martin, *The State and Political Theory* (Princeton, NJ: Princeton University Press, 1984).

Carrithers, M., Collins, Steven and Lukes, S. (eds.), *The Category of the Person: Anthropology, Philosophy, History* (Cambridge: Cambridge University Press, 1985).

Castoriadis, Cornelius, 'Time and Creation', in J. Bender and D. Wellbery (eds.), *Chronotypes: the Construction of Time* (Stanford, CA: Stanford University Press, 1991), pp. 38–64.

Catlin, G. E. G., *The Science and Method of Politics* (New York: Knopf, 1927).

Cerny, Philip, 'Globalization and the Changing Logic of Collective Action', *International Organization*, vol. 49, 1995, no. 4, pp. 595–625.

Clark, Ian, 'Beyond the Great Divide: Globalization and the Theory of International Relations', *Review of International Studies*, vol. 24, 1998, no. 4, pp. 479–98.

Cohen, Jean L. and Arato, Andrew, *Civil Society and Political Theory* (Cambridge, MA: MIT Press, 1992).

Coker, Francis W., 'Pluralism', *Encyclopedia of the Social Sciences* (New York: Macmillan, 1934).

'The Technique of the Pluralist State', *American Political Science Review*, vol. 15, 1921, no. 2, pp. 186–213.

Cole, G. D. H., *Essays in Social Theory* (London: Macmillan, 1950).

Collini, Stephan, Winch, Donald and Burrow, John, *That Noble Science of Politics: a Study in Nineteenth-Century Intellectual History* (Cambridge: Cambridge University Press, 1983).

Collins, Steven, 'Categories, Concepts or Predicaments? Remarks on Mauss's Use of Philosophical Terminology', in M. Carrithers, Steven Collins and S. Lukes (eds.), *The Category of the Person: Anthropology, Philosophy, History* (Cambridge: Cambridge University Press, 1985), pp. 46–82.

Comte, Auguste, *Cours de Philosophie Positive*, vols. I and IV (Paris: Bachelier, 1830/9).

The contemporary Crisis of the Nation State, *Political Studies*, special issue, vol. 42, 1994.

Connolly, William E., 'Identity and Difference in Global Politics', in James Der Derian and Michael J. Shapiro (eds.), *International/Intertextual Relations: Postmodern Readings of World Politics* (Lexington, MA: Lexington Books, 1989), pp. 323–42.

Political Theory and Modernity (Oxford: Basil Blackwell, 1988).

Cornell, D., Rosenfeld, M. and Carlson, D. G. (eds.), *Deconstruction and the Possibility of Justice* (New York and London: Routledge, 1992).

Cox, Robert W., 'Social Forces, States, and World Orders: beyond International Relations Theory', in Robert O. Keohane (ed.), *Neorealism and its Critics* (New York: Columbia University Press, 1986), pp. 204–54.

Crick, Bernard, *The American Science of Politics: its Origins and Conditions* (London: Routledge, 1959).

Cumming, Robert D., *Human Nature and History: a Study of the Development of Liberal Political Thought*, vol. I (Chicago: University of Chicago Press, 1969).

Cunningham, Andrew and Jardine, Nicholas (eds.), *Romanticism and the Sciences* (Cambridge: Cambridge University Press, 1990).

Czempiel, E.-O. and Rosenau, James N. (eds.), *Global Changes and Theoretical Challenges: Approaches to World Politics for the 1990s* (Lexington, MA: Lexington Books, 1989).

Dahl, Robert, 'The Behavioral Approach in Political Science: Epitaph for a Monument of a Successful Protest', *American Political Science Review*, vol. 55, 1961, no. 4, pp. 763–72.

Dallamayr, Fred R., *G. W. F. Hegel: Modernity and Politics* (London: Sage, 1993).

Deleuze, Gilles, *Foucault*, trans. S. Hand (Minneapolis, MN: University of Minnesota Press, 1988).

Deleuze, Gilles and Guattari, Felix, *What is Philosophy?* (London: Verso, 1994).

Der Derian, James (ed.), *International Theory: Critical Investigations* (London: Macmillan, 1995).

Der Derian, James and Shapiro, Michael J. (eds.), *International/Intertextual Relations: Postmodern Readings of World Politics* (Lexington, MA: Lexington Books, 1989).

Derrida, Jacques, 'Force of Law: the "Mystical Foundation of Authority"', in D. Cornell, M. Rosenfeld and D. G. Carlson (eds.), *Deconstruction and the Possibility of Justice* (New York and London: Routledge, 1992), pp. 3–67.

Spectres of Marx: the State of the Debt, the Work of Mourning, and the New International (London: Routledge, 1994).

'Structure, Sign and Play in the Discourse of the Human Sciences', in *Writing and Difference* (London: Routledge, 1978), pp. 278–93.

Deslandres, M., *La Crise de la Science Politique et le Problème de la Methode* (Paris: Chevalier-Maresq, 1902).

Dessler, David, 'What's at Stake in the Agent–Structure Debate?', *International Organization*, vol. 43, 1989, no. 3, pp. 441–73.

Dewey, John, *Outlines of a Critical Theory of Ethics* [1891] (New York: Hilary House, 1957).

Problems of Men (New York: Philosophical Library, 1946).

Dickey, Lawrence, *Hegel: Religion, Economics, and the Politics of Spirit 1770–1807* (Cambridge: Cambridge University Press, 1987).

Dierkes, M. and Biervert, B. (eds.), *European Social Science in Transition: Assessment and Outlook* (Boulder, CO: Westview, 1992).

Domhoff, G. William, *Who Rules America?* (Englewood Cliffs, NJ: Prentice-Hall, 1967).

Donnelly, Jack, 'Realism and the Academic Study of International Relations', in James Farr, John S. Dryzek and Stephen T. Leonard (eds.), *Political Science in History: Research Programs and Political Traditions* (Cambridge: Cambridge University Press, 1995), pp. 175–97.

Donzelot, Jacques, *L'invention des Social* (Paris: 1984).

'The Mobilization of Society', in Graham Burchell, Colin Gordon and Peter Miller (eds.), *The Foucault Effect: Studies in Governmentality* (London: Harvester, 1991), pp. 169–79.

Draper, Hal, *Karl Marx's Theory of Revolution. Vol. I: State and Bureaucracy* (New York: Monthly Review Press, 1977).

Dreyfus, Hubert L. and Rabinow, Paul, *Michel Foucault: beyond Structuralism and Hermeneutics* (Chicago, IL: University of Chicago Press, 1982).

Dryzek, John S., 'The Progress of Political Science', *Journal of Politics*, vol. 48, 1986, no. 2, pp. 301–20.

Dryzek, John S. and Leonard, Stephen T., 'History and Discipline in Political Science', *American Political Science Review*, vol. 82, 1988, no. 4, pp. 1245–59.

Dryzek, John S. and Schlosberg, David, 'Disciplining Darwin: Biology in the History of Political Science', pp. 130–1, in James Farr, John S. Dryzek and Stephen T. Leonard (eds.), *Political Science in History: Research Programs and Political Traditions* (Cambridge: Cambridge University Press, 1995), pp. 123–44.

Duguit, Leon, *Law in the Modern State* (New York: Huebsch, 1919).

Dunn, John, 'The Identity of the History of Ideas', in P. Lasslett, W. G. Runciman and Q. Skinner (eds.), *Philosophy, Politics and Society*, 4th series (Oxford: Blackwell, 1972).

Dupré, Louis, *Passage to Modernity: an Essay in the Hermeneutics of Nature* (New Haven, CT: Yale University Press, 1993).

Dyer, H. C. and Mangasarian, L. (eds.), *The Study of International Relations* (London: Macmillan, 1989).

Dyson, Kenneth H. F., *The State Tradition in Western Europe: a Study of an Idea and an Institution* (Oxford: Martin Robertson, 1980).

Easton, David, *The Political System: an Inquiry into the State of Political Science* (New York: Knopf, 1953).

'The Political System Besieged by the State', *Political Theory*, vol. 9, 1981, no. 3, pp. 303–25.

Elliot, W. Y., 'The Pragmatic Politics of Mr H. J. Laski', *American Political Science Review*, vol. 18, 1924, no. 2, pp. 251–75.

'Sovereign State or Sovereign Group?', *American Political Science Review*, vol. 19, 1925, no. 3, pp. 475–97.

Ellis, Ellen Deborah, 'The Pluralistic State', *American Political Science Review*, vol. 14, 1920, no. 3, pp. 393–407.

Engelhardt, Dietrich von, 'Historical Consciousness in the German Romantic Naturforschung', in Andrew Cunningham and Nicholas Jardine (eds.), *Romanticism and the Sciences* (Cambridge: Cambridge University Press, 1990), pp. 55–68.

Engels, Friedrich, *The Origin of the Family, Private Property, and the State* (London: Lawrence and Wishart, 1972).

Eulau, Heinz, Eldersveld, Samuel J. and Janowitz, Morris (eds.), *Political Behaviour: a Reader in Theory and Research* (Glencoe, IL: The Free Press, 1956).

Evans, Peter B., Rueschemeyer, Dietrich and Skocpol, Theda (eds.), *Bringing the State Back In* (Cambridge: Cambridge University Press, 1985).

Ewald, François, 'Insurance and Risk', in Graham Burchell, C. Gordon and P. Miller (eds.), *The Foucault Effect: Studies in Governmentality* (London: Harvester, 1991), pp. 197–210.

Fabbrini, Sergio and Massari, Oreste, 'The State: the Western Experience', paper presented at 17th IPSA Congress, Seoul, 1997.

Farr, James, 'Francis Lieber and the Interpretation of American Political Science', *Journal of Politics*, vol. 52, 1990, no. 4, pp. 1027–49.

'The History of Political Science', *American Journal of Political Science*, vol. 32, 1988, no. 4, pp. 1175–95.

'Political Science and the Enlightenment of Enthusiasm', *American Political Science Review*, vol. 82, 1988, no. 1, pp. 51–69.

'Political Science and the State', in J. Brown and D. K. van Keuren (eds.), *The Estate of Social Knowledge* (Baltimore, MD: Johns Hopkins, 1991), pp. 1–21.

'Understanding Conceptual Change Politically', in Terence Ball, Russell L. Hanson and James Farr (eds.), *Political Innovation and Conceptual Change* (Cambridge: Cambridge University Press, 1989), pp. 24–49.

Farr, James, Dryzek, John S. and Leonard, Stephen T. (eds.), *Political Science in History: Research Programs and Political Traditions* (Cambridge: Cambridge University Press, 1995).

Ferguson, Yale H. and Mansbach, Richard W., *Polities: Authority, Identities, and Change* (Columbia, SC: University of South Carolina Press, 1996).

Figgis, John N., *Churches in the Modern State* (London, 1913).

Follett, M. P., *The New State: Group Organization for the Solution of Popular Government* (London: Longmans, Green, 1918).

Foucault, Michel, *The Archaeology of Knowledge* (New York: Pantheon Books, 1972).

'The Discourse on Language', in *The Archaeology of Knowledge* (New York: Pantheon Books, 1972), pp. 215–37.

'Governmentality', in Graham Burchell, Colin Gordon and Peter Miller (eds.), *The Foucault Effect: Studies in Governmentality* (London: Harvester, 1991), pp. 87–104.

'Nietzsche, Genealogy, History', in Donald F. Bouchard (ed.), *Language, Counter-memory, Practice: Selected Essays and Interviews by Michel Foucault* (Ithaca, NY: Cornell University Press, 1977), pp. 139–64.

'Omnes et Singulatim: towards a Criticism of "Political Reason" ', *The Tanner Lectures on Human Values 1981* (Salt Lake City, UT: University of Utah Press, 1981), pp. 221–54.

The Order of Things: an Archaeology of the Human Sciences (London: Routledge, 1991).

'The Political Technology of Individuals', in Luther H. Martin, Huck Gutman and Patrick H. Hutton (eds.), *Technologies of the Self: a Seminar with Michel Foucault* (London: Tavistock, 1988), pp. 145–62.

'Politics and the Study of Discourse', in Graham Burchell, Colin Gordon and Peter Miller (eds.), *The Foucault Effect: Studies in Governmentality* (London: Harvester, 1991), pp. 53–72.

'The Subject and Power', afterword to Hubert L. Dreyfus and Paul Rabinow, *Michel Foucault: Beyond Structuralism and Hermeneutics* (Berkeley, CA: University of California Press, 1982), pp. 208–26.

'Truth and Power', in Colin Gordon (ed.), *Power/Knowledge: Selected Interviews and Writings 1972–1977* (New York: Pantheon, 1980), pp. 109–33.

Frankel, Boris, 'On the State of the State: Marxist Theories of the State after Leninism', *Theory and Society*, vol. 7, 1979, nos. 1–2, pp. 199–242.

Freeman, E. A., *Comparative Politics: Six Lectures Read Before the Royal Institution in January and February, 1873* (London: Macmillan, 1873).

Fried, Morton H., 'The State', *Encyclopedia of the Social Science* (New York: Macmillan, 1968).

Friedrich, C. J., 'The Deification of the State', *Review of Politics*, vol. 1, 1939, pp. 18–30.

Fuller, Steve, 'Disciplinary Boundaries and the Rhetoric of the Social Sciences', in Ellen Messer-Davidow, David R. Shumway and David J. Sylvan (eds.), *Knowledges: Historical and Critical Studies in Disciplinarity* (Charlottesville, VA: University Press of Virginia, 1993), pp. 125–49.

Social Epistemology (Bloomington, IN: Indiana University Press, 1988).

Gadamer, Hans-Georg, *Hegel's Dialectic: Five Hermeneutical Studies* (New Haven, CT: Yale University Press, 1976).

Gettell, Raymond G., *History of Political Thought* (New York: Century, 1925).

Giddens, Anthony, *A Contemporary Critique of Historical Materialism* vol. II: *The Nation-State and Violence* (Cambridge: Polity Press, 1985).

Gierke, O., *Political Theories of the Middle Age*, trans. F. Maitland (Cambridge: Cambridge University Press, 1900).

Gill, Stephen, 'Reflections on Global Order and Sociohistorical Time', *Alternatives*, vol. 16, 1991, no. 3, pp. 275–314.

Gillespie, Charles C., *Genesis and Geology: the Impact of Scientific Discoveries upon Religious Belief in the Decades Before Darwin* (New York: Harper & Row, 1959).

Gilpin, Robert G., 'The Richness of the Tradition of Neorealism', in Robert O. Keohane (ed.), *Neorealism and its Critics* (New York: Columbia University Press, 1986), pp. 301–21.

Godelier, Maurice, 'System, Structure, and Contradiction in *Capital*', *Socialist Register*, 1967.

Gold, David A., Lo, Clarence Y. H. and Wright, Erik Olin, 'Recent Developments in Marxist Theories of the Capitalist State', *Monthly Review*, vol. 27, 1975, no. 5, pp. 29–43, no. 6, pp. 37–51.

Goldmann, Kjell, Hannerz, Ulf and Westin, Charles, *Nationalism and Internationalism in the Post-Cold War Era* (London: Routledge, 2000).

Goldstein, D. S., 'History at Oxford and Cambridge: Professionalization and the Influence of Ranke', in Georg G. Iggers and J. M. Powell (eds.), *Leopold von Ranke and the Shaping of the Historical Discipline* (Syracuse, NY: Syracuse University Press, 1990), pp. 141–53.

Gordon, Colin, Afterword to *Power/Knowledge*, in Colin Gordon (ed.), *Power/Knowledge: Selected Interviews and Writings 1972–1977* (New York: Pantheon, 1980), pp. 229–59.

'Governmental Rationality: an Introduction', in Graham Burchell, Colin Gordon and Peter Miller (eds.), *The Foucault Effect: Studies in Governmentality* (London: Harvester, 1991), pp. 1–51.

Gordon, Colin, (ed.), *Power/Knowledge: Selected Interviews and Writings 1972–1977* (New York: Pantheon, 1980).

Gourevitch, Peter, 'The Second Image Reversed: the International Sources of Domestic Politics', *International Organization*, vol. 32 , 1978, no. 4, pp. 881–911.

Gracia, Jorge J. E., *Philosophy and its History: Issues in Philosophical Historiography* (New York: SUNY, 1992).

Greenfeld, Liah, *Nationalism: Five Roads to Modernity* (Cambridge, MA: Harvard University Press, 1992).

Grimm, Dieter, 'The Modern State: Continental Traditions', in F.-X. Kaufmann, Giandomenico Majone and Vincent Ostrom (eds.), *Guidance, Control, and Evaluation in the Public Sector* (Berlin: De Gruyter, 1986), pp. 89–109.

Gross, David, 'The Temporality of the Modern State', *Theory and Society*, vol. 14, 1985, no. 2, pp. 53–82.

Gunnell, John G., *Between Philosophy and Politics: the Alienation of Political Theory* (Amherst, MA: University of Massachusetts Press, 1986).

'The Declination of the State and the Origins of American Pluralism', in James Farr, John S. Dryzek and Stephen Leonard (eds.), *Political Science in History: Research Programs and Political Traditions* (Cambridge: Cambridge University Press, 1995), pp. 19–40.

The Descent of Political Theory: a Genealogy of an American Vocation (Chicago, IL: University of Chicago Press, 1993).

'The Myth of the Tradition', *American Political Science Review*, vol. 72, 1978, no. 11, pp. 122–34.

Political Philosophy and Time: Plato and the Origins of Political Vision (Chicago, IL: University of Chicago Press, 1987).

'In Search of the State: Political Science as an Emerging Discipline in the US', in P. Wagner, B. Wittrock and R. Whitley (eds.), *Discourses on Society* (Dordrecht: Kluwer, 1990), pp. 123–61.

Hacking, Ian, 'Nineteenth-Century Cracks in the Concept of Determinism', *Journal of the History of Ideas*, vol. 44, 1983, no. 3, pp. 455–75.

The Taming of Chance (Cambridge: Cambridge University Press, 1990).

Hall, J. A. (ed.), *States in History* (Oxford: Basil Blackwell, 1986).

Halliday, Fred, 'State and Society in International Relations: a Second Agenda', in H. C. Dyer and L. Mangasarian (eds.), *The Study of International Relations* (London: Macmillan, 1989), pp. 40–59.

Hansen, Lene, 'R. B. J. Walker and International Relations: Deconstructing a Discipline', in Iver B. Neumann and Ole Wæver (eds.), *The Future of International Relations: Masters in the Making* (London: Routledge, 1997), pp. 316–36.

Hegel, G .W. F., *The Philosophy of History* (Buffalo, NJ: Prometheus, 1991).

The Philosophy of Right (Cambridge: Cambridge University Press, 1991).

Heilbron, John, Magnusson, Lars and Wittrock, Björn (eds.), *The Rise of the Social Sciences and the Formation of Modernity* (Dordrecht: Kluwer, 1998).

Held, David, 'Central Perspectives on the Modern State', in G. McLennan, David Held and S. Hall (eds.), *The Idea of the Modern State* (Milton Keynes: Open University Press, 1984), pp. 29–79.

'Democracy, the Nation-State and the Global System', *Economy and Society*, vol. 20, 1991, no. 2, pp. 138–72.

Political Theory and the Modern State: Essays on State, Power, and Democracy (Oxford: Polity Press, 1989).

Hempel, Carl G., *Aspects of Scientific Explanation and Other Essays in the Philosophy of Science* (New York: The Free Press, 1965).

Herbst, Jürgen, *The German Historical School in American Scholarship* (Ithaca, NY: Cornell University Press, 1965).

Herder, Johann Gottfried, 'Yet Another Philosophy of History', in F. M. Barnard (ed.), *J. G. Herder on Social and Political Culture* (Cambridge: Cambridge University Press, 1969).

Herschel, J., *Preliminary Study of Natural Philosophy* (London, 1831).

Higham, J. and Conkin, P. K., *New Directions in American Intellectual History* (Baltimore, MD: Johns Hopkins, 1979).

Hintze, Otto, 'The State in Historical Perspective', in R. Bendix (ed.), *State and Society: a Reader in Comparative Political Sociology* (Berkeley, CA: University of California Press, 1973), pp. 154–167.

Hobhouse, L. T., *The Metaphysical Theory of the State* (London: Allen and Unwin, 1918).

Hoffman, John, *Beyond the State: an Introductory Critique* (Cambridge: Polity Press, 1995).

Holloway, John and Picciotto, Sol, *State and Capital: a Marxist Debate* (London: Edward Arnold, 1978).

Holt, Stull W. 'The Idea of Scientific History in America', *Journal of the History of Ideas*, vol. 1, 1940, no. 3, pp. 352–62.

Holzgrefe, J. L., 'The Origins of International Relations Theory', *Review of International Studies*, vol. 15, 1989, no. 1, pp. 11–26.

Hont, István, 'The Permanent Crisis of a Divided Mankind: "Contemporary Crisis of the Nation State" in Historical Perspective', *Political Studies*, vol. 42, special issue, 1994, pp. 166–231.

Hsiao, Kung Chuan, *Political Pluralism: a Study in Contemporary Political Theory* (New York: Harcourt Brace, 1927).

Hughes, H. Stuart, *Consciousness and Society: the Reorientation of European Social Thought 1890–1930* (New York: Vintage, 1977).

Humboldt, Wilhelm von, 'On the Historian's Task', *History and Theory*, vol. 6, 1967, no. 1, pp. 57–71.

Iggers, Georg G., *The German Conception of History: the National Tradition of Historical Thought from Herder to the Present* (Middletown, NJ: Wesleyan University Press, 1968).

Iggers, Georg G. and Powell, J. M. (eds.), *Leopold von Ranke and the Shaping of the Historical Discipline* (Syracuse, NY: Syracuse University Press, 1990).

Jellinek, Georg, *Allgemeine Staatslehre* [1900] (Berlin: O. Häring, 1905).

Jessop, Bob, *Nicos Poulantzas: Marxist Theory and Political Strategy* (New York: St Martin's, 1985).

'On the Originality, Legacy, and Actuality of Nicos Poulantzas', *Studies in Political Economy*, vol. 34, 1991, no. 1, pp. 75–107.

'Recent Theories of the Capitalist State', *Cambridge Journal of Economics*, vol. 1, 1977, no. 4, pp. 353–73.

State Theory: Putting the Capitalist State in Its Place (Cambridge: Polity Press, 1990).

Kant, Immanuel, 'The Metaphysics of Morals', in Hans Reiss (ed.), *Kant's Political Writings* (Cambridge: Cambridge University Press, 1991), pp. 131–75.

Kantorowicz, Ernst, *The King's Two Bodies: a Study in Medieval Political Theology* (Princeton, NJ: Princeton University Press, 1957).

Kaufmann, F.-X., Majone, Giandomenico and Ostrom, Vincent (eds.), *Guidance, Control, and Evaluation in the Public Sector* (Berlin: De Gruyter, 1986).

Keane, John, 'Despotism and Democracy: the Origins and Development of the Distinction between Civil Society and the State 1750–1850', in John Keane (ed.), *Civil Society and the State: New European Perspectives* (London: Verso, 1988), pp. 35–71.

'Introduction', in John Keane (ed.), *Civil Society and the State: New European Perspectives* (London: Verso, 1988).

Keane, John (ed.), *Civil Society and the State: New European Perspectives* (London: Verso, 1988).

Kelley, Donald R., 'Mythistory in the Age of Ranke', in Georg G. Iggers and J. M. Powell (eds.), *Leopold von Ranke and the Shaping of the Historical Discipline* (Syracuse, NY: Syracuse University Press, 1990), pp. 3–20.

'What is Happening to the History of Ideas?', *Journal of the History of Ideas*, vol. 51, 1990, no. 1, pp. 3–25.

Kelsen, Hans, *General Theory of Law and State* (Cambridge, MA: Harvard University Press, 1945).

Keohane, Robert O. and Nye, Joseph, *Power and Interdependence: World Politics in Transition* (Boston, MA: Little, Brown, 1977).

Keohane, Robert O. (ed.), *Neorealism and its Critics* (New York: Columbia University Press, 1986).

King, R., *The State in Modern Society* (Chatham, NJ: Chatham House, 1986).

Knutsen, Torbjørn L., *A History of International Relations Theory* (Manchester: Manchester University Press, 1997).

Koselleck, Reinhart, *'Begriffsgeschichte* and Social History', in Reinhart Koselleck, *Futures Past: on the Semantics of Historical Time* (Boston, MA: MIT Press, 1985), pp. 73–91.

Critique and Crisis: Enlightenment and the Pathogenesis of Modern Society (Oxford: Berg, 1988).

'Einleitung', in O. Brunner, W. Conze and Reinhart Koselleck (eds.), *Geschichtliche Grundbegriffe. Historisches Lexicon zur Politisch-Sozialen Sprache in Deutschland* (Stuttgart: Klett-Cotta, 1972–1997), vol. I, pp. xvi–xvii.

Futures Past: on the Semantics of Historical Time (Boston, MA: MIT Press, 1985).

'Linguistic Change and the History of Events', *Journal of Modern History*, vol. 61, 1989, no. 4, pp. 649–68.

' "Neuzeit": Remarks on the Semantics of the Modern Concepts of Movement', in Reinhart Koselleck, *Futures Past: on the Semantics of Historical Time* (Boston, MA: MIT Press, 1985), pp. 231–66.

' "Space of Experience" and "Horizon of Expectation": Two Historical Categories', in Reinhart Koselleck, *Futures Past: on the Semantics of Historical Time* (Boston, MA: MIT Press, 1985), pp. 267–88.

'Staat und Souveränitet', in O. Brunner, W. Conze and Reinhart Koselleck (eds.), *Geschichtliche Grund Begriffe Historisches Lexicon zur Politisch-Sozialen Sprache in Deutschland* (Stuttgart: Klett-Colta, 1972–1997), vol. VI.

Koselleck, Reinhart and Gadamer, Hans-Georg, *Hermeneutik und Historik* (Heidelberg: Carl Winter, 1987).

La Capra, Dominick, 'History, Language, and Reading: Waiting for Crillon', *American Historical Review*, vol. 100, 1995, no. 3, pp. 799–828.

Lalor, J. F., *Cycloedaedia of Political Science, Political Economy, and the Political History of the United States* (New York: Charles E. Merrill, 1888).

Laski, Harold J., *Authority in the Modern State* (New Haven, CT: Yale University Press, 1919).

Foundations of Sovereignty and Other Essays (New Haven, CT: Yale University Press, 1921).

Studies in the Problem of Sovereignty (New Haven, CT: Yale University Press, 1917).

Laslett, P. and Runciman, W. G. (eds.), *Philosophy, Politics and Society*, 2nd series (Oxford: Blackwell, 1964).

Laslett, P., Runciman, W. G. and Skinner, Q. (eds.), *Philosophy, Politics and Society*, 4th series (Oxford: Blackwell, 1972).

Lasswell, Harold D. and Kaplan, Abraham, *Power and Society: a Framework for Political Inquiry* (New Haven, CT: Yale University Press, 1950).

Lenz, M., *Die Großen Mächte. Ein Rückblick auf unser Jahrhundert* (Berlin: Paetel, 1900).

Lieb, I. C., 'The Ontological Status of the Laws of Nature', *Review of Metaphysics*, vol. 29, 1985, no. 2, pp. 227–41.

Lieber, Francis, (ed.), *Encyclopedia Americana* (Philadelphia, PA: Thomas Desilver, 1835).

Lindberg, Leon N., Alford, Robert, Crouch, Colin and Offe, Claus (eds.), *Stress and Contradiction in Modern Capitalism* (Lexington, MA: D. C. Heath, 1973).

Lindsay, A. D., 'The State in Modern Political Theory', *Political Quarterly*, vol. 1, 1914, no. 1, pp. 128–45.

Lord, A. R., *The Principles of Politics: an Introduction to the Study of the Evolution of Political Ideas* (Oxford: Clarendon, 1921).

Luhmann, Niklas, *Essays on Self-Reference* (New York: Columbia University Press, 1990).

Luke, Timothy W., 'Discourses of Disintegration, Texts of Transformation: Re-Reading Realism in the New World Order', *Alternatives*, vol. 18, 1993, no. 2, pp. 229–58.

MacIver, R. M., *The Modern State* (London: Oxford University Press, 1926).

Maine, Henry S., *Lectures on the Early History of Institutions* (London: John Murray, 1875).

Maitland, Frederic W., 'The Body Politic', in H. D. Hazeltine, G. Lapsley and P. H. Winfield (eds.), *Maitland: Selected Essays* [1899] (Cambridge: Cambridge University Press, 1936), pp. 240–56.

translator's introduction to Otto Gierke, *Political Theories of the Middle Age* (Cambridge: Cambridge University Press, 1900).

Mandel, Ernst, *Late Capitalism* (London: New Left Books, 1975).

Mandelbaum, Maurice, *History, Man, and Reason* (Baltimore, MD: Johns Hopkins, 1974).

Manicas, Peter T., *A History and Philosophy of the Social Sciences* (Oxford: Basil Blackwell, 1987).

Mann, Michael, 'The Autonomous Power of the State: its Origins, Mechanisms and Results', in J. A. Hall (ed.), *States in History* (Oxford: Basil Blackwell, 1986).

Maritain, Jacques, *Man and the State* (Chicago, IL: University of Chicago Press, 1951).

Martin, L. H., Gutman, H. and Hutton, P. H. (eds.), *Technologies of the Self: a Seminar with Michel Foucault* (London: Tavistock, 1988).

Marx, Karl, *Critique of Hegel's 'Philosophy of Right'*, trans. A. Jolin and J. O'Malley (Cambridge: Cambridge University Press, 1970).

Marx, Karl and Engels, Friedrich, *The German Ideology* [1932] (New York: International Publishers, 1947).

McIlwain, C. H., *The Growth of Political Thought in the West* (New York: Macmillan, 1932).

McLennan, G., Held, David and Hall, S. (eds.), *The Idea of the Modern State* (Milton Keynes: Open University Press, 1984).

Meier, Christian, *The Greek Discovery of Politics*, trans. D. McLintock (Cambridge, MA: Harvard University Press, 1990).

Meinecke, Friedrich, *Machiavellism: the Doctrine of Raison d'Etat and its Place in Modern History*, trans. D. Scott (Boulder, CO and London: Westview, 1984).

Merriam, Charles E., *New Aspects of Politics* (Chicago, IL: University of Chicago Press, 1931).

'The Present State of the Study of Politics', *American Political Science Review*, vol. 15, 1921, no. 2, pp. 173–85.

Messer-Davidow, Ellen, Shumway, David R. and Sylvan, David J., 'Disciplinary Ways of Knowing', in Ellen Messer-Davidow, David R. Shumway and David J. Sylvan (eds.), *Knowledges: Historical and Critical Studies in Disciplinarity* (Charlottesville, VA: University Press of Virginia, 1993), pp. 1–21.

Messer-Davidow, Ellen, Shumway, David R. and Sylvan, David J. (eds.), *Knowledges: Historical and Critical Studies in Disciplinarity* (Charlottesville, VA: University Press of Virginia, 1993).

Meuret, Denis, 'A Political Genealogy of Political Economy', *Economy and Society*, vol. 17, 1988, no. 2, pp. 225–50.

Miliband, Ralph, *The State in Capitalist Society: the Analysis of the Western System of Power* (London: Quartet Books, 1973).

'State Power and Class Interests', *New Left Review*, no. 138, 1983, pp. 57–68.

Mill, John Stuart, *A System of Logic Ratiocinative and Inductive. Being a Connected View of the Principles of Evidence and the Methods of Scientific Investigation*, vol. II, 8th edn (London: Longmans, Green, Reader and Dyer, 1872).

Mills, C. Wright, *The Power Elite* (New York: Oxford University Press, 1956).

Mommsen, Wolfgang J., 'Ranke and the Neo-Rankean School in Imperial Germany', in Georg G. Iggers and J. M. Powell (eds.), *Leopold von Ranke and the Shaping of the Historical Discipline* (Syracuse, NY: Syracuse University Press, 1990), pp. 124–40.

Morgenthau, Hans, *Politics Among Nations: the Struggle for Power and Peace* (New York: Knopf, 1985).

Nederman, Cary J., 'Aristotelianism and the Origin of "Political Science" in the Twelfth Century', *Journal of the History of Ideas*, vol. 52, 1991, no. 2. pp. 179–94.

Neumann, Iver B. and Wæver, Ole (eds.), *The Future of International Relations: Masters in the Making* (London: Routledge, 1997).

Nietzsche, Friedrich, ' "Guilt", "Bad Conscience" and the Like', in *On the Genealogy of Morals* (New York: Vintage, 1969), pp. 57–96.

The Will to Power, ed. Walter Kaufmann (New York: Vintage, 1968).

Nordlinger, Eric A., *On the Autonomy of the Democratic State* (Cambridge, MA: Harvard University Press, 1981).

Nowotny, Helga, *Time: the Modern and Postmodern Experiences* (Oxford: Polity Press, 1994).

Offe, Claus, 'Advanced Capitalism and the Welfare State', *Politics and Society*, vol. 2, 1976, no. 4, pp. 479–88.

'The Capitalist State and the Problem of Policy Formation', in Leon N. Lindberg, Robert Alford, Colin Crouch and Claus Offe (eds.), *Stress and Contradiction in Modern Capitalism* (Lexington, MA: D. C. Heath, 1973).

'The Crisis of Crisis Management: Elements of a Political Crisis Theory' *International Journal of Politics*, vol. 6, 1976, no. 3, pp. 29–67.

Offe, Claus, and Ronge, W., 'Theses on the Theory of the State', *New German Critique*, 1975, no. 6, pp. 137–47.

'Structural Problems of the Capitalist State, Class Rule and the Political System', in Klaus von Beyme, *German Political Studies*, vol. I (London: Sage, 1974), pp. 31–57.

Pagden, Anthony, (ed.), *The Languages of Political Theory in Early Modern Europe* (Cambridge: Cambridge University Press, 1987).

Parekh, Bhikhu, 'When Will the State Wither Away?', *Alternatives*, vol. 15, 1990, no. 3, pp. 247–62.

Pasquino, Pasquale, 'Emmanuel Sieyès, Benjamin Constant et le "Gouvernement de Modernes" ', *Revue Française de Science Politique*, vol. 37, 1987, pp. 214–28.

'Theatrum Politicum: the Genealogy of Capital-Police and the State of Prosperity', in Graham Burchell, Colin Gordon and Peter Miller (eds.), *The Foucault Effect: Studies in Governmentality* (London: Harvester, 1991), pp. 105–18.

Pizzorno, Alessandro, 'Politics Unbound', in C. S. Maier (ed.), *Changing Boundaries of the Political* (Cambridge: Cambridge University Press, 1987), pp. 27–62.

Pocock, J. G. A., 'The Concept of Language and the *Métier d'Historien*: some Considerations on Practice', in A. Pagden (ed.), *The Languages of Political Theory in Early Modern Europe* (Cambridge: Cambridge University Press, 1987), pp. 19–38.

'The History of Political Thought: a Methodological Inquiry', in P. Laslett and W. G. Runciman, *Philosophy, Politics and Society*, 2nd series (Oxford: Basil Blackwell, 1964), pp. 183–202.

The Machiavellian Moment: Florentine Political Thought and the Atlantic Republican Tradition (Princeton, NJ: Princeton University Press, 1975).

'Modes of Political and Historical Time in Early Eighteenth-Century England', in J. G. A. Pocock, *Virtue, Commerce, and History: Essays on Political Thought and History, Chiefly in the Eighteenth Century* (Cambridge: Cambridge University Press, 1985), pp. 91–102.

'The State of the Art', in J. G. A. Pocock, *Virtue, Commerce, and History* (Cambridge: Cambridge University Press, 1985), pp. 1–33.

Virtue, Commerce, and History: Essays on Political Thought and History, Chiefly in the Eighteenth Century (Cambridge: Cambridge University Press, 1985).

Pogge, Thomas W., 'Cosmopolitanism and Sovereignty', *Ethics*, vol. 103, 1992, pp. 48–75.

Pollock, Frederick, *An Introduction to the History of the Science of Politics* (London, 1890).

Poulantzas, Nicos, 'The Capitalist State: a Reply to Miliband and Laclau', *New Left Review*, 1976, no. 95, pp. 63–83.

Classes in Contemporary Socialism (London: New Left Books, 1975).

Political Power and Social Classes (London: New Left Books, 1973).

'The Problems of the Capitalist State', *New Left Review*, no. 58, 1969, pp. 67–78.

State, Power, and Socialism (London: New Left Books, 1978).

Putnam, Hilary, *Reason, Truth, and History* (Cambridge: Cambridge University Press, 1981).

Ranke, Leopold von , 'The Great Powers', trans. by H. Hunt-von Laue, in T. H. von Laue, *Leopold Ranke: the Formative Years*, Princeton Studies in History, vol. IV (Princeton, NJ: Princeton University Press, 1950).

Reill, P. H. 'History and the Life Sciences in the Early Nineteenth Century', in Georg G. Iggers and J. M. Powell (eds.), *Leopold von Ranke and the Shaping of the Historical Discipline* (Syracuse, NY: Syracuse University Press, 1990), pp. 21–35.

Rice, Stuart A., *Quantitative Methods in Politics* (New York: Knopf, 1928).

Richter, Melvin, 'Conceptual History (*Begriffsgeschichte*) and Political Theory', *Political Theory*, vol. 14, 1986, no. 4, pp. 604–37.

The History of Political and Social Concepts: a Critical Introduction (New York: Oxford University Press, 1995).

'Reconstructing the History of Political Languages: Pocock, Skinner and the *Geschichtliche Grundbegriffe*', *History and Theory*, vol. 24, 1990, no. 1, pp. 38–70.

Ricœur, P., *Time and Narrative* (Chicago, IL: University of Chicago Press, 1988), vol. III.

Ringmar, Eric, 'On the Ontological Status of the State', *European Journal of International Relations*, vol. 2, 1996, no. 4, pp. 439–66.

Rockman, B. A., 'Minding the State – or a State of Mind?', in J. A. Caporaso (ed.), *The Elusive State: International and Comparative Perspectives* (Newbury Park, CA: Sage, 1989), pp. 173–203.

Rockmore, Tom, 'Subjectivity and the Ontology of History', *The Monist*, vol. 74, 1991, no. 2, pp. 187–205.

Roger, Jacques, 'The Living World', in G. S. Rousseau and Roy Porter (eds.), *The Ferment of Knowledge: Studies in the Historiography of Eighteenth-Century Science* (Cambridge: Cambridge University Press, 1980), pp. 255–83.

Rorty, Richard, *Contingency, Irony, and Solidarity* (Cambridge: Cambridge University Press, 1989).

Philosophy and the Mirror of Nature (Oxford: Basil Blackwell, 1980).

Rose, Nikolas, 'Government, Authority and Expertise in Advanced Liberalism', *Economy and Society*, vol. 22, 1993, no. 3, pp. 283–99.

Rose, Nikolas and Miller, Peter, 'Political Power Beyond the State: Problematics of Government', *British Journal of Sociology*, vol. 43, 1992, no. 2, pp. 173–205.

Rosenau, James N., 'The State in an Era of Cascading Politics: Wavering Concept, Widening Competence, Withering Colossus, or Weathering Change?', in J. A. Caporaso (ed.), *The Elusive State: International and Comparative Perspectives* (Newbury Park, CA: Sage, 1989), pp. 17–48.

Ross, Dorothy, 'The Liberal Tradition Revisited and the Republican Tradition Addressed', in J. Higham and P. K. Conkin (eds.), *New Directions in American Intellectual History* (Baltimore, MD: Johns Hopkins, 1979).

'On the Misunderstandings of Ranke and the Origins of the Historical Profession in America', in Georg G. Iggers and J. M. Powell (eds.), *Leopold von Ranke and the Shaping of the Historical Discipline* (Syracuse, NJ: Syracuse University Press, 1990), pp. 154–69.

The Origins of American Social Science (Cambridge: Cambridge University Press, 1991).

Rossini, Gigliola, 'The Criticism of Rhetorical Historiography and the Ideal of Scientific Method: History, Nature, and Science in the Political Language of Thomas Hobbes', in Anthony Pagden (ed.), *The Languages of Political Theory in Early Modern Europe* (Cambridge: Cambridge University Press, 1987), pp. 303–24.

Roth, Michael S., *Knowing and History: Appropriations of Hegel in Twentieth-Century France* (Ithaca, NY: Cornell University Press, 1988).

Rousseau, G. S. and Porter, Roy (eds.), *The Ferment of Knowledge: Studies in the Historiography of Eighteenth-Century Science* (Cambridge: Cambridge University Press, 1980).

Rousseau, Jean-Jacques, 'L'État de Guerre', in C. E. Vaughn (ed.), *The Political Writings of Jean-Jacques Rousseau*, vol. I (Cambridge: Cambridge University Press, 1915).

Rêveries (Paris: Larousse, 1993).

Rubinstein, Nicolai, 'A History of the Word *"Politicus"* in Early-Modern Europe', in Anthony Pagden (ed.), *The Languages of Political Theory in Early Modern Europe* (Cambridge, Cambridge University Press, 1987), pp. 41–56.

Ruby, J. E., 'The Origins of Scientific "Law"', *Journal of the History of Ideas*, vol. 47, 1986, no. 3, pp. 341–59.

Rudner, R. S., *Philosophy of the Social Science* (Englewood Cliffs, NJ: Prentice-Hall, 1966).

Ruggie, John Gerald, 'Continuity and Transformation in the World Polity: towards a Neorealist Synthesis', in Robert O. Keohane (ed.), *Neorealism and its Critics* (New York: Columbia University Press, 1986), pp. 131–57.

Runciman, David, *Pluralism and the Personality of the State* (Cambridge: Cambridge University Press, 1997).

Runciman, W. G., *Social Science and Political Theory* (Cambridge: Cambridge University Press, 1969).

Rundell, John F., *Origins of Modernity: the Origins of Modern Social Theory from Kant to Hegel to Marx* (Cambridge: Polity Press, 1987).

Sabine, George H. 'The Concept of the State as Power', *Philosophical Review*, vol. 29, 1920, no. 4, pp. 301–18.

'Pluralism: a Point of View', *American Political Science Review*, vol. 17, 1923, no. 1, pp. 34–50.

'The State', *Encyclopedia of the Social Sciences* (New York: Macmillan, 1934).

Saint-Amand, Pierre, *The Laws of Hostility: Politics, Violence and the Enlightenment* (Minneapolis: University of Minnesota Press, 1996).

Schluchter, Wolfgang, *Paradoxes of Modernity* (Stanford, CA: Stanford University Press, 1997).

Schmidt, Brian C., 'The Historiography of Academic International Relations', *Review of International Studies*, vol. 20, 1994, no. 4, pp. 349–67.

'Lessons from the Past: Reassessing the Interwar Disciplinary History of International Relations', *International Studies Quarterly*, vol. 42, 1998, no. 3, pp. 433–59.

The Political Discourse of Anarchy: a Disciplinary History of International Relations (Albany, NY: SUNY, 1998).

Seeley, John R. *Introduction to Political Science* [1885] (London: Macmillan, 1911).

Seidelman, R. and Harpham, E. J., *Disenchanted Realists: Political Science and the American Crisis 1884–1984* (New York: SUNY, 1985).

Shapin, S. and Shaffer, S., *Leviathan and the Air-Pump* (Princeton, NJ: Princeton University Press, 1985).

Shaw, Martin, 'The Theory of the State and Politics: a Central Paradox of Marxism', *Economy and Society*, vol. 3, 1974, no. 4, pp. 429–50.

Shöttler, Peter, 'Historians and Discourse Analysis', *History Workshop*, 1989, no. 27, pp. 37–62.

Sidgwick, Henry, *The Elements of Politics* (London: Macmillan, 1891).

'The Historical Method', *Mind*, vol. 11, 1886, pp. 203–19.

Sieyès, Emmanuel Joseph, *What is the Third Estate?*, trans. M. Blondel (London: Pall Mall Press, 1963).

Skinner, Quentin, 'Conventions and the Understanding of Speech-acts', *Philosophical Quarterly*, vol. 20, 1970, no. 79, pp. 118–38.

The Foundations of Modern Political Thought, 2 vols. (Cambridge: Cambridge University Press, 1978).

'Language and Social Change', in James Tully (ed.), *Meaning and Context: Quentin Skinner and his Critics* (Cambridge: Polity Press, 1988), pp. 119–32.

Liberty before Liberalism (Cambridge: Cambridge University Press, 1998).

'Meaning and Understanding in the History of Ideas', in James Tully (ed.), *Meaning and Context: Quentin Skinner and his Critics* (Cambridge: Polity Press, 1988), pp. 29–67.

'On Performing and Explaining Linguistic Actions', *Philosophical Quarterly*, vol. 21, 1971, no. 82, pp. 1–21.

'Some Problems in the Analysis of Political Thought and Action', in James Tully (ed.), *Meaning and Context: Quentin Skinner and his Critics* (Cambridge: Polity Press, 1988), pp. 97–118.

'A Reply to My Critics', in James Tully (ed.), *Meaning and Context: Quentin Skinner and his Critics* (Cambridge: Polity Press, 1988), pp. 231–88.

'The State', in Terence Ball, Russell L. Hanson and James Farr (eds.), *Political Innovation and Conceptual Change* (Cambridge: Cambridge University Press, 1989), pp. 90–131.

Skocpol, Theda, 'Bringing the State Back In: Strategies of Analysis in Current Research', in Peter B. Evans, Dietrich Rueschemeyer and Theda Skocpol (eds.), *Bringing the State Back In* (Cambridge: Cambridge University Press, 1985), pp. 3–37.

States and Social Revolutions (Cambridge: Cambridge University Press, 1979).

Smith, Munroe, 'Introduction: the Domain of Political Science', *Political Science Quarterly*, vol. 1, 1886, no. 1.

Spencer, Herbert, *Essays: Scientific, Political and Speculative* (New York: Appleton, 1892).

Spruyt, Hendrik, *The Sovereign State and its Competitors: an Analysis of Systems Change* (Princeton, NJ: Princeton University Press, 1994).

Strauss, Leo, *Natural Right and History* (Chicago, IL: The Free Press, 1953).

Strayer, Joseph R., *On the Medieval Origins of the Modern State* (Princeton, NJ: Princeton University Press, 1970).

Stråth, Bo and Torstendahl, Rolf, 'State Theory and State Development: States as Network Structures in Change in Modern European History', in Rolf Torstendahl (ed.), *State Theory and State History* (London: Sage, 1992), pp. 12–37.

Tamir, Yael, 'Who's Afraid of a Global State?', in Kjell Goldmann, Ulf Hannerz and Charles Westin (eds.), *Nationalism and Internationalism in the Post-Cold War Era* (London: Routledge, 2000), pp. 244–67.

Tilly, Charles, *Coercion , Capital and European States AD 990–1992* (Oxford: Basil Blackwell, 1992).

Tilly, Charles, 'Reflections on the History of European State-Making', in Charles Tilly (ed.), *The Formation of National States in Western Europe* (Princeton, NJ: Princeton University Press, 1975), pp. 27–32.

Tilly, Charles (ed.), *The Formation of National States in Western Europe* (Princeton, NJ: Princeton University Press, 1975).

Tivey, L., 'Introduction: Philosophy, Science, Ideology', in L. Tivey and A. Wright (eds.), *Political Thought since 1945: Philosophy, Science, Ideology* (Aldershot: Edward Elgar, 1992), pp. 1–71.

Tivey, L. and Wright, A. (eds.), *Political Thought since 1945: Philosophy, Science, Ideology* (Aldershot: Edward Elgar, 1992).

Toews, John E., 'Intellectual History after the Linguistic Turn: the Autonomy of Meaning and the Irreducibility of Experience', *American Historical Review*, vol. 92, 1987, no. 4, pp. 879–907.

Torstendahl, R. (ed.), *State Theory and State History* (London: Sage, 1992).

Truman, David B., *The Governmental Process: Political Interests and Public Opinion* (New York: Knopf, 1951).

'The Implications of Political Behavior Research', Social Science Research Council, *Items*, December 1951.

Tully, James (ed.), *Meaning and Context: Quentin Skinner and his Critics* (Cambridge: Polity Press, 1988).

Ullmann, Walter, *A History of Political Thought: the Middle Ages* (Harmondsworth: Penguin, 1965).

Principles of Government and Politics in the Middle Ages (London: Methuen, 1974).

Van den Berg, A., *The Immanent Utopia: from Marxism on the State to the State of Marxism* (Princeton, NJ: Princeton University Press, 1988).

Vaughn, C. E., *Studies in the History of Political Philosophy before and after Rousseau* (Manchester: Manchester University Press, 1925).

Vico, Giambattista, *The New Science* [1725] (Ithaca, NY: Cornell University Press, 1968).

Vincent, Andrew, *Theories of the State* (Oxford: Basil Blackwell, 1987).

Viroli, Maurizio, 'The Concept of *Ordre* and the Language of Classical Republicanism in Jean-Jacques Rousseau', in Anthony Pagden (ed.), *The Languages of Political Theory in Early Modern Europe* (Cambridge: Cambridge University Press, 1987), pp. 159–78.

From Politics to Reason of State: the Acquisition and Transformation of the Language of Politics, 1250–1600 (Cambridge: Cambridge University Press, 1992).

'The Revolution in the Concept of Politics', *Political Theory*, vol. 20, 1992, no. 3. pp. 473–95.

Wagner, P., *A Sociology of Modernity: Liberty and Discipline* (London, Routledge, 1994).

Wagner, P., Wittrock, B. and Whitley, R. (eds.), *Discourses on Society* (Dordrecht: Kluwer, 1990).

Walker, R. B. J., 'East Wind, West Wind: Civilizations, Hegemonies, and World Order', in R. B. J. Walker (ed.), *Culture, Ideology and World Order* (Boulder, CO: Westview, 1984), pp. 2–22.

Inside/Outside: International Relations as Political Theory (Cambridge: Cambridge University Press, 1993).

'From International Relations to World Politics', in J. A. Camilleri, A. P. Jarvis and A. J. Paolini (eds.), *The State in Transition: Reimagining Political Space* (Boulder, CO: Lynne Rienner, 1995), pp. 21–38.

'The Prince and "The Pauper": Tradition, Modernity, and Practice in the Theory of International Relations', in James Der Derian and Michael J. Shapiro (eds.), *International/Intertextual Relations: Postmodern Readings of World Politics* (Lexington, MA: Lexington Books, 1989), pp. 25–48.

'Security, Sovereignty, and the Challenge of World Politics', *Alternatives*, vol. 15, 1990, no. 1, pp. 3–27.

'Sovereignty, Identity, Community: Reflections on the Horizons of Contemporary Political Practice', in R. B. J. Walker and S. H. Mendlovitz (eds.), *Contending Sovereignties: Redefining Political Community* (Boulder, CO: Lynne Rienner, 1990), pp. 159–85.

'Violence, Modernity, Silence: from Max Weber to International Relations', in D. Campbell and M. Dillon (eds.), *The Political Subject of Violence* (Manchester: Manchester University Press, 1993), pp. 137–60.

'World Politics and Western Reason: Universalism, Pluralism, and Hegemony', in R. B. J. Walker (ed.), *Culture, Ideology and World Order* (Boulder, CO: Westview, 1984), pp. 182–216.

Walker, R. B. J. (ed.), *Culture, Ideology and World Order* (Boulder, CO: Westview, 1984).

Walker, R. B. J. and Mendlovitz, S. H. (eds.), *Contending Sovereignties. Redefining Political Community* (Boulder: Lynne Rienner, 1990).

Waltz, Kenneth N., *Theory of International Politics* (Reading, MA: Addison-Wesley, 1979).

Warren, Mark, *Nietzsche and Political Thought* (Boston, MA: MIT Press, 1988).

Weber, M., *The Methodology of the Social Sciences*, ed. E. A. Shils and H. A. Finch (New York: The Free Press, 1949).

'Politics as a Vocation', in H. H. Gerth and C. Wright Mills (eds.), *From Max Weber: Essays in Sociology* (London: Routledge, 1948), pp. 77–128.

Wendt, Alexander, 'The Agent–Structure Problem in International Relations Theory', *International Organization*, vol. 41, 1987, no. 3, pp. 335–70.

Social Theory of International Politics (Cambridge: Cambridge University Press, 1999).

Wendt, Alexander and Duvall, Raymond, 'Institutions and International Order', in E.-O. Czempiel and J. N. Rosenau (eds.), *Global Changes and Theoretical Challenges: Approaches to World Politics for the 1990s* (Lexington, MA: Lexington Books, 1989), pp. 51–73.

White, Hayden, *Metahistory: the Historical Imagination in Nineteenth-Century Europe* (London and Baltimore, MD: Johns Hopkins, 1973).

Wight, Martin, 'Why is there no International Theory?', in Martin Wight and Herbert Butterfield (eds.), *Diplomatic Investigations* (London: Allen & Unwin, 1966).

Wight, Martin and Butterfield, Herbert (eds.), *Diplomatic Investigations* (London: Allen & Unwin, 1966).

Willoughby, W. F., *Introduction to the Study of the Government of Modern States* (New York: Century, 1919).

Willoughby, Westel W., *Political Theories of the Ancient World* [1903] (Freeport, New York: Books for Libraries Press, 1969).

'The Prussian Theory of the State', *American Journal of International Law*, vol. 12, 1918, no. 2.

Wilson, Woodrow, *The State: Elements of Historical and Practical Politics* (London: Heath, 1899).

Wittgenstein, L., *Philosophical Grammar* (Oxford: Blackwell, 1974).

Wittrock, Björn, 'Discourse and Discipline: Political Science as Project and Profession', in M. Dierkes and B. Biervert (eds.), *European Social Science in Transition: Assessment and Outlook* (Boulder, CO: Westview, 1992), pp. 268–308.

'Political Science', in UNESCO, *The Scientific and Cultural Development of Humanity*, Vol. VII: *The Social Sciences* (London: Routledge, 1997).

Wokler, Robert, 'Contextualizing Hegel's Phenomenology of the French Revolution and the Terror', *Political Theory*, vol. 26, 1998, no. 1, pp. 33–55.

'The Enlightenment and the French Revolutionary Birth Pangs of Modernity', in Johan Heilbron, Lars Magnusson and Björn Wittrock (eds.), *The Rise of the Social Sciences and the Formation of Modernity* (Dordrecht: Kluwer, 1998).

Woolsey, Theodore W., *Political Science or the State Theoretically and Practically Considered* (London: Sampson Low, Marston, Searly and Rivington, 1877).

Wormell, D., *Sir John Seeley and the Uses of History* (Cambridge: Cambridge University Press, 1980).

Yates, Frances A. *Astraea: the Imperial Theme in the Sixteenth Century* (London: Routledge and Kegan Paul, 1975).

Zilsel, E., 'The Genesis of the Concept of Scientific Law', *The Philosophical Review*, vol. 51, 1941, pp. 245–67.

Zizek, Slavoj, *For They Do Not Know What They Do: Enjoyment as a Political Factor* (London: Verso, 1991).

Zizek, Slavoj, *The Plague of Fantasies* (London: Verso, 1997).

Index